Know Your Child

By the Same Author

Pre-Primary Education Philosophy and Practice

About the Author

Professor G. Pankajam (M.Sc., M.A., M.Ed., Ph.D.) has the experience of teaching Child Development, Exceptional Children and Pre-school Education since 1965. Starting her career as a lecturer in Lakshmi College of Education, she rose upto the Principal of the College for 16 years and then the Vice-Chancellor of Gandhigram Rural Institute (Deemed University), Gandhigram.

Prof. Pankajam received Alumni Achievement Award from M.S. University, Baroda and the Best Principal Award from Government of Tamil Nadu. She has ten books to her credit on pre-primary education, child development, higher education, and women and child welfare.

KNOW YOUR CHILD

PROF. G. PANKAJAM
Former Vice-Chancellor
Gandhigram Rural Institute
Deemed University
Gandhigram

CONCEPT PUBLISHING COMPANY, NEW DELHI-110059

Cataloging in Publication Data—DK
Courtesy: D.K. Agencies (P) Ltd. <docinfo@dkagencies.com>

Pankajam, G. (Gnanasundaram), 1939-
Know your child / G. Pankajam.
p. cm.
Includes bibliographical references (p.)
Includes index.
ISBN 8180692124

1. Child development. I. Title.

DDC 305.231 21

ISBN: 81-8069-213-2 (P.B.)

First Published 2005

Published and Printed by
Ashok Kumar Mittal
Concept Publishing Company
A/15-16, Commercial Block, Mohan Garden
New Delhi-110059 (INDIA)

Phones : 25351460, 25351794
Fax : 091-11-25357103
Email : publishing@conceptpub.com

CHILDREN LEARN WHAT THEY LIVE

If a child lives with criticism, he learns to condemn
If a child lives with hostility, he learns to fight
If a child lives with ridicule, he learns to be shy
If a child lives with shame, he learns to feel guilty
If a child lives with tolerance, he learns to be patient
If a child lives with encouragement, he learns to confidence
If a child lives with praise, he learns to appreciate
If a child lives with security, he learns justice
If a child lives with security, he learns to have faith
If a child lives with approval, he learns to like himself
If a child lives with acceptance and friendship,
he learns to find love in the world

—Dorothy Law Holtz

Preface

I developed a desire to learn about children when I was doing my undergraduate programme. This desire was responsible for my pursuing the post-graduate course (M.Sc.) in Child Development and Human Relationship in Maharaja Sayaji Rao University, Baroda. The atmosphere—both physical and social atmosphere which include my Professors, Library and Chetan Balwadi—the Laboratory, Nursery school made me enjoy the study of Child Development and Human Relationship.

It was my luck that I was appointed as the Lecturer in Child Development to teach the post-graduate course in Early Childhood Education sponsored by NCERT, New Delhi. My two years of experience gave me the opportunity to have an indepth knowledge of a child's growth and development while teaching the course, to the experienced field supervisors, teacher educators, and children in Balwadies—the Pre-Primary Centres in rural and urban areas. Then my position as a Lecturer, Professor and Principal in Lakshmi College of Education, teaching and research in Early Childhood Care and Education (ECCE) for three decades convinced me that I am for the child and my contribution to the ECCE should be a permanent one.

Challenges I encountered with children and my students made me think, reasonout and plan for solving them. My desire to share my experiences resulted in organizing a number of training programmes, seminars, workshops and conferences to the people who work with children and love children—the Anganwadi workers. teacher educators, supervisors, inspecting officers and administrators. All these experiences are responsible for my writing about Children and Pre-Primary Education.

This book "Know Your Child" has been written with a hope that those who are interested and love children will enjoy reading it and be benefitted. Students who learn child development will certainly get what they require from this book, become the real lovers of children and promote wholesome childhood. Parents will definitely get information as to how the child is to be brought up. These are the objectives of this book "KNOW YOUR CHILD".

I will be happy and thankful to the readers if they could interact with me after reading it with their suggestions to improve further my approach to writing this book.

G. PANKAJAM

Contents

Preface vii

1. How to Study the Child 1
2. Evaluation 18
3. Conception, Prenatal Development and Birth 41
4. Physical Development 58
5. Motor Development 70
6. Social Development 80
7. Emotional Development 94
8. Cognitive Development 104
9. Concept Formation 116
10. Language Development 136
11. Habit-formation in Children 151
12. Behaviour Problems of Children 160
13. Children with Special Needs 169
14. Health and Nutrition of Pre-schoolers 203
15. Deficiency Diseases among Pre-schoolers 225
16. Common Ailments and Their Prevention 231
17. Common Childhood Illnesses 235
18. First Aid for Minor Injuries and Common Ailments 245
19. Home Stimulation 253

Bibliography 258

Index 261

1

How to Study the Child

The importance of the earliest years and their effect upon the subsequent development of character and personality is now generally understood. True pattern of personality is drawn in infancy, early childhood and early adolescence. The modern psychologists have emphasized the importance of recognizing differences as well as likenesses among individuals. The individual differences are very clearly noted during childhood and early adolescence than at any other periods. The impact of culture on biologically inherited potentialities is extremely strong during these years. For these reasons it is important that techniques of guidance in earliest period be constantly refined and improved that they be based upon careful study of child nature, and directed towards wisely conceived and realistic ends. It also helps the parents and the teachers not to be shocked or over-ambitious to see their children's growth pattern and behaviours.

Many of the problems of home and family adjustment could be avoided if parents and other relatives possessed a greater understanding of the nature of the child, and its growth and development. This understanding also helps them to know the problems that beset the child, when she should be helped, and when she should be left alone. It helps us to understand what happy, well-adjusted childhood really means and knowing what can they do for their children during these growing years. The assistance which these people can give after understanding the child will help to grow into a healthy and well adjusted child.

In a pre-primary school, the atmosphere and attitudes of the teachers should meet children's needs for security, sense of belonging and affection, for achievements, creativity and recognition; for social interaction, motor manipulation, and language exploration; and for emotional release. These general goals to be achieved through pre-primary school programme and the teacher's attitudes towards the children. Knowledge about the individual children and group differences will be helpful in planning the programmes. Understanding of the maturity levels, interests, problems, and skills of the group members is essential if teachers are to plan effectively for learning experiences and for guiding children in wholesome development. The goal in planning any group activity should be attended to the individual and group needs and capacities.

The above discussions show clearly the importance of adults understanding the child, his growth and development, and behaviour in different situations. Adults must also understand their problems and fulfil their responsibilities towards solving and satisfying their needs.

Child Development Specialists and Child Psychologists have found out many tools to study child – his developmental characteristics and behaviours. Now the teachers of young children, parents and others who are interested in the welfare of children can get a large body of information concerning child's growth, development and behaviour patterns. A teacher or parent can observe their children and compare his observations with the findings of others who had already done some research on the same.

A Brief History of the Child Study Movement

Down through the ages, however, our ways of dealing with children have been influenced not only by philosophical consideration but also by economic demands, military and political affairs, religious precepts, birth and death rate, and by famine and diseases. We have varying conceptions of the fundamental nature of the child, held by different people at different times in history of child study.

Till Nineteenth Century there was, speculative, non-scientific approach to the study of the child. The first significant efforts to get away from the speculative philosophical approach and turn more towards a child study based on direct observation were situated by the early biographers of the late Nineteenth Century. Darwin and Preyer kept careful notes on the development and behaviour of individual children over a period of months and years. They used longitudinal method to study the children. Only afterwards in the late Nineteenth and early Twentieth Centuries the first scientific investigations of children were carried out by G. Stanley Hall (1844-1924) in America, and Alfred Binet (1857-1911) in France. They were mostly concerned with finding out causes of behaviour. Their findings and writings helped the people to understand, to some extent the causes of children's behaviours. Hall used questionnaire to gain information about child's behaviour and published "The Content of Children's Minds", a study of concepts held by children upon their entrance in school. Binet's professional contributions were many, including the development of a method of testing the intelligence of children.

Gasell of Yale University, utilized Clinical developmental examination, surveys and observations of home life, school life, and nursery school behaviour, and interviews with parents of the children in reporting on "The Infant and Child in the Culture of Today". They described their findings in terms of behaviour apt to occur in a child at a particular age level. These descriptions constitute norms to each side of which extends the variety of behaviours which made up the normal range of behaviour.

From the work of these people has come a tradition that statements and generations about child behaviour and development must be based on observable evidences. This has led to reliance on standardized, controlled situations in which a child may be observed in order to detect his special reaction to these situations. The dramatic change, which took place after these studies was from thinking of the child as a miniature adult, whose behaviour was primarily a matter of his normal fibre and will, to think of him as having certain psychological resources at his disposal. The child has some basic psychological needs, the satisfaction of which leads to enhanced development, and the frustration of which leads to family development.

General Approaches to the Study of the Child

Although there are many approaches to the study and evaluation of child behaviour and development, the Layman's evaluation is conducted informally and reflects his own attitudes and values. If we want the result to be more accurate and valid, we must follow scientific procedures and represent an objective approach. To be valid one must observe very carefully, measure accurately, classify obtained data objectively and completely, and verify conclusions.

There are four major approaches to the study of the child: (*i*) the behaviouristic approaches, (*ii*) the normative-descriptive approach, (*iii*) the field theory approach, and (*iv*) the psychoanalytic approach. Though we have classified them into four approaches they are not independent of each other. These developments were overlapping and concurrent rather than sequential. They should be considered as illustrations of the varying types of emphasis that have been placed on the central question of the nature and causes of a child's development and behaviour.

A SHORT DESCRIPTION ON THE APPROACHES

The Behaviouristic Approach

Contributions of Ivan Pavlov (1849-1936), a Russian Psychologist, and John B. Watson (1878-1958) and American Psychologist are very great. Pavlov demonstrated that animals can learn – that is acquire new habits – by forming a new association between a stimulus and a response. He illustrated the principle of conditioned learning. Watson was much concerned not only with the basic nature of the child, but also with influence of learning experiences. He was mainly interested in knowing how the child's observable behaviour could be modified by the presentation of special experiences. He recognized the importance of biological processes as well as psychological processes as the basis for human behaviour. He felt that new habits are the modification of old ones through conditioning and experiences. His major philosophy of child rearing is expressed by the term "habit training". Watson has made us aware of the need to study children objectively and in so doing, we have learned much we could not have learned in any other way.

The Normative-Descriptive Approach

Parents, teachers, psychologists, social workers and all others who are working with children must know the relative and normal development and behaviour of children. They must be able to find out to what extent specific members of the group deviate from established norms based on accurate measurement and evaluation of many individuals. These large group investigations generally are referred to as normative studies.

These studies have given a wealth of information concerning the probable general rate and kind of changes that can be expected to take place during childhood. They have observed a large number of children, individually as well as in groups and carefully catalogued the behaviour typical of each age level. Contribution of General, his colleagues and students is greater in this field. They have provided information on development from conception to adolescence – their motor behaviours, personal-social behaviour, language-behaviour and adoptive or intelligent behaviour. They describe the kinds of behaviour typical for each age, and which might reasonably be expected of normal children and given age norms. Though norms are merely average and as such, they tell us nothing the rightness or wrongness, the healthiness or unhealthiness of behaviour. Comparable information has been prepared by Gasell for other age, beginning with early infancy.

Another significant contribution on this line of study has been the emphasis on stages of readiness of the child which has helped us to outline the stages through which a child normally progresses from infancy to maturity. The normative approach to child development has enabled us to set up reasonable levels of expectation for children. It has fostered the acceptance of the current philosophy that children are individuals who require at each stage of development, experiences appropriate to their levels of readiness. Through this approach to child study we have learned that many stages of growth are accompanied by behaviour that can be difficult, but that is perfectly normal for the stage. It has also taught us that children revise their behaviour as they proceed from one stage to the next and as new stages emerge, old problems tend to disappear.

The Psychoanalytic Approach

For greater insight into motives, causes, and reasons for growth and behaviour, many Scientists have found it profitable to turn to more dynamic approaches to the study of the child. Sigmund Freud (1856-1939) has contributed much towards this approach. He has developed an extensive and elaborate theory of the nature of human personality, based on fundamental instincts and drives. He has also helped us to see that human behaviour is often motivated at an unconscious level. According to Freud, personality consists of 3 major divisions: (*i*) the Id, the reservoir of basic energy giving rise to all forms of instinctual striving; (*ii*) the Ego, that part of the personality concerned with among other things, reality and the child's position in relation to the realistic elements of his world; and (*iii*) the superego, concerned with normal values and the rightness or wrongness of behaviour.

The Field Theory Approach

Kurt Lewin (1890-1947) was the first person who related the theory to the growth and behaviour of children. Like Watson, Lewin was concerned with the environment. But there is slight difference in their approaches. While Watson was mainly concerned with the effects of external environmental forces on the child, Lewin argued that a child was more than a passive receiver of stimulation from the outside. In his view the child's personality included numerous psychological systems which interacted with his environment included objects and persons having powers of attraction and repulsion for the child. He tried to explain human behaviour in accordance with principles of mathematics and physics. His description of conflict situations are of special interest in the understanding of child's behaviour. According to him there are three basic kinds of conflicts, all of them in terms of interaction of the individual with his environment.

The Cross-Sectional Approach (Horizontal Study)

In the cross-sectional approach different children are studied at different ages. Any number of children, of any age can be studied at the same time. This approach refers to that type of study in which specific characteristics of a large group of the same age or same status subjects are investigated to discover the average of general trends of specific characteristics for the group. When averages (norms) have been ascertained, comparisons can be made between the individual's characteristics studied and the norms for the group. The cross-sectional approach is valuable in that it is a convenient technique that can be used to evaluate the status of young person at any stage of his development.

The Longitudinal Approach (Vertical Study)

Complete data about children can be obtained only by means of a continuous study of individual from the pre-natal period through maturity. The study of the same children at different stages is known as the longitudinal approach. Studies like this may be time consuming, costly, and difficult to complete. Though it is a difficult task, it is very useful to understand each in individual, his growth, development and behaviour at each age level.

Other sources through which we can gather information are: (*i*) verbal and non-verbal behaviour of children, (*ii*) past records of the child that have been compiled and preserved, (*iii*) memories of the child concerning his past interests, activities and behaviour or his introspections, (*iv*) available materials that the child has produced in the past, (*v*) memories of parents or other adults concerning the child's behaviour, and (*vi*) records of evaluation or measurements made of the child.

TECHNIQUES OF COLLECTING INFORMATION

The procedures of instruments that are issued in collecting information about the child's growth and development and his behaviour are as follows: (*i*) observation, (*ii*) the interview—with parents, play mates, teachers and the child himself, (*iii*) questionnaire, (*iv*) standardized testing instruments, (*v*) projective techniques, (*vi*) experimentation, and (*vii*) the case study or case history.

Observation of Children

Observation is the earliest, the most widely used, and in the long run probably the most valuable method of child study. As a technique it is the simplest and most natural way of learning about child's behaviour, although from the scientific standpoint it has very serious limitations. Observation cannot but be partly subjective. Because this is the simplest method; students, parents and teachers use this method.

An individual's displayed behaviour is constantly being observed by others. Observation of children, at home, on the street, in school, at play ground, at the market or at any place is informal, natural and are not very scientific. But through these observations we can form ideas, attitudes and opinions about children. These ideas and opinions may or may not be accurate. One of the very serious problems with informal observation is that what we consciously want to see may easily influence our perceptions of what is actually going on. It is not safe to generalize about children on the strength of our informal observation with a clear recognition that our present reactions to children are very much influenced by our past experiences with them.

To improve our observation we must observe every detailed movement of the child's behaviour and record them. Keeping records serves the dual purpose of forcing us to organize our observations into meaningful statements about a child. This provides a permanent record which can be referred to at a later time without having to rely solely on memory in future.

Recording the actual behaviour of a child and interpretations help us to distinguish between "facts" on the one hand, and "interpretations" on the other. We can easily observe the child's overt behaviour. From the overt behaviours we can make reasonable inferences about the existence of emotions, mental processes, attitudes, wishes, motives, etc., which are difficult to observe outwardly. But this making of inferences is based on our interpretation of the child's behaviour. As observers it is necessary that we keep a descriptive, objective record of events as they occur among children. Interpretations, personal reactions, feelings about the child's behaviour, etc., may be noted separately with full awareness on our part that these are not the same as observations.

Methods of Recording the Observations

An adequate observation record begins with the necessary descriptive information on the setting—date, time, place, the situation, name, age and the sex of the child. Observations of the students, are frequently based on a particular topic, or aspect of development. This might include topics like physical or motor characteristics of children, emotional behaviour, language development, intellectual development, personal-social behaviour or his participation in school activities.

The Running Record or the Diary

We can maintain the observation record in the form of daily diary record or running record. This is a running account of the behaviour of a particular child for a stated period of time. With practice however, one learns to record the most significant events that relate to a child's use of objects and materials in his environment, and the nature of his contact with the people around him. Records like this should be completely factual, with conscientious efforts to eliminate opinions, values, judgements, and personal attitudes. Only the facts are noted while recording and the interpretations are to be made later.

How to Interpret Child Behaviour

It is better to observe children from two points of view and interpret on the basis of these two. The following two questions are to be considered while observing:

1. How does the child's present status compare with that of others in his age group?
2. How does the child's present status compared with his past?

Every parent wants to know whether his child is normal; whether he is developing continuously. A teacher is interested in knowing whether each child is mature or immature for his age; he is developing as rapidly as most children of his age; so that she can plan her programme effectively.

As Kawin says:

"Every prospective teacher should be trained to be his own investigator of children, since every good teacher must be continuously alert to recognize likenesses and differences in children in all areas of development – physical, intellectual, social and emotional. To understand and guide any child effectively the adults who deal with him must first learn to see that child in all his uniqueness, recognizing him as a person who must be studied and understood both in terms of his own individual make-up and his relationship to others.

There is no substitute for direct observation as the foundation for such an understanding of a child."

Achievement Checklist for Pre-primary Schoolers

Directions for Using: Below is a list of items which may be for three, four and five-year old children. Put a tick (✓) in the appropriate column to indicate how frequently, in your experience with this child, he or she has achieved in each item:

Development	*Always*	*Some-times*	*Never*	*Does not Apply*
Motor Development				
Eats with spoon				
Holds spoon correctly				
Holds cup with one hand				
Spills food or drink only once during meal				
Spills food or drink more than once during meal				
Goes to toilet without help with clothing				
Flushes toilet				
Puts on dress				
Buttons dress				
Manages zipper				
Ties shoe laces				
Climbs jungle gym				
Jumps from 12-inch height				
Skips				
Catches ball				
Pedals tricycle				
Climbs steps with alternate feet				
Puts three-piece puzzle together				
Puts puzzle of five or more pieces together				
Holds scissors correctly				
Cuts on a line				
Writes given name				
Folds paper (simple)				
Folds diagonally				
Cognitive Development				
Follows simple directions				
Sits and listens to story for at least 5 minutes				
Sits and listens to story for at least 10 minutes				

(*Contd.*)

Development	*Always*	*Sometimes*	*Never*	*Does not Apply*
Puts away blocks or toys when finished				
Responds to own name				
Recognizes locker				
Leaves mother after one says "good bye"				
Rides to school in car with someone other parent				
Chooses to look at picture books				
Looks at page from top to bottom				
Looks at books from front to back				
Recognizes name				
Recognizes name of at least one other child				
Contributes to experience story				
Read experience story with group				
Cognitive Development				
Identifies words in experience story				
Can identify rhyming words				
Can match beginning consonant sounds				
Counts by rote 1—5				
Counts by rote 1—10				
Counts rationally 1—5				
Counts rationally 1—10				
Uses ordinal numbers first through third				
Recognizes money – Rupee, Paise				
Recognizes geometric shapes-circle, square, triangle, rectangle				

(*Contd.*)

Development	*Always*	*Some-times*	*Never*	*Does not Apply*
Solves problem without number				
Uses number in problem solving				
Writes numerals 1—5				
Language Development				
Speaks without baby talk				
Uses personal pronouns				
Speaks in sentences (uses sentences of at least five words)				
Tells events or story in sequence				
Engages in conversation with other children				
Engages in conversation with adults				
Speaks in group situation				
Aesthetic Development				
Sings alone				
Sings songs of at least two phrases				
Recognizes songs sung or played by others				
Manipulates and experiments with instruments				
Uses instrument as accompaniment to movements				
Knows names of at least two better known musical instruments				
Listens and identifies sounds of different instruments				
Matches tones				
Draws or paints lines and circles				

(*Contd.*)

Development	*Always*	*Some-times*	*Never*	*Does not Apply*
Draws or paints squares				
Shows ground line in painting or drawing				
Names paintings or drawings				
Names (or recognizes) primary colours				
Names at least five colours				
Adjusts bodily movement to accompaniment of regular beat (can keep time to music)				
Adjusts bodily movements to accompaniment which involves contrasts (slow-fast, light-heavy)				

Directions for Scoring: Note items in which the pupil has achieved, the items that need continued practice, and those that need to be introduced. Plan learning opportunities in terms of analysis of achievement items. Ignore those items which do not apply.

Courtesy: Sara Hammond Leepeer, *et al.*

Case Study

Systematic biographies of children from birth or early childhood constitute the source of data for case studies. Case study methods are the most flexible tools we have in the scientific research, because they impose the fewest constraints on the way observation is to be made and can be pursued in any situation. Case studies are often useful for didactic purposes.

Most frequently used technique to study the child is case study method. All the information gathered by observing the individual child is brought together in an organized way in case study. Usually the children who are exceptional socially, emotionally, who do not get along with other children are closely observed for case studies. Careful collection of necessary correct and accurate information will help a teacher to understand the problems and difficulties of children and take necessary corrective measures to overcome those problems and get over the difficulties.

If a teacher observes the talented children and tries to make case studies of these children. She tries to identify the factors which contribute to the talents. She records the behaviour profiles of children. One or two anecdotes which reveal the extraordinary behaviours of children may be recorded to interpret the child's behaviour. Teacher's observation may also reveal the progress made by children in various aspects of growth and development, which will help her guide the children, provide remedial measures and guidance and counselling could also be provided for furthering their development.

Along with the observation of growth and development of children the following aspects could also be observed:

(*i*) Favourite activities, (*ii*) Special interest, (*iii*) Self concept, (*iv*) Approaches to new situations, (*v*) Response to strangers, (*vi*) Development problems, (*vii*) Approach to solve problems, (*viii*) Relationship with other children, (*ix*) Play habits, (*x*) Relationship with teachers and other adults, (*xi*) Ability to explore new environment, (*xii*) How does the child make friendship, (*xiii*) Quarrel with others etc.

Sources of Data

Case study data may emerge from many kinds of sources:

1. School records—address, date of birth, name of parents, occupation, nationality of parents, academic subjects, child achievement etc.
2. Interviews with child—both formal and informal.
3. Interviews with parents, teachers and other people who know the child.
4. Observation and interviews in the home.
5. Observation of child in school, on the play ground, on the street etc.
6. Results of standardized tests of intelligence, achievement tests etc.
7. Cumulative records sent from other schools. Daily schedules of the child.

Outline of Case Study

Name...................... School........................ Date of birth...................
Age........................ Parents' Nationality..
Occupation.................... Address..................... Religion..................
Mother Tongue ....Referral Source......................

Reason for referral	(Specific problems including observable symptoms)
Family background	(Family relationships, home environment, socio-economic status)
Physical history	(Special defect, vision, height, scholastic achievement)
Aptitudes	(Test data including mental ability)
Personality and Social adjustment	(General behaviour pattern)

Interests, hobbies and experience

Plans (Vocational or Educational)

General appraisal, interpretation and hypothesis

Merits

1. It provides a basis for more complete understanding and gives a more accurate evaluation of events and thus prevents superficiality and quick judgments.
2. The knowledge that a particular condition exists in a unique instance would suggest factors to look for in other case as well.
3. Case study is an extremely useful method to study rare and unusual cases of human behaviour. Some of the case study data cannot be obtained by any other techniques.

Limitations

1. The case study requires much time for gathering extensive data.

2. Human beings are constantly interacting with diverse environmental factors. Therefore human behaviour cannot be explained without examining environmental factors in relation to the individuals.
3. Element of subjectivity can enter into a report when judgments are made about an individual's character and motives.

An experienced teacher in a pre-primary school who is also interested in the welfare of children deepens her understanding of all her children through intensive study of her children. By creating a file of case studies she is able to have a better understanding of her children and at the same time contributes to the child study.

Reporting to the Parents

Every parent is interested in knowing how far their children are progressing and whether they are comparable with other children. They depend on the pre-primary school teachers for this information. Hence, regular observation of the developmental profile of children and systematic maintenance of case studies would be of immense help to teachers. They could send periodical report about child's progress and the guidance to be provided to the child.

The regular and periodical reports about children to the parents may be either orally given during the parents visits to pre-primary schools or when the teachers make home visit. If parents are literate they may prefer periodical written reports or tellers from the teachers. Parents may also consider this as a very good opportunity to know not only about their children but to know the developmental patterns of children in general. They are interested to understand what happens to their children in their first school experience. Their observation in the school, their child behaviour helps them to have a better first hand information to compare the growth and development of their children with other children in the pre-primary school.

A wise teacher should remember that the relationship between a parent and a child is heavy loaded with feelings and she has to respect these feelings while contacting the parents. She should help the parents understand their children without hurting their feelings. As she approaches her children in the pre-primary school, she should approach so that she could build the confidence on them and the parents will also have the confidence on the teacher who takes care of their children. Her reporting about the child's growth and development and behaviour patterns should be done without any bias so that she will be an accepted person by the parents.

2

Evaluation

Evaluation is a word that has come into prominence in recent years in education. It plays a vital role inasmuch as they try to act as a determinant for several decisions to be made during the process of education. Until the middle of the 19th century, recitation was almost the only method of evaluation in the classroom.

In the later half of the century, educators began to understand certain shortcomings in depending solely on recitation but invariably insisted that this must be supplemented through the use of written test.

Tests

In every day life, the terms test, examination, measurement and evaluation are often used. According to the dictionary, test is defined as a series of questions on the basis of which some information is sought. In education, the meaning of test is something more than this. An educational test is a standardized procedure to measure quantitatively or qualitatively one or more than one aspect of trait by means of a sample of verbal or non-verbal behaviours. In the words of Bean (1953), a test is "an organized succession of stimuli designed to measure quantitatively or to evaluate qualitatively some mental process, trait or characteristics". This definition reveals two important characteristics of an educational test. First, test is an organized succession of stimuli which means that the stimuli (popularly known as items) in the test are organized in a certain sequence and are based upon some principles of test constructions. Second, both quantitative and qualitative measurements are possible through educational test. Thus, in general, test is a device or procedure for confronting a subject with a standard set of questions or tasks to which the student is to respond independently and the results of which can be treated as to provide a quantitative as well as qualitative comparison of the performance of different students.

Measurement

It is an act or a process of assigning numerals to events, objects etc., according to certain rules. Tyler (1963) defines measurement as, "assignment of numerals, according to rules". A still more elaborate and wider definition has been given by Nunnally (1970) "as measurement consists of rules for assigning numbers to objects in such a way as to represent quantities of attributes". An analysis of the definition of measurement given by Nunnally reveals the following main properties of measurement. They are:

1. In the process of measurement numbers are assigned according to some rules. A number is a kind of numeral which is assigned some quantitative meaning. In the process of measurement, the investigator does not assign numbers of his own choice, but according to certain fixed and explicit rules,
2. Measurement is always concerned with certain attributes or features of the object. It is these attributes or features of the object which are measured and not the object itself,
3. In the process of measurement, numerals are used to represent quantities of the attribute.

There are three types of measurement: (*i*) Direct, (*ii*) Indirect, (*iii*) Relative.

However, measurement in education is more complex than measurement in physical situation. Educational measurement involves the mental processes of individual which are not visible and which are interpreted in terms of the behaviour of the individual in certain situations.

Evaluation

It is an act or process that allows one to make a judgment about the desirability or value of a measure.

Evaluation— Quantitative description of pupils' achievement + Qualitative description of pupils' abilities + Value judgment about achievement and abilities.

Evaluation is a continuous and comprehensive process covering every aspect of the educative programme. It is an integral part of education in which pupil and teacher are partners. Thus, evaluation signifies a wider process of judging students' programmes.

The Aspects of Educational Evaluation

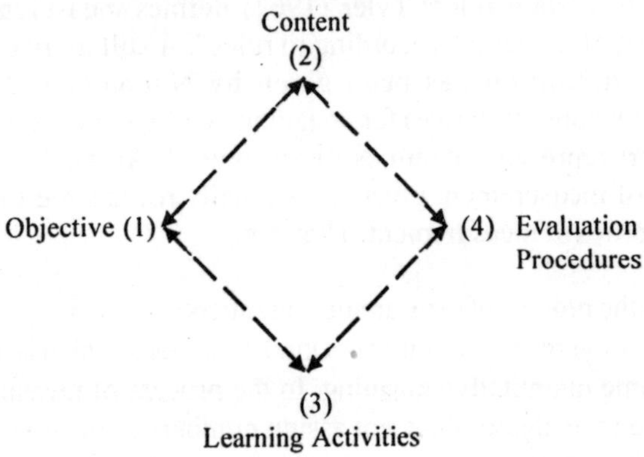

Steps Involved in Evaluation

To understand the relation among the four aspects of evaluation, it is necessary to study the various steps in the process of evaluation. They are:

1. identifying and defining general objectives;
2. identifying and defining specific objectives;
3. selecting teaching points;
4. planning the suitable learning activities;
5. implementing the suitable learning activities;
6. evaluating;
7. using the results as feedback.

Purpose of Measurement and Evaluation

Educational measurement of:

1. academic achievement of a student by a teacher to aid in selecting a learning experience;

2. individual differences of a student by a teacher to aid in selecting the most effective of alternative learning experience for each;
3. vocational interests of a student by that student to help in planning an academic programme;
4. to gain in level of achievement of a group of students by a teacher to determine the effectiveness of a learning experience;
5. the efficiency of a curriculum by a curriculum team to help determine whether it is preferable to alternative curricula;
6. the potential value of a course by a student to assist in arriving at a decision as to whether or not to enroll.
7. levels of achievement of groups of students by a legislative body to aid in allocation of funds;
8. accomplishment of a teacher by an administrator to assist in arriving at a recommendation regarding continued employment;
9. the needs of a school system by tax payers to aid in marking a ballot on a bond issue;
10. attitudes of teachers by a student to aid in selecting among sections of a course;
11. the potential effectiveness of schools by parents to aid them in selecting a school in which to enroll their child;
12. parents' perceptions of school programmes by an administrator to aid in planning information dissemination activities.

The major role of the school and the individual classroom teacher is to facilitate certain types of student learning. The teacher should encourage those activities that promote desirable student learning and discourage those that do not. Sometimes teachers feel that evaluation is the antithesis of instruction. It is never true under the broader definition of evaluation. Evaluation correctly done should enhance learning because it aids both the teacher in teaching and the student in learning. The relationship between instruction and evaluation is presented as follows:

Relationship between Instruction and Evaluation

Instruction	*Evaluation*
1. Instruction is effective when it leads to desired changes in students.	1. Evaluation is effective when it provides evidence of the extent of the change in students.
2. New behavioural patterns are best learned by students when the inadequacy of present behaviour is understood and the significance of the new behavioural patterns thereby made clear.	2. Evaluation is most conducive to learning when it provides for and encourages self-evaluation.
3. New behavioural patterns can be more efficiently developed by teachers who know the existing behavioural patterns of individual students and the reasons for them.	3. Evaluation is conducive to good instruction when it reveals major types of inadequate behaviour and the contributory causes.
4. Learning is encouraged by problems and activities that require thought and/or action by each individual student.	4. Evaluation is most significant in learning when it permits and encourages the exercise of individual initiative.
5. Activities that provide the basis for the teaching and learning of specified behaviour are also the most suitable activities for evoking and evaluating the adequacy of that behaviour.	5. Activities or exercises developed for the purpose of evaluating specified behaviour are also useful for teaching and learning of the behaviour.

Measurement is the hand maiden of instruction without measurement, there cannot be evaluation, without evaluation there cannot be feedback, without feedback, there cannot be good knowledge of results, without knowledge of results, there cannot be systematic improvement in learning. Measurement and evaluation can help both the teacher and the student. Let us look at both aspects.

1. Evaluation procedure help the teacher by:
   (*a*) providing knowledge concerning the students' entry behaviour;
   (*b*) setting, refining and clarifying realistic goals for each student;
   (*c*) evaluating the degree to which the objective have been achieved;
   (*d*) determining, evaluating and refining his instructional techniques.

2. Evaluation procedures help the student by:
   (*a*) communicating the teacher's goals;
   (*b*) increasing motivation;
   (*c*) encouraging good study habits;
   (*d*) providing feedback that identifies strengths and weaknesses.
3. Evaluation procedures help in the administrative decisions of:
   (*a*) selection,
   (*b*) classification,
   (*c*) placement.

In selection decision, one decides whether to accept or reject a student for a particular programme or treatment. In classification one decides the type of programme or treatment and in placement one decides the level of treatment.

Characteristics of a Good Measuring Instrument

Many aspect of student behaviour are evaluated to serve a variety of uses. Achievement may be evaluated in order to diagnose learning difficulties or to determine progress towards instructional objectives. Regardless of the area of behaviour to be evaluated, however, to be used or to be made of the results, of all the various procedures used, an evaluation programme should possess certain common characteristics like planning validity, reliability, objectivity, discriminating power, adequacy, practicability, comparability and utility. All of these qualities are criteria that must be given serious thought when a teacher selects a measuring instrument.

TYPES OF EVALUATION

Formative Evaluation

Formative evaluation refers to tests that are administered at intervals throughout a given unit. The teacher conducts formative tests during the instructional period to assess student progress. The teacher repeats giving the formative test until mastery is achieved.

According to Scriven (1980) formative evaluation is conducted during the development or improvement of a programme or product (or person).

It is an evaluation conducted for in-house staff and normally remains in house, but it may be done by internal or external evaluation or a combination.

The purpose of a formative evaluation is to obtain data necessary for making revisions and refinements of the instructional materials during the design and development phases. Data collection for this evaluation are derived from qualitative and quantitative sources. These sources are mainly subject matter consultants and learners for whom the instruction is intended.

Formative evaluation starts during the design phase with a review and critique during content structure by subject matter consultants. The content structure refers to the scope and sequence of the subject matter to be included in the instructional materials. This procedure is more qualitative than quantitative. Much of the content that is learned is determined by consensus. Having subject matter consultants review the content and offer. Suggestions can help to answer that the content structure reflects the consensus. This form of evaluation is particularly useful in making refinements on the content since learners often contribute little to this part of the evaluation.

One-to-One Tryout

The second part of the evaluation takes place concurrently with the development of the instructional materials. This procedure involves a tryout of the product between the teacher and a person for whom the instructor is intended. While the learner works through the instructional materials. The teacher observes and takes notes. The purpose of the one-to-one tryout are to identify editorial problems, any nuclear-directions and those content areas which are nuclear.

Group-Tryout

The final step in formative evaluation involves a group tryout. The purpose is to obtain information for making any major refinements before beginning production of the materials. Variables to be considered for refinement here include learner time for direct use of instructional materials and indirect study, *e.g.*, home work, pre-test scores to assess prerequisite skill levels, and pre-test, post-test scoring patterns.

A group can include from 5-10 learners. Refinements usually change resulting from variations in the learner population. Certain learner may need additional instruction or perhaps more help in understanding certain parts of the content or it could be that some amount of practice is redundant and should be left out. In all refinements in the instructional materials represent changes associated with individual differences found in the learner population. Certainly, the identification of such differences that might necessitate refinement is only possible with a group tryout.

Summative Evaluation

Summative evaluation refers to tests that are given immediately after the completion of an instructional unit, a programme, or a course of study.

The third evaluation phase, summative, takes place in the environment or setting where the instruction is to be normally used. Its purpose is to determine to what degree the instructional materials meet the goals and objectives of development project.

The basic instrumental goal to be evaluated states that learners will learn the defined content and behaviours in an effective and efficient manner. Data of this evaluation should include student performance, gain in learning, student time expanded in learning attitudes, comparison with a central group and costs.

Summative evaluation tends to emphasise administrative decisions relating to discontinuation of programme, allocation of staff and other resources and dismissal or re-assignment of teachers. Such evaluations call for much more elaborate data gathering focusing on inputs, processes and products in relation to each other.

According to Scriven (1980), summative evaluation is conducted after completion of a programme (or a study course) and for the benefit of same external audience or decision maker, though it too may be done either by an internal or an external or by combination.

Measurement Devices

The nature of the reference group against which results are to be compared is critical in determining whether the available data are useful. Reference groups are usually by test developers in the form of test norms that indicate the distribution of scores from other groups. Ideally users want a reference group to be similar to the group that they are evaluating. For this reason, conscientious test developers provide test users with norms from a variety of reference groups from large cities, various regions of the country, inner cities, specific status or the entire nation.

Recently some educators have been seeking a form of reference not based on norm groups. The new references are criteria established by the teacher or evaluator before data collection. This form of referencing is called criterion referenced testing. From previous experience and expectations, the educator states the requirements that would define success with respect to a particular objective. The data that is obtained can then be compared with these previously stated requirements.

Reference System

Reference system in educational measurement are used to provide a basis for interpreting results obtained from a measuring device. Reference systems are the key to making useful the information that is obtained from tests. There are primarily two types of reference system available in educational measurement. The most commonly used reference system involves the use of information collected from some known group. The group is well described and its characteristics are known to the people who use it as a reference. This reference group is commonly called a norm group and the reference of system is called a 'norm referenced system'.

Another commonly used reference system is called a criterion-referenced system. In this there is no specifically defined group. Instead the measuring device or test is the reference. A criterion-referenced test is constructed in such a way that either it represents the information or skills necessary to be successful at the next stage of whatever area is being assessed or it represents the terminal skills necessary to show competence.

Norm-referenced and criterion-referenced measurements are both useful in educational evaluations, and they can be used separately or simultaneously to provide useful information for an evaluation process. In general, a reference system helps the teacher interpret reported scores.

Norm Referenced Groups

In evaluations in which the reference system to be used is a norm group, the usefulness of test information depends on the nature of the norm group. Its characteristics must be similar to those of the group that is being evaluated.

A teacher is usually dealing with a heterogeneous group that cannot be described adequately by a single set of categories. The children in a heterogeneous classroom usually have a wide variety of experimental backgrounds. The teacher should select the most common characteristic; probably grade level, and use this characteristic to determine the appropriate norm group.

A teacher selects a reference groups from a standardized reference because it is believed to be representative of the conventional classroom most like that teacher's class. Quite often this norm group is characterized as a national norm group because it is believed to represent children throughout the nation at a particular grade level.

Criterion-Referenced Testing

Norm-referenced measurement can provide a teacher or evaluator with a great deal of valuable information about a student's abilities and achievements. All the information provided by norm-referenced measurement is relative to the norm-group, however, when norm-referenced tests are administered, the resulting raw sources are conversion made in order to determine how particular raw scores compare to the raw scores of some known group of students.

The fact that norm-referenced measurement provides only information relative to norm groups must be considered a limitation. Criterion-referenced measurement has been developed in an attempt to overcome this limitation. The purpose of criterion-referenced measurement is to determine whether an individual possesses the skills and knowledge for success at the next level of whatever attribute is being measured. A criterion-referenced test would have completely revealed the skills and knowledge of each person. The test results would have indicated the limitation also.

Comparison of Criterion and Norm-referenced Tests

1. Criterion-referenced and norm-referenced tests are similar in some aspects. Either one may be a written or a performance test, taken with paper and pencil form or as an activity requiring completion of specified tasks.
2. They may be either achievement tests or aptitude tests. An achievement test intended to provide an indication of what a student has already accomplished. An aptitude test is intended to provide an indication of what the student may be expected to accomplish in the future.

3. Both are providing information about the success of the instructional system. There are also some marked differences between these measurement system.

One arises from the difference in their purpose: Norm-referenced tests are constructed to show which individuals in a group possess the most knowledge about the content being tested. Such tests are designed to force a distribution of scores, the highest score indicating the best performance and the lowest score indicating the poorest performance. A norm-referenced test's purpose is to discriminate between the best students and the poorer students.

A criterion referenced test on the other hand, attempts to assess the behaviour possessed by the individuals being tested. There is no attempt to discriminate between individuals. All may get one item right, which would mean that they all possess the behaviour being measured by that item.

A major difference between these two is the precision required in determining the best items. Very precise mathematical procedures has been established and accepted for determining the quality of a norm-referenced test and the result is that we are able to place some degree of confidence in the test scores. Similar procedure have not been used. So, interpretation of the quality of the test depends on the judgment of the individual evaluator.

Both measurements provide the teacher and evaluator with a great deal of information. Norm-referenced measurement indicates how a student's test performance compares to that of students who comprise the norm group. Criterion-referenced measurement provides information as to what behaviour the student possess at the time the test is administered. Each is different in purpose, but both play an important role in the evaluation of the educational system.

Power Test

A power test is a measure of the student's ability to answer the questions correctly, given generous time limits. It usually presents a series of problems of increasing difficulty, allowing reasonable time for individual to complete as many as he can. In power test the examiner's score depends on how much he is able to do, how readily he is able to do it. Hence, in a power test there is either no time at all or a very generous time limit. The tasks in a power test are sometimes arranged in order of increasing difficulty with the expectation that the examiner will stop when he reaches task of a level of difficulty beyond his capabilities.

Examples: Co-operative Reading Test or
Henmon-Nelson Test of Mental Ability

Speed Test

A speed test is one that is in part a measure of the student's ability to answer questions quickly: stick time limits are set. It requires the individual to complete as many problems or tasks as he can at a maximum speed.

In a speed test the rapidity with which a task is completed is an important factor determining the score in the test. Some speed tests consists of tasks of uniform and relatively low difficulty. So the student's score is determined almost entirely by how fast he works, not by the difficulty of the tasks he accomplishes. Any test with a time limit short enough to prevent many examinees from finishing is at least partially a speed test.

Example: Purdue peg-board test.

TEACHER MADE ACHIEVEMENT TESTS

Achievement Test

A teacher in a classroom after teaching a unit would like to know how far her pupils have understood what has she taught so that she could modify her way of teaching. She herself constructs the tests and administers to her pupils. These tests are also called teacher made tests.

Types of Teacher Made Tests

Essay type, short answer type, objective type, oral and practical tests are some of the types of tests which a teacher uses in her class to test the comprehension of the subjects taught. Usually our tests evaluate the cognitive domain and very little of affective and psycho motor domains. Whereas when a teacher gives oral and practical tests these two dimensions could also be tested.

General Principles of Test Construction

Test construction requires a systematic, organized approach if positive results are to be forthcoming. The following steps will serve as a guide to the test maker who would strive to make his examination as valid as possible:

1. List the major objectives for which an appraisal is desired.
2. Examine the course content for additional objectives.
3. Analyze and define each objective in terms of expected student outcomes.
4. Establish a table of specifications.
5. Construct one or more test item for each objective listed.
6. Assemble the items for the test.
7. Write clear and concise direction for each type of questions.
8. Study every aspect of the assembled test.
9. Construct the key.
10. Have other instructions criticize and if possible, actually take the test.
11. Make any necessary revisions.
12. After the test has been administered to one or two groups of students, analyze and improve it.

A helpful means for constructing tests is a card file of effective test items. Such a file can be developed over a period of time and the busy instructor will find it has various tests. There are several ways in which such a file can be organized but the important point is for the instructor to get into the habit of systematically contributing items to his file.

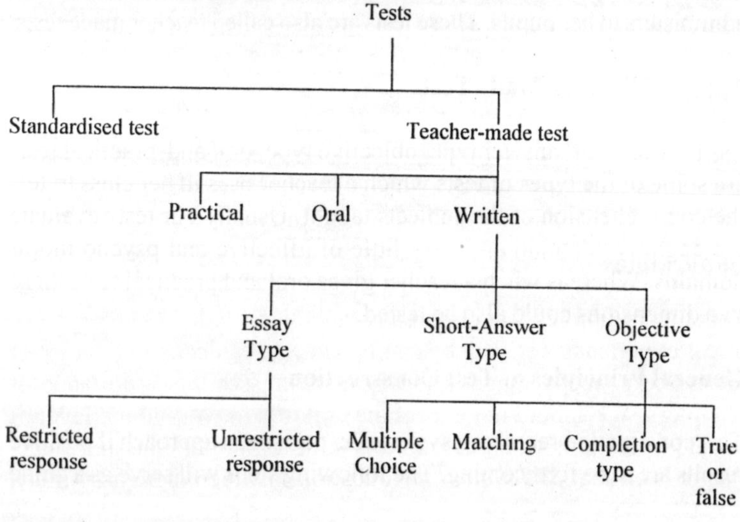

There are numerous points to be observed in constructing a test. Some of more important are listed below. Others will be included in the discussion of specific types of test items:

1. It is not possible to measure all outcomes of instruction with one type of test.
2. Make the test comprehensive but exclude insignificant and trivial items.
3. Devise your items so that they require the student actually to apply things learned rather than merely recall or recognize facts.
4. Make certain that the type of item used for measuring each objective is the one that will measure best that objective.
5. Avoid trick or "catch" questions.
6. Include a large number of items in the test.
7. Do not 'lift' statements directly items, books as test items.
8. Whenever possible, avoid items with only two choices from which the student selects one.
9. Check to make sure that no item can be answered simply by referring to other items.
10. Make each item independent of the others.
11. Include no item for which the response is obvious to a person who does not know the subject matter.
12. Word the items in the simplest possible manner.
13. State questions clearly. Eliminate ambiguous items.
14. Keep the method of recording responses as simple as possible (keep the student in mind).
15. Leave sufficient space for all responses without crowding.
16. Arrange blanks for responses along one side of the page, if possible.
17. Arrange the items so that responses will not form a particular pattern.
18. Arrange the items in such a manner that it will not be necessary for the student to refer to more than one page in answering a given item.
19. Number the responses consecutively from the beginning to the end of the test.
20. The practice of underlining crucial words, if not done too

frequently and indiscriminately, tends to increase the objectivity of test items.
21. Avoid the weighing of items.
22. If certain items are to be corrected for guessing, this could be clearly indicated in the directions.
23. Make sure the directions are clear and complete.
24. Prepare a proper heading for the test.

Test items can be classified in several ways. One method is to divide them into two groups; those which demand recall [completion, listing, etc., and those which call only for recognition of the correct answer (multiple-choice, true false etc.)]. It is difficult to draw a fine line of demarcation between the two. Either type can be a good item if it is designed to measure application of things learned. This is the important criterion to keep in mind.

For the purpose of this discussion test items have been classified under five main headings: (*i*) multiple-choice; (*ii*) true or false; (*iii*) matching; (*iv*) recall; (*v*) miscellaneous (Essay). There are many adoptions, modifications and combinations of these main type.

Essay Type Test

It consists of questions or instructions which require the examinee to compose a more or less extension original written response. Essay test questions frequently begin with words like 'discuss', 'explain' and 'describe'. The examinee is allowed relative freedom in composing his response. This requires that its quality must be judged subjectively by one skilled and informal in the subject.

Example:

1. From the observation made bring out the symptoms of deficiency diseases and suggest remedial measures.
2. What criteria you will follow to select dress for young children? Why?
3. How will you assess the suitability of food for any age group?
   (*a*) The student organizes his own answers with a minimum constraint.
   (*b*) Uses his own words and his own style of writing.

(*c*) Answers a small number of questions.
(*d*) Produces answers having all degrees of completeness and accuracy. A well prepared essay question requires that the student:
   (*i*) Determines what the problem is.
   (*ii*) Reviews the body of knowledge that he has and selects.
   (*iii*) Relates these to one another and organizes them into a coherent whole.
   (*iv*) Produces a well edited answer.

The distinctive features are:

1. It provides opportunity to show either how logical or how innovative and original a student can be in dealing with a topic.
2. It shows how well he can express his ideas.
3. It shows how well he can think, reason and argue.

But most of the examiner-made tests are not constructed to bring out their claimed advantages.

Major Defects of the Essay Type of Examination

1. They encourage rote memory.
2. They produce unwholesome influence on learning habits and teaching.
3. There is great deal of subjectivity in scoring.
4. They suffer seriously regarding reliability and validity.
5. The sampling of content is poor and lumpy.
6. There is scope for bluffing.
7. Essay type tests are easy to construct but answers are difficult to evaluate.
8. Chance factors play a crucial role.
9. Evaluation consumes much of the teacher's time-sincerity.
10. Evaluation becomes more difficult when the number of students is too large.
11. Students' poor language ability have a great disadvantage.
12. Poor handwriting and slow writing may produce adverse conditions.

Multiple-Choice Items

Multiple-choice items consist of a question or incomplete statement followed by several possible answers, from which the tastee selects the correct one. The item may take several forms. The student may be required to select the one correct answer, he may be asked to choose the best answer, the worst, or both. The item may be constructed, in the form of an analogy, or it may call for association. When well constructed, the multiple-choice item is one of the best if not the best, of the objective tests. Some suggestions follow for use in constructing multiple-choice items:

1. The step of the item should contain a central problem.
2. The item should be practical and realistic.
3. The stated problem should be specific, clear and as brief as possible.
4. Illustrations are sometimes useful in presenting the central problem.
5. Have at least four and preferably five answers (choices).
6. Include no response that are obviously wrong.
7. Avoid the inclusion of irrelevant clues.
8. Place the choices at the end of the incomplete statement.
9. List each choice on a separate line.
10. When the choices include a series of figures, put these in order.
11. Scatter the correct responses.
12. When a negative response is desired be sure to make this clear.
13. Do not use a multiple-choice item if a simpler type will be sufficient.

(Extract from "Measurement of Educational Achievement" by Michess and Karness Megram Book Company)

The test maker is expected to choose the right answer from the given choices. For example:

For each statement choose the most relevant answer and write the appropriate letter in the box.

For proper social development it is necessary for a child to have:

(*a*) a very secure home
(*b*) exact parents

(*c*) outside group experience
(*d*) opportunity to play with other children of the same age.

Which is the best method of cooking the rice to conserve the nutrients:

(*a*) absorption
(*b*) pressure cooking
(*c*) boiling and draining the water
(*d*) use of hay box.

True/False Items

The true/false item consists of a declaratory statement that is either true or false (right or wrong). It is used widely and often abused. There are numerous variations and modifications that help to correct some of the inherent weaknesses.

This type of item is relatively easy to construct, although the quality is often doubtful. It can be used to sample a wide range of subject matter. Students can usually answer three to five true/false items per minute. The item can be scored readily in an objective manner. It is especially useful when there are only two choices governing a particular point.

The true/false item is of doubtful value for measuring achievement. It encourages guessing. Difficulty is encountered in constructing items that are completely true or false without being obvious. Ambiguities, unimportant details, irrelevant clues these are added weaknesses of the typical true/false item.

The following points will prove helpful on constructing true/false items:

1. Make approximately half the items true and half false.
2. Make the method of indicating response as simple as possible.
3. Whenever possible, construct the items to make application of things learned.
4. Do not "lift" statements directly from books.
5. Use direct statements. Avoid words with general meanings.
6. Do not make the statements consistently longer than the false statements.
7. Avoid negative statements.
8. Be careful with specific determiners.

9. Make the point of the item obvious.
10. Avoid catch questions.
11. If you plan to correct for guessing, be sure to emphasize, this is the direction.
12. Wherever possible, use modified true/false items rather than the plain type.

Write whether the following statements are True (T) or False (F):

1. Wood pulp is used to prepare cellulose. (T/F)
2. Woolen garments should be washed in hot water. (T/F)
3. Solitary play is common to all pre-school children at all ages. (T/F)

Matching Items

Matching items require the matching of two sets of materials in accordance with given directions. In a sense they are a variations of the multiple-choice item. They are especially applicable for measuring the "Who", "What", "Where", "When" type of subject matter. They are relatively easy to construct, can be made objective, and can be scored quickly.

The typical matching item provides a poor indication of complete understanding and is inferior to the multiple-choice items for measuring judgment and application. It is apt to stress the memorization of facts and will often contain subtle, irrelevant clues to the correct response.

The following suggestions will prove helpful in constructing matching items:

1. Have at least five and not more than twelve responses in each matching exercise.
2. Include at least three extra choices from which response must be chosen.
3. Use only homogeneous or related materials in any one exercise.
4. Include at least possible choices from which the correct response must be selected.
5. Place the column containing the longer statements on the left side of the page.
6. Use illustration whenever possible.
7. Arrange the selection column in a logical order.

8. Keep the student in mind as the item is prepared.
9. Make sure the entire exercise appears on one page.
10. Make the directions specific.
11. Use capital letters to label the parts in the column from which the responses are to be selected.

Match the Vitamins in list A with their function in the list B.

List A		*List B*
1. Thiamine	(*a*)	For reproduction
2. Biotin	(*b*)	For clotting
3. Vitamin K	(*c*)	For proper appetite
4. Vitamin D	(*d*)	Formation of red blood cells
5. Folic acid	(*e*)	Metabolism of carbohydrate
6. Vitamin E	(*f*)	Normal functioning of nerve tissues
	(*g*)	For healthy bones
	(*h*)	For oxidation of carbohydrate

Recall Items

In a recall item the student supplies the answer. There are various kinds and types of recall item, including simple recall sentencecompletion, problems or situations, identification, listing or enumeration, and the like. The essay type item might also be considered a recall item.

The recall item is useful in measuring the retention of specific points. It is relatively easy to construct. The several variations can be used effectively in obtaining a wide sampling and they tend to have a high discriminative value.

Because the simple recall types are easy to construct they tend to be used excessively. This results in an over emphasis on memorization and verbal facility. Care must be exercised if subjectivity in scoring is to be avoided. Some points are being given below that will be helpful in constructing recall items:

1. Use direct questions whenever possible.
2. Make sentence completion items as specific as possible.
3. Do not copy statements directly from textbooks.
4. In simple recall and sentence-completion items place the blanks at or near the end of statement.
5. Avoid the inclusion of irrelevant clues.

6. Construct the item so that there is only one correct response.
7. Design enumeration items to call for specific facts.
8. Rarely should one question call for more than six or eight things to be listed if the student is required to list things in a given order.
9. Make all sketches or illustration clear and of sufficient size.
10. Whenever possible, make the student to solve problems by using previous learning.
11. Be sure there is plenty of room or space to indicate responses.

Comparison of Objective Type and Essay Type Questions

Objective Type	*Essay Type*
1. Requires pupils to choose among two or more alternatives.	1. Requires the pupils to plan their own answer and express in their own words.
2. Consists of many specific questions requiring only brief answers.	2. Consists of relatively few more general questions which call for extend answers.
3. Pupils spend most of their time in reading and thinking.	3. Pupils spend most of their time in thinking and writing.
4. Quality is determined by the skill of the test constructed.	4. Quality is determined largely by the skill of grade reading.
5. It is relatively tedious and difficult to prepare but easy to score.	5. It is easy to prepare but relatively tedious and difficult to score.
6. Offers freedom to the test constructor to demonstrate her knowledge and values but limits the pupils in their expression.	6. Offers freedom to the pupils to express their answer indirectly and freedom to the scores to score preferentially.
7. States pupils' tasks and the basis for judgment more clearly.	7. States pupils' tasks and the basis judgment less clearly.
8. Permits and occasionally encourages guessing.	8. Permits and occasionally encourages bluffing.
9. Distribution of scores is determined by the tests.	9. Distribution of scores is controlled largely by the scorer.

Similarities

1. Both tests can measure almost any important instructional objectives that any written test can measure.
2. Both tests can encourage pupils to learn concepts, principles and problem solving.
3. Both tests involve the use of subjective judgment.

4. Both tests yield scores whose value is dependant on subjectivity and reliability.

Blue-Print

While constructing an achievement test it is essential that the teacher has a blue-print so that she is assured that her question paper evaluates all the important learning outcomes of the instruction. She also decides the type of evaluation tool she is going to use to test the performance of her students.

The teacher is expected to give weightage for each objective and for each item included in her question paper.

TABLE I

Weightage to Objectives

Sl. No.	*Objectives*	*Marks (Weightage)*
K	Knowledge	15
U	Understanding	20
A	Application	10
S	Skill	5

In a unit there may be sub-topics. We may either test the whole unit or a sub-topic or there may be many units in the lesson which are to be tested. Each sub-unit or topic should be given some weightage as given in Table II for a unit in Child Development.

TABLE II

Sl. No.	*Content (Units)*	*Marks (Weightage)*
1.	Principles of growth and development and its significance	15
2.	Characteristics of childhood emotions	10
3.	Physical growth	15
4.	Motor development	10

Weightage to Type of Questions

The teacher should also decide how much weightage is to be given to different types of questions such as Essay, Short answer, and Objective type. More number of objective type questions could be asked to cover a larger area.

Sl. No.	*Type of Questions*	*No. of Questions*	*Marks*
1.	Objectivè type	20	20
2.	Short answer type	5	10
3.	Essay type	4	20

On the basis of knowledge of the above classification and analysis we can prepare a blue-print for the question paper.

Sl. No.	*Unit/Content*	*Knowledge Understanding*	*Application*	*Skill*	*Total*
		O S A E	O S A E	O S A E	O S A E
1.	Growth and Development				
2.	Physical Development				
3.	Motor Development				
4.	Emotional Development				
	Total				

In bracket the marks allotted for each question may be mentioned.

3

Conception, Prenatal Development and Birth

Evolution could have taken many courses with our species and other mammals, the requirement that there be a mother and father for conception being only one of them. Who knows, perhaps people could have evolved to self fertilize like some fungi or fission like bacteria. But this complex mammalian arrangement of mixing genes from two parents to produce an offspring appears to have evolved because it leads to diversification, and diversification gives a species better chances of surviving the natural selection process.

Conception

Conception or fertilization occurs when a father's sperm cell joins with a mother's egg cell, called an ovum. The ovum is much larger than the sperm. The sperm is, microscopic, while the ovum is about half the size of the period at the end of this sentence.

Conception typically takes place within one of the fallopian tubes, which are part of the female reproductive system. Sometimes though not often, an ovum is fertilized before it enters a fallopian tube or after it enters the uterus. The instant that a sperm penetrates an ovum, a special reduction occurs that immediately makes the ovum impervious to other sperm.

The probabilities vary from couple to couple, depending on the fertility of the woman and the sperm production of the man. If we assume that both partners are healthy the one variable that seems the most influential is the woman's age. It was found that the chances of becoming pregnant over a period of 12 menstrual cycles were 73 per cent for women aged 25 years or younger, 70 per cent for women aged

26 years to 30 years, 61 per cent for women aged 31 to 35 years, and 54 per cent for women over 35 years (Federation CECOS, Schwartz of Meraux, 1982).

The primary reason why older women conceive less frequently is that they often fail to ovulate. This most likely is due to changes in hormone levels associated with aging and the simple fact that the body's metabolism tends to slow down as we get older (Silberner, 1980).

The chance of conception is also influenced by the woman's ratio of body fat to lean tissue. Loss of fat owing to diet on exercise can lead to infertility which is restored once the fat is regained (Frisch, 1988). This particular mechanism probably evolved because of the survival advantages of preventing pregnancy during stressful times.

Multiple Births

Sometimes the new born has company, a twin brother or sister. Sometimes, although less often, the new born is just one of a crowd — triplets, quadruplets, or more.

A number of factors affect the probability of a multiple birth. Such a birth is more common among mothers between the ages of 35 and 39 years and among the mothers who have had previously, are more likely use to have a multiple birth in their current pregnancy.

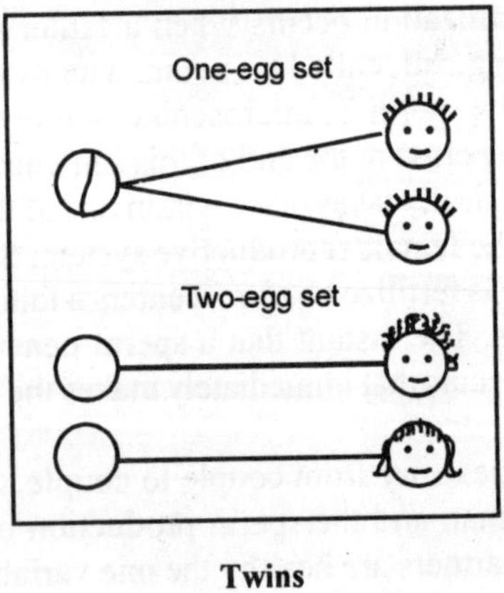

Twins

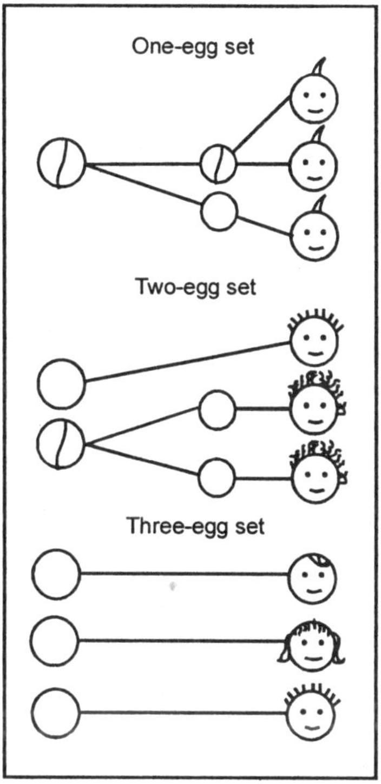

Triplets

Fraternal offspring result when two or more ova are fertilized separately. Identical offspring result when one zygote splits, fissions into two identical zygotes.

STAGES OF DEVELOPMENT

The Three Stages of Prenatal Development

The average length of pregnancy or gestation is 266 days. After fertilization and throughout the prenatal (gestational) period an immensely complicated genetic programme begins to direct the development of billions of specialized cells. The single fertilized cell quickly divides, grows and divides again. The three stages of prenatal development—germinal, embryonic and fetal are all marked by a rapid increases in the number of cells making up new being, which becomes increasingly complex.

The Period of the Ovum (Fertilization to 2 Weeks)

The ovum, once fertilized is called a zygote. Assuming that fertilization has occurred in a fallopian tube, it usually takes 3 to 4 days for the zygote to make its way to the uterus. By the time it reaches the uterus, the zygote has a fluid filled sphere called a blastocyst, the blastocyst may float unattached in the uterus for approximately 48 hours.

An inner cell mass then forms to one side of the interior to the blastocyst. This mass will begin to differentiate into two layers. The outside layer, or ectoderm, will later form the skin, teeth, hair, nails and nervous system of the fetus. The inner layer, or endoderm, will eventually develop most of the body organs. At a later time, a mesoderm or middle layer will develop eventually creating the muscles, the skeletal system, and the circulatory system.

Once the blastocyst enters the uterus, it attaches itself to the uterine wall, and a series of complex connections between the blastocyst and the mother's body begins to form. The trophoblast, which is the external cellular layer of the blastocyst, produces fine spindle like structures that penetrate the uterine epithelium or lining of the uterus and begins to develop nurturing connections with the mother's body. The time from conception until the blastocyst is attached within the uterus or womb, is called the period of the ovum, it lasts approximately 2 weeks.

The Period of the Embryo (2 to 8-12 Weeks)

The period of the embryo lasts from the time of the blastocyst's attachment to the uterine wall until the first occurrence of classification in the embryo. This period usually lasts from 2 weeks following fertilization to the eighth week.

Once implantation has occurred, the trophoblast, plays a very important role. It provides signals that tell the mother's body "a baby is forming" which in turn, trigger a protective 'dampening' response from her, preventing her antibodies from attacking the newly forming embryo (Foulkcal, & Billington, 1988).

Interestingly, about one out of every 300 women spontaneously abort, because their immune system does in fact attack the embryo. Researchers have discovered that such an occurrence is most likely if the father is genetically similar to the mother. In such a case, the trophoblast, which of course, is a combination of the father's and mother's genes, will appear only slightly different from the mother's own body cells.

This similarity may result in the failure of the mother's immune system to distinguish the trophoblast from the mother. If that happens, the mother's immune system may miss the initial "a baby is forming" message, because the message is too weak. If that message is not received, the mother's immune system will attack when it finally detects that something foreign is forming.

Doctors have been successful at helping such couples to have children by inoculating women with cells from their husbands, thereby sensitizing them to their husband's body cells, which in turn, makes them more sensitive to the trophoblast's 'a baby is forming' message (Sliberner, 1986).

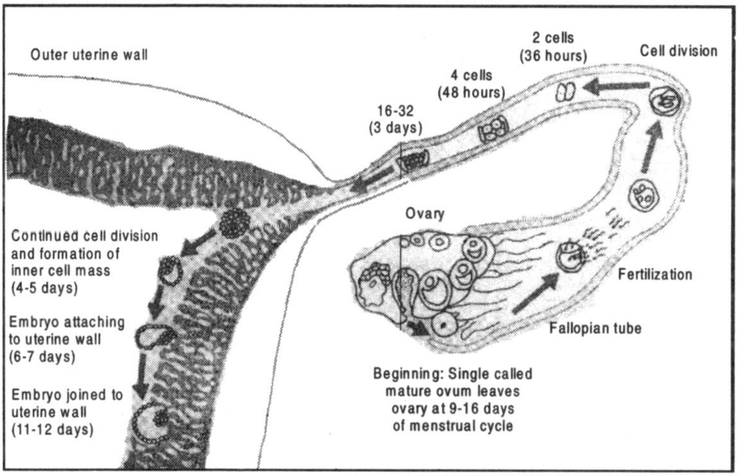

Period of Embryo

During the period of the embryo, cellular divisions continues at a very rapid rate, and cellular specialization occurs. Although each cell in a body carries the DNA blueprint for that entire body, during cellular specialization or differentiation, different portions of the DNA code in each cell becomes active, while other portions go dormant, depending on which kind of cell is to be created. The forces that determine how cells differentiate or specialize, are not fully understood. This specialization of cells, however, becomes apparent as skin, hair, sensory organs, a cartilage skeleton, a nervous system, a digestive system, a circulatory system, and other internal organs develop.

By the fourth week following conception, heart begins to pulse even though the embryo is approximately one inch long and is beginning to resembling a human-being.

As the embryo grows, additional by supporting auxiliary structures continue to develop. Among these are connection with the mother's body through which the embryo obtains nutrients and expels wastes. The umbilical cord placenta enroute to and from the mother's body. The placenta consists of a number of semi-permeable membranes that allow only molecules of relatively small size to pass. For this reason, the red blood cells of the mother and those of the unborn infant never mix prior to birth. This separation of blood is essential because the mother's blood type may be different from—and incompatible with—that of the embryo. Moreover, nutrients and wastes can pass through the placental barrier so a shared bloodstream is unnecessary.

During the period of the embryo, research has shown the spontaneous abortion rate to be relatively high. Approximately 31 per cent of all pregnancies and in spontaneous end in abortion. About two-third of the time, the women who undergo spontaneous abortion are unaware that they were ever pregnant, because the spontaneous abortion may seem to be nothing more than an unusually heavy flow during, menstruation.

It is assumed that the spontaneously aborted embryos are most often abnormal, not that there is something wrong with the women, because 95 per cent of women who have spontaneous abortions eventually have normal pregnancies.

The Period of the Fetus (8-12 Weeks to Birth)

From the time of ossification (approximately 8 weeks after conception) until birth, the developing prenatal organism is called a fetus.

Fetal Development

The period of the fetus is marked by continued and rapid growth of the specialized systems that emerged during the embryonic phase. Cellular differentiation is quite well advanced by the time ossification begins. As the fetus develops, the muscular and nervous system grow at great speed. Often before the twentieth week following conception, the mother is able to feel the fetus move. By the fifth month, reflexes such as swallowing or sucking occur.

By the end of the sixth month, the fetus is a little over foot long, and weighs almost 2 pounds, its skin is thin and there is, as yet, no underlying layer of fat. Fingerprints are visible, the eyelids have developed and become functional. As the fetus grows, it becomes more active (Darker and Rosen, 1982).

By the end of the seventh month of pregnancy, a layer of fat is deposited beneath the skin of the fetus. The fetus can easily respond to stimuli. Should a bright light be surgically passed into the womb, the fetus will close its eyes and perhaps block the light by shading its eyes with its hands. During this time ultra high frequency sound scans of a pregnant woman's womb may produce a moving image of the fetus sucking its thumb or even hiccupping. The most sensitive of these scanners can resolve objects as small as 1 millimetre in length, enabling physicians to see detail as fine as the pupil of the fetus's eye. The chance that a fetus will survive if born at this time is high.

By the end of the eighth month, the fetus is about 18 inches long and weighs about 5 pounds. Development of the brain is especially rapid. Most systems are matured but the lungs may still need more time in the womb.

By the end of the ninth month, the fetus becomes less active probably because it is feeling confined. The lungs are matured. The length of fetus is about 20 inches and the weight approximately 7½ pounds. The infant is now ready to be born.

ADVERSE INFLUENCES ON PRENATAL DEVELOPMENT

A number of adverse influences can seriously harm an unborn child. Psychologists are especially interested in these potential dangers because they may seriously affect the child's psychological development or upset the family or to social structure on which the child will have to depend. Unfortunately the reaction of others to a child's handicap can often be the most damaging result of any birth defect or disability because many of these dangers to the unborn can be prevented by changing parental behaviour, or by altering the environment, it is essential that prospective parents be made aware of them.

Often, though not always, the greatest burden lies with the mother because she has the greatest control over the intra-uterine environment, substances capable of producing fetal abnormalities are classified as teratogens.

Smoking

By smoking, the mother can create a dangerous environment for her unborn child. When a mother smokes carbon-monoxide level in her blood increase rapidly. The carrier molecule that normally takes oxygen across the placental barrier to the embryo or fetus will choose carbon-monoxide over oxygen whenever possible, and the unborn child will begin to suffocate. This lack of vital oxygen may result in damage to the fetus that is expressed later as a learning or memory deficit.

In addition to this danger from the carbon-monoxide, there is a threat if the 3,000 or so other chemicals contained in the smoke that enter the mother's body. One of the most serious of these is nicotine. Nicotine is vasoconstrictor, it causes constriction of the capillaries in the mother's body. This, in turn, further deprives the fetus of oxygen by reducing blood flow.

Maternal smoking may also affect the ability of the fetus' lungs to grow and mature children born to smoking mothers were found, even at the age of 5 years, to have lungs with significantly less capacity than children born to non-smoking mothers.

Smoking may contribute to the malformation of the heart or other organs in the fetus, increase chance of the placenta's separating, from the womb too soon and causing miscarraige. There are possibilities of sudden infant death.

If the father smokes, he may cause the mother to become a passive smoker as she will be living in the smoky environment that he has created. This may be a hazard to the fetus. Also smoking can effect sperm production. A significantly greater number of abnormal sperm were found among men who smoked than among non-smokers. Abnormally shaped sperm are less likely to be able to reach the ovum and fertilize it.

Alcohol

Intake of alcohol can endanger the embryo or fetus. Even a safe dosage for a mother may be a huge dose for an embryo, children may suffer from fetal alcohol syndrome, which is associated with facial, lungs or organ defects. They also exhibit abnormal behaviour pattern such as irritability, short attention span, or some of the repetition body motion's associated with autistic behaviour.

Alcohol consumed during pregnancy has also been found to affect adversely the developing brain of the fetus. The brain weight of the affected fetus is generally lower and specific areas in the brain may adversely be affected.

Alcohol can also damage the muscles of the fetus. Alcohol can cause the umbilical cord to construct, cutting off needed oxygen to the fetus (Altura *et al.* 1982)

Caffeine

The lower birth weight among infants whose mothers had been heavy coffee drinkers throughout their pregnancies. To be on the safe side, the pregnant women should probably avoid caffeine until the issue has been further clarified.

Other Drugs

Alcohol and nicotine are drugs, of course and so is caffeine. But there are many drugs introduced into the embryonic or fetal environment that may cause damage.

Mothers addicted to heroin or cocaine will give birth to infants. Similarly, many other common drugs, such as tranquilizers, antibiotics, and anticonvulsants, can seriously affect the unborn child. Researchers have concluded that pregnant women should avoid taking aspirin (which is an anticoagulant, a substance that hinders blood clotting) because of the danger of creating blood disorders in the fetus.

Some antibiotics, especially tetracycline and streptomycin, have also been found to cause damage to the embryo or fetus.

Anesthesia and Analgesia

During the few hours prior to birth, while the fetus is still attached to the respiratory and circulatory system of the mother, it is not uncommon for anesthetics or analgesics to be given to the mother to ease obstetrical pain. These pain killers may cross the placental barrier and cause a depression of the central nervous system in the fetus, making the fetus prone to anoxia (complete oxygen deprivation) and creating potential, source of dangerous complications. Many infants who were born of mothers who received pain-killing medication show no adverse effects but, because of the possible unwanted consequences, obstetricians and anesthesiologists use pain killing medications judiciously during delivery and often monitor fetal oxygen levels during labour via sensors passed to the scalp of the fetus through the birth canal.

Contraceptive Foams

Contraceptive jellies, foams and creams are spermicidal, that is, they are designed to kill sperm and are used to prevent pregnancy. It is not known whether the spermicidal agent damages the sperm that eventually fertilizes the egg or whether the agent is absorbed into the blood stream through which it somehow harm the embryo.

Environmental Hazards

During the last decade, people have become increasingly aware of the potential danger from environmental hazards such as radiation or pollution.

Chemical Waste

Inadequately managed chemical wastes can pervade an environment and make it unhealthy. Of course, pregnant women should not drink contaminated water or live neighbourhoods suspected of being contaminated, if they can avoid doing so, contact with contaminated water may lower a man's sperm count as well.

Heavy Metals

Heavy metals such as cadmium, mercury and lead have also been found to cause damage to the unborn. In small amounts, they can be quite harmful to the fetus. This is especially true for lead.

Heat

Overheat at 102°F (39°C) or 10 minutes at 106°F (41°C) is sufficient to cause fetal damage.

Radiation

Pregnant women in contact with X-rays or radioactive materials must be extremely cautious. As you can well imagine, given the rapid cell-division occurring in the Zygote, embryo or fetus, disruption by ionizing radiation can be especially hazardous.

Pathogens

Many disease processes can threaten the unborn child. Following up are some of those which cause the most concern.

Taxoplasmosis

One of the many common infections caused by microscopic parasites is taxoplasmosis. It is often found in humans and other mammals. It has a devoting effect on an unborn child's nervous system, often resulting in retardation, epilepsy, or blindness.

Viruses

Maternal contact with the rubella Virus (German Measles) can be disastrous for the fetus, especially during the first 3 months of pregnancy. Apparently, the virus interrupts some early development. Although the mother suffers only the mild symptoms of the disease, deaf or blind, contact with the virus later in the pregnancy does not usually result in such severe damage.

Rh Factor Incompatibility

Sometimes the disease process may be caused by genetics rather from external pathogens. One such example Rh factor incompatibility. 'Rh' stands for rhesus, the species of monkey in which this protein factor was first discovered. 85 per cent of population is Rh positive that is the factor exists in their blood. Positive is a dominant trait while negative is recessive. A problem may occur only if father is Rh positive and the mother is Rh negative. If, through a blood test, physicians are aware of the problem ahead of time, they may use drugs to minimize any damage from Rh incompatibility.

Maternal Diet

Malnourishment, as a single variable is quite difficult to separate from generally poor paternal care, poor sanitation and lack of adequate shelter. It leads to have children that weigh less at birth as well as poorly developed nervous system.

Emotional Stress

It is extremely difficult to evaluate the effects of the maternal emotional stress on the developing fetus because, it is too hard to eliminate this one factor from all the others associated with women under stress. Such as malnutrition, poor health, or drug use. It is known that stress in the mother stimulates the production of adrenaline which causes capillary constriction and diverts the blood flow from the uterus to other organs of the body, sufficient stress over enough time might conceivably deprive the fetus of needed oxygen and cause damage in that way.

THE BIRTH PROCESS

Labour and Delivery

For 9 months, the unborn child has been developing within the womb. Now the fetus is prepared to make an exit. One of the first mysterious in human life is precisely what mechanism triggers the contractions of the uterus to expel a fetus. Shortly before birth, the fetus usually rotates in to a head downward positions. This movement is referred to as lightening because it releases pressure on the mother's abdomen.

For women giving birth for the first time, labour will usually last between 12 and 24 hours, with an average of 14 hours. However, for women who have given birth before, labour usually averages only 6 hours.

The Phases of Childbirth

Childbirth or labour, takes place in three overlapping phases. The first stage is the longest, lasting an average 12 to 24 hours for a women having her first child. To this stage, uterine constrictions cause the cervix, the opening of the uterus, to widen until it becomes large enough for the baby's head to pass through. At first, the constrictions tend to be fairly mild. Towards the end of this stage, they become more severe and more uncomfortable, even though the mother's pituitary gland, secretes a painkiller, beta endorphin, which ceases the pain.

The second stage typically lasts about 1½ hours. It begins when the baby's head begins to move through the cervix and the vaginal canal, and it ends when the baby emerges completely from the mother's body. At the end of the second stage, the baby is born but is still attached by the umbilical cord to the placenta, which is inside the mother's body.

During the third stage, which lasts only a few minutes, the umbilical cord and the placenta are expelled. The placenta and other expelled materials are called the afterbirth.

Birth

During birth, the human fetus is forced through the birth canal under extreme pressure and is intermittently deprived of oxygen. During this time, the baby secretes the hormones adrenaline and noradrenaline, collectively classified as catecholamines, at levels that are higher than they are likely to be at any other time throughout its life. Adrenaline helps to open up the lungs, to dry out the bronchi and thus to achieve the switch from a liquid to an air environment, noradrenaline which is especially prevalent slows the heart beat, enabling the fetus to withstand fairly lengthy oxygen deprivation.

Natural and Prepared Child-Birth

Natural child-birth which involves educating women in the physiology of reproduction and delivery and training them in breathing, relaxation and physical fitness, that seeks to prevent pain by eliminating the mother's fear of child-birth. An anxious, frightened women in labour tenses muscles, throughout her body, including those of the uterus. This turns the mild pain that sometimes accompanies strong contractions into a great deal of pain.

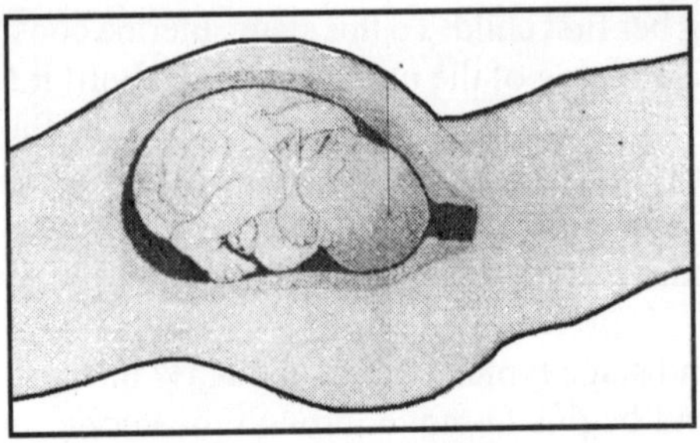

(a) First stage

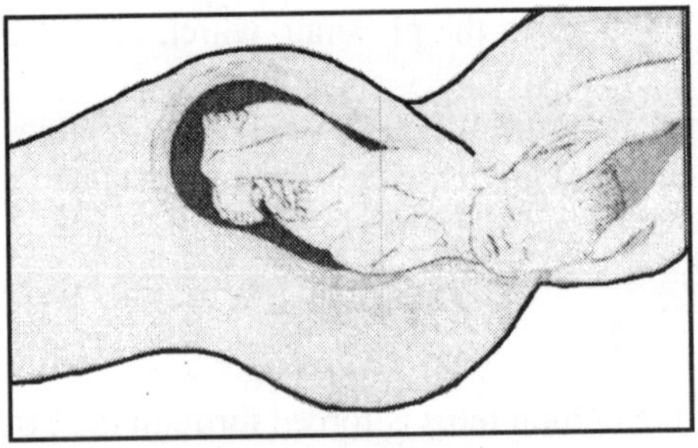

(b) Second stage

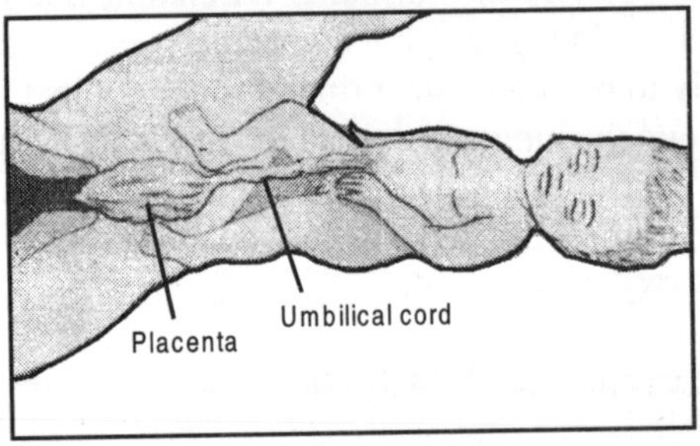

(c) Third stage

Gentle-Birth

The controversial technique of gentle-birth sometimes called the laboyer method, after its developer, involves delivering babies in dimly lit, quiet rooms. No forceps are used, and the umbilical cord is not clamped immediately. No anesthesia or only a local anesthetic, is used. The baby is bathed in warm water and calmly placed on the mother's belly right after birth such practices eliminate much birth trauma and result in happier mothers and babies.

Breech Birth

About 97 per cent of babies are born in the head-first position. However, 2.4 per cent are born rump first, this is called a breech birth. During a breech birth, great care must be taken to avoid damage to the baby's head which is largest and most difficult part of the infant's body to pass through the birth canal.

Cesarean delivery which is a surgical procedure to remove the baby from the uterus, without passing through the vaginal canal the operation is commonly performed when labour is not progressing as quickly as it should, often because the baby is in the breech position. (from which legs or buttocks would emerge before the head) or in the transverse position (lying crosswise in the uterus). It is also done, when the baby's head is too big to pass through the mother's pelvis, the baby seems to be in trouble or the mother is bleeding vaginally.

Also, if the mother has had a cesarean delivery before, her next delivery will probably be by cesarean. Only 5 per cent who have had cesareans have vaginal deliveries afterward.

Instrument Delivery

Forceps, metal clamps placed around the baby's head to pull the infant from the birth canal, have been used since the sixteenth century to speed up delivery. A more recent instrument the vacuum extractor, consists of a plastic cup (placed on the baby's head) attached to a suction tube. Instrument delivery is appropriate if the mother's pushing during the second stage of labour does not cause the baby to move through the birth canal in a reasonable period of time. When a doctor uses forceps (or) vacuum extractions, to pull the baby through the birth canal, deliveries are associated with higher rates of brain damage. As a result, neither method should be used when the mother can still be encouraged to deliver normally and there is no special reason to hurry the birth.

Induced Labour

An induced labour is one that is started artificially. This is usually done by breaking the amnion or bag of waters, and giving the mother synthetic oxytocin, a hormone involved in stimulating contractions. The contractions are longer, harder and closer together, and there is a greater chance of instrument delivery.

Birth Complications

Mothers who are in poor health, who do not receive good medical care, or who have a history of pregnancy problems—are especially likely to experience birth complications.

Inadequate oxygen, a pregnancy that ends too early, and a baby who is born underweight are serious complications. Another risk factor is a pregnancy in which the baby remains in the uterus too long.

Oxygen Deprivation

The oxygen deprivation caused by prenatal damage to the baby's respiratory system, or it may have happened because the infant's lungs were not yet mature enough to breathe. For example, infants born more than 6 weeks early commonly have a disorder called respiratory distress syndrome (otherwise known as hyaline membrane disease). Their tiny lungs are so poorly developed that the air sac collapse, causing serious breathing difficulties and sometimes death. Today, mechanical ventilators keep many such infants alive.

Cerebral palsy, which is a general term for a variety of problems that result from brain damage before, during or just after birth. Difficulties in muscle co-ordination are always involved, such as a clumsy walk, uncontrolled movements, and unclear speech. The disorder can range from very mild tremors to severe crippling accompanied by mental retardation. Many youngsters experienced anoxia, or inadequate oxygen supply, during labour and delivery.

Pre-Term and Low-Birth-Weight Infants

Babies born 3 weeks or more before the end of a full 38 week pregnancy or who weigh less than 5½ pounds (2,500 grams) have for many years been referred to as 'pre-mature'. A wealth of research indicates that premature babies are at risk for many problems. Frequent illness, visual impairments, inattention overactivity, low intelligence test scores and school learning problems are some of the difficulties that extend into the childhood years.

Post-Term Infants

The normal length of pregnancy is 38 weeks. Infants born after 42 weeks are post-terms. Most of these late arriving new borns are quite normal. However, a small number start to lose weight at the end of pregnancy because the placenta no longer functions properly. The possibility of oxygen deprivation and head injuries.

The New-Born

The first four weeks of life mark the neonatal period, a time of transition from intrauterine life — when the fetus is supported entirely by its mother — to an independent existence.

An average new-born or neonate, is about 20 inches long and weighs about 7½ pounds and measures between 18 and 22 inches in length. In their first few days, neonates lose as much as 10 per cent of body weight, because of a loss of fluids. On about the fifth day, they begin to gain, and usually they are back to birth weight by the tenth to fourteenth day.

All new-born babies are covered with vernix caseosa, an oily protection against infection that dries over a few days time. Sleep dominates the neonatal period. Newborn have about six to eight hours sleep period.

As babies become more awake, alert and active, they develop according to their own unique patterns.

4

Physical Development

Physical development refers to increase in bodily tissue. Generally, it denotes height and weight and weight changes, changes in body proportion, bone growth, muscular development and development of nervous system.

Even casual observation reveals that the first two or three years of life are a period of very rapid growth for the human organism. Though many use the two terms growth and development interchangeably, there is a distinct difference between the two.

Growth means increase of body tissue, specifically, it refers to increase in height and weights. It is the quantitative change occurring in the body.

Development. According to Hurlock, development is a progressive series of orderly, coherent changes leading towards the goal of maturity. The term progressive indicates that development is always forward. The term orderly and coherent suggests that there is a definite relationship between a given stage and the stages which have preceded or followed it. It also suggests that development follows an orderly pattern and not haphazard.

STAGES OF DEVELOPMENT

Human life span upto pre-school years has been divided into certain major development stages: (*i*) Infancy, (*ii*) Babyhood, (*iii*) Early childhood. In each of these stages individuals undergo mainly four kinds of developmental changes. They include physical and motor, emotional and cognitive (mental) changes. Description of physical development in each of the life stages upto 6 years is as follows:

Infancy

The baby during the first fifteen days is known as neonate. The physical development of neonate are as follows:

Neonate: The average weight of the new born in India is six pounds (2.87 kg); but weight may range from 3 to 12 pounds. Boys are heavier and larger than girls. Variability in birth weight is dependent upon many factors like maternal diet, economic status of the family, ordinal position of the child, sex etc. The average length of the neonates is about 18 inches.

Physical Proportions

The physical proportions of the infant differ greatly from those of the adult. The infant's head is about one-fourth of the entire body length, while in the adult it is one-seventh. The arms, legs and trunk are small in relation to the head. The abdominal region of the trunk is large and bulging, while the shoulders are narrow.

Babyhood

For the first two weeks, the baby is known as a neonate and infant. From then on, until he completes his second year, he is referred to as a baby. Hurlock calls these period the period of babyhood. There is a lot of changes in the baby between the new-born stage and the time he completes his second years. The new-born is quite helpless and is totally dependent on others. But by two years, he can do a number of activities and is less dependent than before. His development is quite rapid during the period of babyhood.

Patterns of Physical Development During Babyhood

Weight

At the age of four months, the baby's weight has normally doubled. At one year, babies' weight, on the average, three times as much as they did at birth or approximately 21 pounds. At the age of two, increase in weight during babyhood comes mainly from an increase in fat tissue.

Height

At four months, the baby measures between 23 and 24 inches, at one year, between 28 and 30 inches, and at two years between 32 and 34 inches.

Physical Proportions

Head growth slows down in babyhood, while trunk and limb growth increases. Thus the baby gradually becomes less top-heavy and appears more slender and less chunky by the end of babyhood.

Bones

The number of bones increases during babyhood. Ossification begins in the early part of the first year, but is not completed until puberty. The fontanel, or soft spot on the skull, has closed in approximately 50 per cent of all babies by the age of eighteen months, and in almost all babies by the age of two years.

Muscles and Fat

Muscle fibres are present at birth, but in very undeveloped forms. They grow slowly during babyhood and are weak. By contrast, fat tissue develops rapidly during babyhood, partly due to the high fat content of milk, the main ingredient in a baby's diet.

Body Builds

During the second year of life, as body proportions change, babies begin to show tendencies toward characteristic of body builds. The three most common forms of body build are ectomorphic, which tends to be long and slender, endomorphic, which tends to be round and fat, and mesomorphic which tends to be heavy, hard and rectangular.

Teeth

The average baby has four to six of the twenty temporary teeth by the age of one and sixteen by the age of two. The first teeth to cut through are those in the front, the last to appear are the molars. The last four of the temporary teeth usually erupt during the first year of childhood.

Nervous System

At birth, brain weight is one-eighteenth of the baby's total weight. Gain in brain weight is greatest during the first two years of life, thus accounting for the baby's top-heavy appearance. The cerebellum, which plays an important role in body balance and postural control, triples in weight during the first year of postnatal life. This is true also for the cerebrum. Immature cells, present at birth continue to develop after birth but relatively few new cells are formed.

Development of Sense Organs

By the age of three months, the eye muscles are well-enough coordinated to enable babies to see things clearly and distinctly and the cones are well developed to enable them to see colours. Hearing develops rapidly during this time. Smell and taste, which are well developed at birth, continue to improve during babyhood. Babies are highly responsive to all skin stimuli because of the thin texture of their skin and because all sense organs relating to touch, pressure, pain and temperature are present in well-developed forms.

Early Childhood

This is an important period in the life of an individual. Physical development is an important aspect of development because it influences child's behaviour both directly and indirectly. Directly, it determines what the child can do and indirectly, it influences his attitude towards himself and others. Abnormal physical development tends to develop a feeling of awkwardness and inferiority.

Height and Weight

The average annual increase in height is three inches. By the age of six, the average child measures 46.6 inches. Because, on the whole, the height and weight increase is slower than that of infancy. The average annual increase in weight is 3 to 5 pounds. At age six, children should weigh approximately seven times as much as they did at birth.

The average girl weighs 48.5 pounds, and the average boy weighs 40 pounds.

Body Proportions

Body proportions change markedly, and the "baby look" disappears. Facial features remain small but the chin becomes more pronounced and the neck elongates. There is a gradual decrease in the stockiness, of the trunk, and the body tends to become cone-shaped, with a flattened abdomen, a broader and flatter chest, and shoulders that are broader and more square. The arms and legs lengthen and may become spindly, and the hands and feet grow bigger.

Body Build

Differences in body build become apparent for the first time in early childhood. Some children have an endomorphic or flabby, fat body build, some have a mesomorphic or sturdy, muscular body build, and some have an ectomorphic or relatively thin body build.

Bones and Muscles

The bones ossify at different rates in different parts of the body, following the laws of developmental direction. The muscles become larger, stronger, and heavier, with the result that children look thinner as early childhood progresses, even though they weigh more.

Fat

Children who tend toward endomorphy have more adipose than muscular tissue, those who tend toward mesomorphy have more muscular than adipose tissue, and those with an ectomorphic build small muscles and little adipose tissue.

Development of Teeth

During the first four to six months of early childhood, the last four baby teeth – the back molars erupt. During the last half year of early childhood, the baby teeth begin to be replaced by permanent teeth. The first to come out are the front central incisors – the first baby teeth to appear when early childhood ends, the child generally has one or two permanent teeth in front and some gaps where permanent teeth will eventually erupt.

ROLE OF PRE-PRIMARY SCHOOL AND THE TEACHER IN PROMOTING PHYSICAL DEVELOPMENT

Pre-primary school provides much opportunity for developing large and small muscles of children. The child is helped to perfect his ability to walk, run, jump and climb and to develop new skills. It provides infrastructural facilities, equipment and guidance towards physical development.

For the development of the large muscle the teacher provides opportunity for playing on the ladder, slide, swing, and jungle gym. Children climb, jump, hop and run. Through these activities their large muscles and pelvic girdle develop. See-saw, Balancing Board, tricycle, scooters, etc. help him to acquire balance. Children are engaged in rolling, somersaulting, hopping, catching and throwing ball, skipping, walking, boxing and other such activities in the playground. Children learn graceful movements from these activities. Besides development of large muscle, coordination, of the finer muscles and eye-hand coordination of the muscles also result from these activities. Other outdoor activities including sand box-play, gardening, caring for pets in the pet corner, field trips also help in large muscles, small muscle and eye-hand coordination.

Indoor activities like playing musical instruments, dramatization, threading the beads, easel painting, pasting, crayoning, cutting, rhythmic exercises, dancing and block building help in the small muscles development, muscular control and coordination of eye-hand and the muscles.

Providing snacks and lunch in pre-primary school help and promote physical development. The nutritional needs of children are partly satisfied by the snack and lunch provided at pre-primary school.

The teacher should carefully plan the activities for promoting physical development of children. The teacher has the responsibility of providing suitable and safe equipment. Also, she should see that the equipment are in good condition. She should supervise these activities so that children do not meet with accidents and are benefited maximum.

EQUIPMENT FOR PHYSICAL DEVELOPMENT

As we have seen already equipment play a major role in physical development of pre-primary school children. Let us examine them in detail how each equipment helps, in promoting physical development of children.

Outdoor Equipment

Jungle Gym: This may be made of wood or iron. This enables children to climb and jump. Sometimes sliding arrangements are also provided in the jungle gym which promotes balancing.

Slide: Slide enables children practice climbing and sliding.

Swing: Children learn sense of movement and have a feeling of what it is to rise high from ground level. Children also overcome fear of being in high places.

See-Saw: A sense of rhythm and balance are achieved while playing in see-saw. Leg muscles are strengthened.

Sand Pit: Play in sand pit helps in finer muscular development. Children, make use of fine muscles in the sand pit. Hence eye-hand coordination and finer muscle are strengthened.

Gardening: Children do digging, watering, and planting. These activities give exercise both to large muscles and finer muscles of the body.

Water Play: Children play with floating toys, handle water. Eye-hand coordination, large muscles and fine muscular development are facilitated, through water play.

Tricycle and Scooter: The leg muscles are strengthened by these play equipments.

Pet Corner: Children enjoy to see and to feed animals in the pet corner.

Playing with Balls: Throwing and catching the balls of various sizes balancing the body, etc. provide ample opportunity for large and finer muscle development and eye-hand coordination.

Walking-boards: Sense of rhythm and balance is promoted by the activity of walking on the walking boards.

Rocking Toys: Rocking toys also help to promote sense of balance and rhythm.

Indoor Play Equipment

Indoor play materials and equipment mainly cater to eye-hand coordination and finer muscle development and coordination.

The following indoor equipments promote finer muscular co-ordination and eye-hand co-ordination as well.

Blocks, puzzles, form boards, clay, plasticine, musical instruments, picture books, dolls, crayons, chalk pieces, easel board, and brush, beads, scissors, stencils, slate and pencil, etc.

ACTIVITIES FOR PROMOTING PHYSICAL DEVELOPMENT

Running: In the beginning, running is a little more difficult task than walking. The child runs clumsily and with uneven steps. He falls many times before reaching the target. By the age of 5 to 6 years, the child is also able to adjust his speed and can turn corners.

Jumping: By his fourth birth day, the child can jump from a height of about 12 inches and make a standing jump from a height of about 23 to 33 inches. Jumping over obstacles is difficult for a 4 year-old-child. The five-year-old has no difficulty in running over obstacles. Between the 5th and 6th year most children can jump rope.

Skipping and Hopping: Skipping and hopping are modification of jumping. Hopping on two feet precedes hopping on one. While children attempt to hop before they are 3 years old, they are not skillful until 9 or 7. Most children can hop for short distances around four years, but it is not until they are about six years that they are proficient in hopping.

Skipping is more difficult than hopping. Few children can skip well at the age of 16.

Climbing: Even before the boy can walk, he climbs steps by crawling and creeping. Before a child is two years old, he can climb upstairs and downstairs by holding the railing of the stairs or the hand of a person. The adult manner of step-climbing where the child uses his legs alternately is attained by four years of age if the child has adequate opportunities to learn.

Tricycling and Bicycling: By the age of two years, very few children can ride tricycles. Between 3 and 4, all who have an opportunity to learn can do so. After achieving a skilled performance, children use their tricycles for stunting. By the time the child is 6, the child can ride a bicycle.

Swimming: Learning opportunities play a vital role in determining how soon a child will acquire swimming skills. Few children learn to swim before the age of four years, if the opportunity is provided.

Ball Throwing and Catching: The ability to throw and catch balls requires well-coordinated movements, not only of the arms and hands, but of the entire body and a fine sense of balance. Each at 4, a child may find it difficult to throw well. By 6 years, most children are proficient, though there are marked variation in the skill at every age.

Ball catching is likewise difficult. At 4 years, few children are proficient, while at 6, approximately two-thirds are proficient. In the beginning the child uses his whole body to catch the ball, then he uses his arms, with less random movement. Later, he perfects a coordinated movements of the hands to catch the ball between the palms.

Self-feeding: By the end of the second year, the child tries to eat food by himself. During early years he spills most of the food. By 5 years he can feed himself like an adult.

Self-dressing: The period of most rapid improvement in dressing is between 1½ and 3½ years. By the time the child is 5 years old, he is capable of dressing himself completely. Eye-hand coordination is necessary until the child learns to dress himself. Afterwards he can dress himself without much effort.

Self-grooming: Grooming skills develop along with dressing skill. By the time he reaches 5 years of age, he should be able to comb his hair successfully.

Handwriting: Upto one year the child just scribbles in the middle of a big paper. On the average, the baby is not biologically ready for handwriting before he is six year old. Until that age, the nerves and muscles of the fingers, hand, wrist and arm are not developed and matured enough to make the fine co-ordinations needed in holding a pencil or pen to write. At four years, he can write his name in capital letters. At six years, he can write if opportunity is provided to him to learn the alphabets.

Copying: Copying requires not only control over the finer muscles of the hand and arm but also the ability to perceive relationships. Between the ages of 2½ and 5 years, most children show consistent improvement in their ability to copy simple geometric figures.

Handedness: The preferred use of one hand over the other in day-to-day activities is called handedness. This is believed to be established in early childhood.

PHYSICAL AND MOTOR DEVELOPMENT

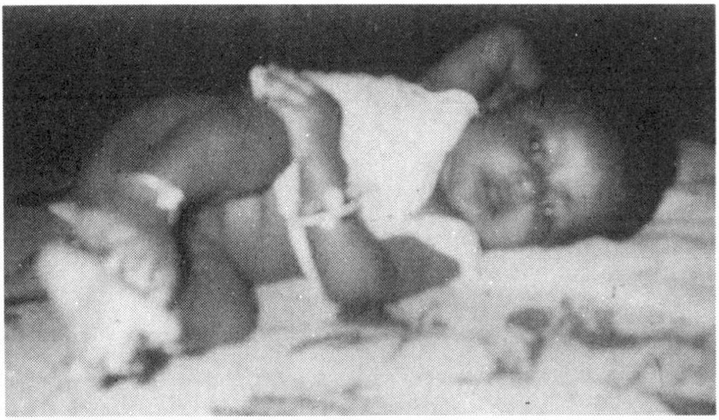

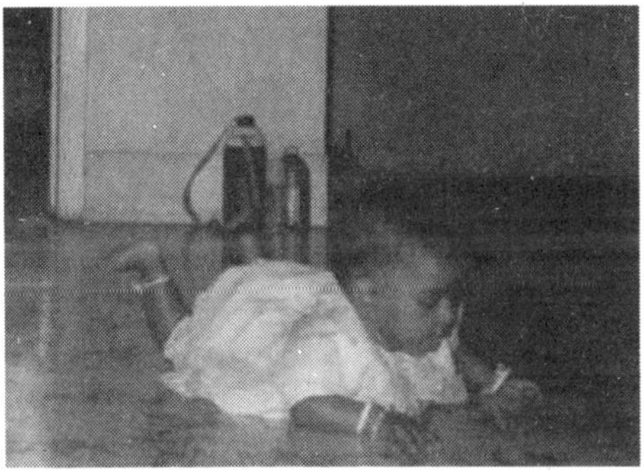

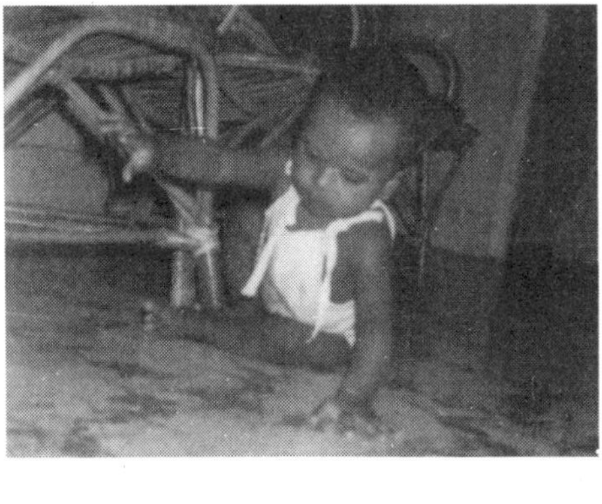

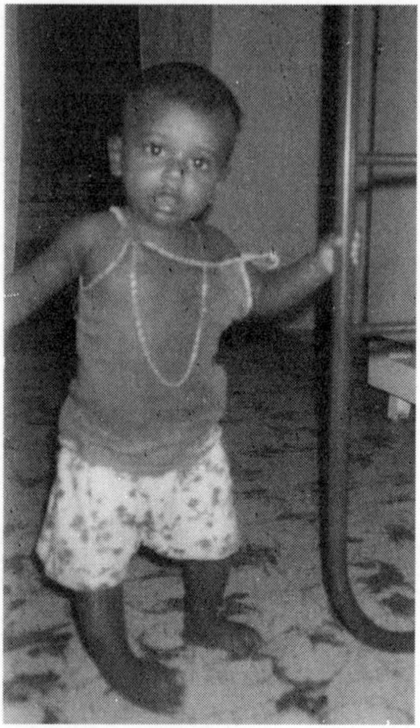

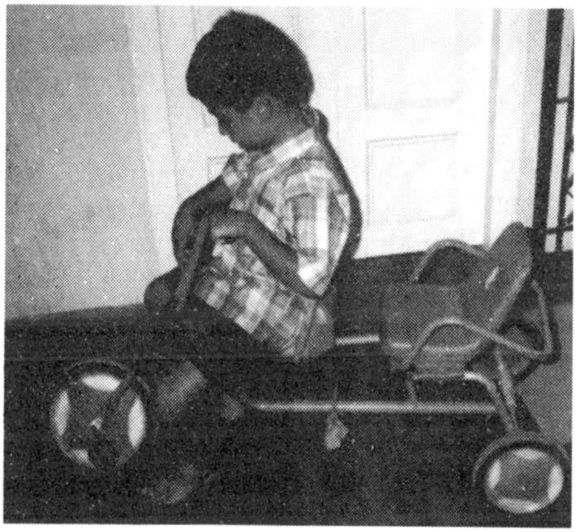

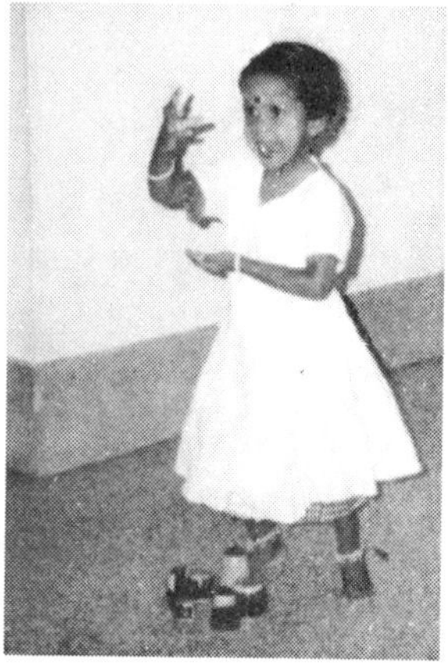

5

Motor Development

The first five years of life are largely concerned with the elaboration of native reactions into a large variety of gross and fine motor skills. The interesting variety of gross and fine motor skills. The interesting feature about the development of these complex movements is that their automatization increases rather than lessens their adaptability to new demands. The rate of improvement in any skill depends to a great extent on the capacity of the organism to anticipate the actual response by appropriate compensatory postural adjustments. Postural skills once acquired and mechanized not only permit greater freedom for adjustments to new situations but serve as an essential preparation for the development of the higher, more refined skills of later years. Writing, for example, is a highly specialized activity which can be successfully undertaken only when certain earlier acquired skills such as fine prehension and sitting balance are so well mechanized that they do not interline with the written activity.

MOTOR CHARACTERISTICS OVER DIFFERENT PERIODS

Four Weeks Old

The 4 weeks old infant when awake lies on his back with head averted, usually to a preferred side. Only momentarily does he bring his head to a mid position. Almost invariably his arm is extended on the side toward which his head is turned. The opposite arm is flexed with the hand resting near or in the head-chest region. This combination of averted head, extended arm, the flexed arm is the so-called tonic-neck-reflex attitude, which dominates the walking life of the infant for some twelve weeks.

Occasionally the 4 week-old infant bursts into startle responses, his head coming momentarily to the mid-line and all his extremities extending abruptly. Occasionally he lashes the air with more or less symmetric windwill movements of the arms. But the symmetric tonic-neck-reflex attitude underlies most of his postural behaviour. Indeed, the tonic-neck-reflex is part of the ground plan of the total reaction system. In partial form it was present parentally, helping the foetus to accommodate to the outline of the utterine cavity. At 16 weeks, it gives way to more symmetric patterns of behaviour, but it is a pre-condition for the growth of these later patterns.

Sixteen Weeks Old

The tonic-neck-reflex is losing its say. The head is more mobile and comes more frequently to the mid-line. Arms and hands likewise, for their movements are in large part correlated with or even controlled by the position of the head and of the eyes.

The dozen directing muscles of the eyes have made enormous gains in the preceding twelve weeks, by virtue of an increasing network of neuro connections. Tiny as these muscles are, the grosser muscles of posture and prehension are becoming obedient to them. Accordingly, a ring dangled before the infant's eye evokes massive movements of incipient approach involving head, shoulders, and arms.

Legs and feet have a very subsidiary status, but there are anticipations of their future responsibilities. When the infant is held in the supported standing position, he extends his legs recurrently and sustains a fraction of his weight.

Trunk musculature is organizing. He enjoys propped-by-pillow sitting, and he enjoys holding up his head which no longer needs a prop. He likes to look around adaptively. This is a good illustration, by the way, of how a single behaviour item (head control) may have a two-fold significance one motor, and adaptive.

Twenty-Eight Weeks Old

The 28-weeks old infant is chronologically and developmentally at a halfway stage on the way to a full attainment of the upright posture. At 56 weeks he will stand quite alone; at 28 weeks he sits alone, erecting his trunk perhaps for a whole minute.

With this improved sedentary balance his prehensory approach upon objects becomes bilateral. He reaches for a cube promptly on sight, he grasps it with tilted hand, thumb participating in the seizure. He transfers the cubes from one hand to other and retransfers. This alternating one-handedness marks a significant motor gain over the bilaterality of 16 weeks.

Gross muscular adjustments are more advanced than finer muscular adjustments. He can perceive a string, but is inept at plucking it. He gives consistent regard to a pellet but places his hand rather crudely over it and usually fails to secure it.

Forty Weeks Old

Forty weeks marks the beginning of the fourth quarter of the first year. The most distal outposts of the organism are being incorporated into the expanding nervous system—tongue tip, finger tips, and toes. In the first quarter, mouth and eyes, in the second quarter, head, neck, arm, shoulders, in the third quarter, trunk, arms and hands; in the fourth quarter, legs, fingers, feet, such is the general order of advance of neuro-motor maturation and of functional emancipation.

His leg now sustains his entire weight, although independent balance will not come until the end of the year. Sitting equilibrium, however, is mastered. While sitting he can turn to the side, lean at varying angles and recover balance. He can shift from sitting to prone and prone to sitting posture. When prone he retrogresses, rocks, or creeps.

Prehension shows new refinements; the index finger and thumb exhibit a specialized extension and mobility for poling, probing, and plucking.

One Year Old

The one year-old child can creep, often with great alacrity. He may creep on hands and knees, or on all fours in full plantigrade fashion. Inspite of his creeping expertness he is under an irrepressible impulse to rise to his two feet and once he has assumed the full plantigrade of attitude, he is almost ready for standing alone. He can pull himself to standing position unassisted, but ordinarily he does not achieve independent equilibrium. Until he is four weeks older. He cruises sidewise as he holds to a support; he walks but not without support. His prehensory patterns are approaching adult facility. His fine prehension is deft and precise, and he has almost acquired the capacity of voluntary release. The flexor or gripping component of prehension is now off set by an inhibitory extensor component of release. A comparable inhibitory control makes it possible for him to release a ball with a throwing thrust.

Eighteen Months Old

The most conspicuous difference between One and Eighteen is postural. Eighteen has gained at least a partial command of his legs, while one can barely stand without holding onto something for support. At 15 months, the infant can attain a standing position quite independently; but not until 36 months does he have sufficient balance to stand on one foot. Eighteen hurries with a stiff, propulsive, flat gait, which is not true running but which is better than walking or toddling. He can sit himself on a child's chair with fairly accurate aim; he can climb into an adult chair. With help he can walk up stairs. He descends stairs unassisted, by the bump method, or he creeps down backward. But in floor locomotion he rarely resorts to creeping. For sometime he has been able to push a chair around; now he can pull a wheeled toy as he walks. Such feats are quite beyond one who still travels best on all fours or on hands and knees, and has not yet fully attained the erect posture. But even during his first steps one may hold a toy as a sure gait support, thus bringing manual and postural behaviour patterns into early co-ordination.

Manually Eighteen is deft enough to place one cube upon another on the first attempt. His prehensory release, however, is exaggerated and it takes repeated trials to build a tower of three. One can hold a single cube in one hand while he grasps for another, he may briefly poise one cube over another. But his adaptive release is crude; so he rarely makes a tower although he can, after a manner, "drop" a cube into a cup. Eighteen can throw a ball, whereas one rolls, projects, or flings it by a simple extensor thrust. Eighteen's elbow is more versatile and he can turn the pages of a book, albeit he seizes two or three folios with each sweep.

Two Years Old

Two years old child is decidedly motor-minded. His most numerous and characteristics satisfactions are muscular. He greatly enjoys gross motor activity. In this respect, he is like eighteen, but he has made important advances in postural control. Two is more flexible at the knees and ankles has a better balance and consequently can run, while Eighteen propels himself with a wobbly, stiff, flat gait. Two no longer needs personal assistance in walking up and down stairs, but he has to shift into "marking time" at each tread. He can jump down from the first tread without help, one foot leading the other as he leaps. He can walk upto a ball and kick it on command. (Eighteen simply walks up to the ball). He can hasten his steps without long equilibrium, but he cannot yet dart about, making short turns and sudden stops.

In his tastes, the 2 year old is to a great extent an acrobat, for he delights in rough and tumble play, both solitary and responsive. Joyful emotions he is likely to express, with dancing, jumping, clapping of hands, screeching, and deep seated laughter. His fundamental muscles tingle with kinesthesia.

His accessory muscles, however, are by no means idle. He can whistle his thumb and his tongue. He likes to talk even when he obviously has nothing to say either to himself or to others. He "burbleson" with his new-found words as once he prattled in the crib and for comparable neuro-motor reasons. His oral musculature has matured. Eighteen masticates with effortful attention; Two, almost automatically.

Manual control has similarly advanced. Eighteen turns the pages of a book, with swift sweeps, a few pages at a time; Two turns them page by page with modulated control and with improved release. Eighteen builds a tower of three. Two builds a tower of six blocks. This is a mathematical index of the advance which has been made in fine motor coordination, both in the flexors of grasp and the extensors of release. Eighteen can not cut with a scissors. Two can skip. He can string beads with a needle. Eighteen holds a glass of milk with two hands and somewhat precariously; Two holds it securely (often with one hand) and even nonchalantly, although the free hand remains poised in sympathetic tension. The spoon is filled excessively as at 18 months but not until it is well in the mouth. Two sizes the handle with thumb and radial fingers and holds it supinely (palm up) as well as by overhead grasp. Two also remains seated for longer periods in a chair. By these fundamental motor tokens he certifies to an increasing readiness for domestic acculturation.

Three Years Old

Three like Two enjoys gross motor activity, but less exclusively so.

He indulges in sedentary play for longer periods; he likes to use crayons and is interested in finer manipulations of play materials. He will for example, work persistently at a puzzle box which imprisons a ball. And, having attained the ball, he prefers to re-solve the puzzle rather than to play with the ball. This reflects a change in motor interests, for two would prefer to play with the ball.

Both in spontaneous and imitative drawings. Three shows an increased capacity to inhibit and delimit movement. His strokes are better defined, less diffuse, and less repetitive. Although he will not draw a man until he is 4 years old, he may make controlled marks, which reveal a growing motor discriminativeness. In tower building, likewise, he shows increased control. Two builds a tower of six or seven, three builds a tower of nine or ten cubes. This increased command of coordinations in the vertical direction is apparently due to the maturation of new neuro-motor equipment, rather than to a prolongation of attention span. Although he has increased control of coordinations in the vertical and horizontal planes, he is curiously input in oblique planes. He can fold a piece of paper lengthwise and crosswise, but not diagonally, even with the aid of a model. A similar inaptitude shows itself in imitative drawing. Nature has not yet matured the requisite neuro-motor girders for oblique movement.

Three is more save and nimble on his feet. He runs with more smoothness; accelerates, and decelerates with greater ease, turns sharper corners, negotiates sudden stops. He can jump down from the bottom freed with both feet together, whereas Two leaps down with one foot leading. Three likewise can jump upward with both feet as much as twelve inches. Three pedals tricycle, while Two and Two and-a-half ride a mere kiddykar with primitive propulsion. An improved sense of balance, as well as the cephalocaudal advance, account for the new attainments. There is less sway and toddle in the gait of Three and he is much nearer to mastery of the upright posture; he can stand on one foot for a precarious second or more.

Four Years Old

Four is a more facile runner than Three. He is also more able to break up the regular rhythms of his stride. He can make a fair running, broad jump and a standing broad jump. Three's jump is usually limited to a downward and upward leap—another instance in which the motor command of the vertical dimension proceeds command of the horizontal. Four can also skip, at least after a lame duck fashion. But he cannot-much less hop-skip-jump in sequence. He can however, maintain a one legged equilibrium much longer than can Three. He can balance himself on one foot for several seconds, and usually in another half-year he can hop.

Four likes to try motor which are not too difficult. He enjoys accomplishment. This well-defined interest in feats and tasks is a somewhat new developmental symptom, which offers a clue to the psychology of the 4 year old.

He finds pleasure in feats of fine coordination well. He can take a knitting-needle spear and thrust it with well-directed aim into a small hole, smiling with success. He can button his clothes and lace his shows with ease. He gestures with more refinement and precision. In his drawing he may give concentrated attention to the representation of an isolated detail.

Five Years Old

Five is more agile than Four and more controlled in general bodily activity. Five has a more mature sense of balance, which makes him seem more sure and less given to caution on the playground.

Four can skip in a lame duck manner. Five skips smoothly and jumps as well. He conducts himself with more self-reliant abandon. He can stand on one foot and even balance himself on his toes for several seconds or more.

These tokens of motor maturity, including a well-developed sense of equilibrium and an increased social adaptability, make Five a more ready pupil than Four in the teaching of dancing and of physical exercises and evaluations.

His spontaneous postural demeanor gives an impression of relative finish and completeness, under wholesome conditions his postural attitudes show natural grace. Ease and economy of movement are present in his finer co-ordinations as well. He can placket a dozen pellets one by one and drop them deftly into a bottle in about twenty seconds, typically with a preferred hand.

Five, in comparison with Four, shows greater precision and command of tools. Five can wield a brush for his teeth and a comb for his hair; he can wash his face. Four needs much more supervision than Five in these domestic activities. Five also dawdles less, party because of his greater motor maturity.

Five likewise wields a crayon with greater assurance and definitiveness. He draws a recognizable man. He has difficulty with the obliques required in the copying of a diamond, but he is quite equal to copying a square and a triangle. He shows interest and some competence in washing dishes. He keeps better time to music when he dances. Such motor abilities suggest that the neuro-motor system is now well advanced in its development. Musical prodigies may approach an adult level of motor virtuosity as early as the fifth year.

Activities for Large Motor Skills

Walking, Jumping off, on and over, Running, Climbing, Crawling, Sliding, Bouncing, Rolling, Stepping on and over, Boundaries.

Things to be Done for Large Motor Skills

(*a*) Provide opportunities for the child to use her body in way.
(*b*) Use the environment-open spaces, features of the building, natural objects and everything around us.
(*c*) Adapt-draw lines on the floor to create patterns, or use low stools or planks to create steps.
(*d*) Suggest games and activities. Let the child always go on to more difficult things when she is ready.

More Motor Skills—Activities

Climbing into and out of, Jumping into and out of, crawling over and under and crawling through, sitting still, Hiding and finding, Arranging, Standing upturning, Imagining.

Things to be Done for More Motor Skills

(*a*) Encourage the child to find or create her own special space or corner;
(*b*) Suggest activities, stimulate and encourage through language;
(*c*) Talk to the child about what she is doing. Name things and activities.

Aids to Motor Activity

(*a*) *Barrow*: Make a small wheel barrow, trolley, or handcraft with the help of packing cases or cartons. If it is big enough, the child can sit in it or let others sit in it for pushing or pulling. Or fill with toys, dolls, or blocks for pushing and pulling.

(*b*) *Swing*: Swinging promotes balancing. Swings can be made from thick rope, suspend—

Small Plank,
Child's Chair,
Thick cushion, and
Section of tyre.

These can be hung even in a tree.

(*c*) *Floor Patterns*: Draw lines and geometrical designs like tiles on the floor. Use—

chalk on cement floor
sticks on wet earth or mad
lines of stones or pebbles
rope or string
hoops
poles and sticks.

(*d*) *Climbing Frame*: Prepare a two or three level set of stairs for climbing with the use of—
Upturned tube, flat bottomed canisters, bricks, Wooden boxes or planks, flower pots, stools and tables.

(*e*) *Balancing Board*: Put two bricks a few feet apart and place a plank across them supported by one brick at each end. Let the child walk on the plank.
As the child gets older, raise the level by using two bricks or upturned flower pots as bases and increase the distance.

(*f*) *Tunnel:* Half bury a tyre in the earth, so that it stands firm and up right and the child can crawl through it.
Make a line of two or three tyres to make a longer tunnel.

You can also use—
Cardboard cartons
Wooden boxes
Large tins, canisters or tubs with the bottom taken out.

Role of a Pre-primary school Teacher: The teacher can play a vital role in promoting the motor development of children by encouraging them to play both outdoor and indoor. She should provide a feeling of security to the children by being with them at play. Some children are afraid of climbing; jumping from certain height, running, swinging and sliding. If the teacher stands near the children, the fear complex will disappear and they will play freely. At the same time she should also see to the safety. The ground and the equipment should be free from hazards and danger. The play ground should be clean. She should plan her activities in such a way that the children don't in crowd and get hurt. Adequate space for children to play outdoor will avoid this mishappening in the play ground.

6

Social Development

Sociologists and Psychologists conceive of human personality as a product of social conditioning. When the baby is born he is as social. He does not exhibit any form of social behaviour. But as he grows, the society expects that he learns to interact with other members in the society in conformity with group, standards, mores and traditions. Learning of these acceptable, forms of interaction is called social development.

During the pre-primary school years, namely from two to six years of age, the child learns how to make social contacts and get along with people outside home, especially with peer group the children of his own age. The child has now acquired, the ability to move from place to place and use his language. As a result, his social contacts widen. These widening social contacts increase the chances for limitation of social behaviour of others. The child's social interactions enable him to acquire new social abilities like being cooperative, sharing with others, having a sense of oneness, developing meaningful relation etc.

STAGE OF SOCIAL DEVELOPMENT

Two to Three Months

Babies can distinguish people from inanimate objects and they discover that people supply their needs. They are content to be with people but discontented when left alone. At this stage, babies show no preference to anyone person.

Four to Five Months

Babies want to be picked up by anyone who approaches them. They react differently while scolded and to smiling faces and to friendly and to angry voices. The baby tries to attract the attention of another baby or a child by bouncing up and down, kicking, laughing or blowing bubbles.

Six to Seven Months

Babies differentiate between familiar and unfamiliar by smiling and reaching out to the former showing fear in the presence of the latter. This is the beginning of the "shy age"—It is also the beginning of the "attachment age—the time when babies become strongly attached to their mothers or mother-substitute and show a warning of indiscriminate friendliness.

The baby smiles at other babies and shows an interest when they cry.

Eight to Nine Months

The baby attempts to imitate the speech, gestures and simple acts of others.

Nine to Thirteen Months

Babies at this stage attempt to explore the clothes and hair of other babies, imitate their behaviour. Vocalization starts they cooperate with other, and share the toys—although they tend to become upset when other babies take one of their toys.

The baby reacts to the warning "no-no".

Thirteen to Eighteen Months

Fighting over toys decreases, and the baby shows more cooperation during play and a willingness to share, with playmates. Negativism, in the form of stubborn resistances to request or demands from adults is manifested in physical withdrawal or angry outbursts, during this period.

Eighteen to Twenty-four Months

The baby cooperates in a number of routine activities, such as being dressed, fed and bathed.

The baby shows more interest in playing with other babies and uses play materials and shares play materials to establish social relationship with them. At this stage he tries to be more sociable with others.

COMMON PLAY PATTERNS OF BABYHOOD

Sensorymotor Play: This is the earliest form of play where in the children display kicking, bouncing, wiggling, moving fingers and toes, climbing, babbling and rolling.

Exploratory Play: As hand and arm co-ordination develop, babies begin to explore their bodies by pulling hair, sucking their fingers, and toes, pushing their fingers in their navels and manipulating their sex organs. They shake, throw, bang, suck and pull their toys and explore by pulling, banging, throwing and tearing any object within their reach.

Initiative Play: During the second year, babies try to imitate the actions of those around them—presenting reading a magazine, sweeping the floor, or writing with a pencil or crayon.

Make-Believe Play: During the second year, most babies attach their toys with the qualities of real life. Stuffed animals are endowed with the qualities of real animals just as dolls and trucks are treated by the baby as if they were real people or real trucks.

Games: Before babies reach one year old, they play the traditional games like peekaboo, pat-a-cake, pigs to market, and hide-and-seek. These are usually played with parents, grandparents or older siblings.

Amusements: Babies like to be sung, to be talked to, and read to be from picture books. Most are fascinated by listening to radio and watching television and enjoy looking at pictures in the picture books.

Early Childhood: The most important forms of social behaviour necessary for successful social adjustment appear and begin to develop at the early childhood years. In the early years of childhood, these forms are not developed well enough to enable the child to get along successfully with others. However this is a crucial stage in development because it is at this time that the basic social attitudes and the pattern of social behaviour are established.

The different forms of behaviour in social situations during the early childhood years are given as follows:

Social Pattern

Imitation: To identify themselves with the group, children imitate the attitudes and behaviour of a person whom they especially admire and want to be like.

Rivalry: The desire to excel or outdo others is apparent as early as the fourth year. Rivalry begins at home first and later develops while playing with other children outside the home.

Cooperation: By the end of the third year, Cooperative play and group activities begin to develop and increase in both frequency and duration as the child's opportunities for play with other children increase.

Sympathy: Because sympathy requires an understanding of the feelings and emotions of others, it appears only occasionally before the third year. If the child is provided with more play contacts with other children he may develop sympathy early.

Empathy: Like sympathy, empathy requires an understanding of the feelings and the emotions of others. It also requires the ability to imagine one self in the place of the other persons to realise their feelings. Relatively few children are able to do this during early childhood years.

Social Approval: As early childhood years draw to a close, approval by the peer group becomes more important that paternal and adult approval. Young children find that naughty and disturbing behaviour is a way of winning peer approval.

Sharing: Young children during early years discover, from experiences with others, that one way to win social approval is to share what they have – especially toys – with others. Thus generosity gradually replaces selfishness.

Attachment Behaviour: When young discover that the satisfaction comes from warm, close, personal association with others, gradually they start attaching their affection to people outside the home. They include pre-primary school teachers, or to some inanimate objects, such as a favourite toys or even a blanket. These then become what are known as attachment objects.

As Social Patterns

Negativism: Negativism, or resistance to adult authority, reaches its peak between three and four years of age and then declines. Physical resistance gradually gives way to verbal resistance and pretending not to hear or not to obey the requests, from elders.

Aggressiveness: Aggressiveness increase between the ages of two to four and then declines. Physical attacks begin to be replaced by verbal attacks in the form of name-calling, tattling, or blaming others for everything.

Ascendant Behaviour: Ascendant behaviour or "bossiness" begins around the age of three and increases as opportunities for social contacts increase. Girls tend to be bossier than boys.

Selfishness: While young children's social horizons are limited mainly to the home, they are often seem to be selfish and egocentric. As their social horizons broader, selfishness gradually disappears but generosity is still undeveloped.

Egocentrism: Like selfishness, egocentrism is gradually replaced by an interest in and concern for others. When will this change occur will depend on number of contacts young children have with people outside the home and how anxious they are to win then acceptance.

Sex Antagonism: Until the children are four years old, boys and girls play together without any discrimination. After that, boys come under social pressures that lead then to withdraw them from those play activities that might be regarded as "girlish" or "sissyish". Many boys tend to engage in aggressive behaviour which antagonizes girls.

Prejudice: Most pre-primary school children show a preference for playmates of their own race, but they seldom refuse to play with children of another race. Racial prejudice begins sooner than religious or socio-economic prejudice, but later than sex prejudice.

Factors in Social Development

Even when young children begin to play with other children outside the home, the family remains the most important socializing agency. Because contacts with family members are closer, warmer, and more emotionally tinged than contact with those outside the home. Those close family relationships exert a great influence over the child than do any other social influence. But, how much each family members influences the child depends on their individual relationship with the child.

(*a*) *Child rearing:* Although no one method of child training can guarantee good or poor adjustments, whether personal or social, there is evidence that children brought up in democratic homes generally make better adjustments to outsiders than children from permissive or authoritarian homes.

(*b*) *Order of birth:* The ordinal position or order of birth of the child influences the time of adjustments the child will make. First born makes better social adjustments than their later born siblings, though not necessarily better personal adjustments.

(*c*) *Parent-Child Relationship:* Perhaps the most important condition influencing the kind of adjustments young children will make, both personal and social is the type of parent-child relationship which a child has during the early childhood years. Then comes their relationship with sibling and relationships with relatives, especially grand parents. The influence comes from the closeness of the relationship, the child has with a specific family member. When young children are attached to one parent than to the other, they imitate the attitude, emotions and behaviour patterns of that parent.

Because young children depend more on their parents for feelings of security and for happiness than on anyone else, poor relationships with their parents have a devastating effect on the child's behaviour. This is especially true when the poor relationship is with the mother, the parent on whom most young children are mostly dependent.

Poor relationships with parents undermines feelings of security of children. It will be especially serious if it is broken, due to death or divorce. Children who are deprived of the parent on whom they depend for security since birth are likely to experience severe emotional trauma can be eased if the missing parent is replaced by a step parent or if the child is adopted into a two-parent family where a satisfactory relationship can be established.

(*d*) *Sibling Relationships:* The pleasant relationship between their siblings starts to deteriorate during the second year of life and by the time babies become young.

The relationship among the siblings is often frictional. This friction not only plays have with the home climate but it also has a detrimental effect on the young child's self-concept. Young children are made to feel inadequate, especially if their achievement are criticized and ridiculed by their older siblings. Consequently sibling relationships are important aids to the young child's personal and social development and adjustment.

From their siblings, young children learn to evaluate their own behaviour as others do, and to think of themselves as others think of them. Older siblings serve as role models to imitate and learn.

(*e*) *Peer group:* In recent years there has been increasing recognition of the importance of extra familial agents in the socialization process. With the rise in maternal employment and the increase in the availability of pre-primary school education, the role of peers and teachers has been brought into sharp focus.

The term "peers" usually refers to children who are social equals, and who are similar on characteristics such as age. However, recently it has been suggested that classifying children who interact at about the same level of behavioural complexity as peers might be more appropriate than just focusing on equal ages. It is frequently stated that the relationship with peers is qualitatively different from that with family members, that the child's relationship with parents is more intense and enduring than that with friends. Some investigators have noted that the more free and egalitarian relationship with peer permits a new kind of interpersonal experimentation and exploration, and most particularly a new kind of sensitivity, which will serve as one of the corner stones for the development of social competence and the capacity to love (Piaget, 1932; Scevillivan, 1953).

DEVELOPMENTAL TRENDS IN PEER INTERACTION

As early as the first year of life infants are responsive to their peers. Babies in the first months of life touch and look at each other and even cry in response to the other's crying. However, it is unlikely that these early responses are really social in the sense of the infant seeking and expecting a social response from the other child. It is not until the second half of the first year that truly social behaviours begin to appear.

It is difficult to think of infants as popular or unpopular, but even in the first year of life there are marked individual differences in the social style and social acceptance of infants. In a study of 8 to 10 month-old infants in a day-care centre, it was observed that one child was avoided by his peers and another child was sought out and appeared to be usually liked. Even 10 month-old infants don't like children who are aggressive or who do not reciprocate their friendly overtones.

BABYHOOD IS THE BEGINNING OF SOCIALIZATION

The ego-centrism, characteristics of the very young baby, quickly gives way to desire to become a part of the social group. Babies show their desire to become a part of the social group by putting up protests when they are left alone for any length of time and by trying to win the attention of others in anyway they can.

One of the ways in which babies show their interest in becoming a part of the social group is by attachment behaviour. Because they can count on the attention and affection of their mothers or mother substitutes more than on other family members or outsiders they develop strong emotionalities with their mothers long before babyhood comes to a close. It is from the satisfaction of this attachment behaviour that the desire to establish warm and lasting relationships with others develops.

Socialization in Early Childhood

One of the important developmental tasks of early childhood is acquiring the preliminary training and experience needed to become a member of a "gang" in late childhood. The foundations for socialization are laid as the number of contacts young children have with their peer increases with each passing year. Not only they play more with other children, but they also talk more with them.

The kind of social contacts young children have is more important than the number of such contacts. If young children enjoy their contacts with others, even if they are only occasional their attitudes toward future social contacts will be more favourable than if they have more frequent social contacts of a favourable kind, children who prefer interacting with people to interacting with objects develop more social know-how and, as a result, are more popular than those who have limited social interactions.

The advantages young children take of the opportunities offered to them for social contacts will be greatly influenced by how pleasurable their past social contacts have been. As a general role, daring the pre-primary school years, children find social contacts with members of their own sex more pleasurable than those with members of the opposite sex.

Patterns of Early Socialization

Between the age of two and three years children show a decided interest in watching other children and they attempt to make social contacts with them. This is known as parallel play, play in which young children play independently beside other children rather than with them. If any contacts are made with other children, they find it to be frictional rather than cooperative. Parallel play is the earliest form of social activity young children have with their peers.

Following this comes associative play, which children engage in similar, if not identical, activities with other children. As social contacts increases, young children engage in cooperative play, play in which they are a part of the group and interact with group members.

Even after children begin to play with other children, they often play the role of onlooker, watching other children learn how others make social contacts and what their behaviour is in social situations.

Early Forms of Behaviour in Social Situations

The most important forms of social behaviour necessary for successful social adjustment appear and begin to develop at this time. In the early years of childhood these forms are not developed well enough to enable the child to get along successfully with others at all times. However, this is a crucial stage in development because it is at this time that the basic social attitudes and the patterns of social behaviour are established. In a longitudinal study of a group of young children, Waldrop and Halverson reported that those children who at age 2½ years were friendly and socially active continued to be so when they reached the age of 7½ years. They concluded that Sociability at 2½ years was predictive of Sociability at 7½ years.

Social Groupings and Social Behaviour in Late Childhood

Late childhood is often referred to as the "gang age" because it is characterized by interest in peer activities, an increasingly strong desire to be an accepted member of gang and discontent when children are not with their friends. Older children are no longer satisfied to play at home alone or with siblings or to do things with family members. They want to be with their peer and they are lonely and dissatisfied when they are not with them.

Even one or two friends are not enough for older children. They want to be with the gang, because only then will there be a sufficient number of individuals to play the games and sports they now enjoy and to give excitement to their play. From the time children enter school, the desire to be with and to be accepted by the gang becomes, increasingly strong. This is just as true of girls as it is of boys.

Characteristics of Children's Gangs

Most people think of gangs of hoodlums or mischief-makers because of the popular association of the team with juvenile delinquents. As used by child psychologists, and sociologists, children's gangs are markedly different from adolescent gangs. For that reason, when speaking of gangs in childhood, it is customary to refer to them as children's gangs to distinguish them from adolescent gangs.

There are many ways in which children's gangs differ from adolescent gangs, four of which are especially common and important. First, the major purpose of children's gangs is to have fun; they are primarily play grounds. By contrast the major purpose of adolescent gangs is to cause for trouble for others in retaliation for real or imagined slights on the part of the social group. Second, children's gangs are made up of children who are popular with the peers, while adolescent gangs are composed of those who have failed to gain peer acceptance and, as a result, hand together in the desire to those who have friend to accept them. Third, children's gangs rarely have members of both sexes, while adolescent gangs are more often composed of members of both sexes than members of one sex. And, fourth, children's gangs are composed of children of the same age and level of development whose interests and abilities are similar, while adolescent gangs are composed of individuals of different age levels and whose abilities and interests are not necessarily similar except that they all want to seek revenge on those who have refused to accept them.

Role of Pre-Primary School in Social Development

Pre-primary school offers plenty of chances for social development. The first group experience is provided in pre-primary school. The child gets his experiences with his contemporaries whose interest and capacities are of the same level as his own. The child gets a change of experiencing variety of experiences like friendliness, sharing, taking turns etc.

In group relationship and experience children are enabled to build a realistic self-concept. They learn about themselves from the estimation of others.

Children build-up self-confidence in a social group. They find strength and safety through group membership. The feeling that they belong to a group gives them a great sense of confidence to the child. The child overcomes the feeling of helplessness in a social group of the same age group.

SOCIO-EMOTIONAL DEVELOPMENT

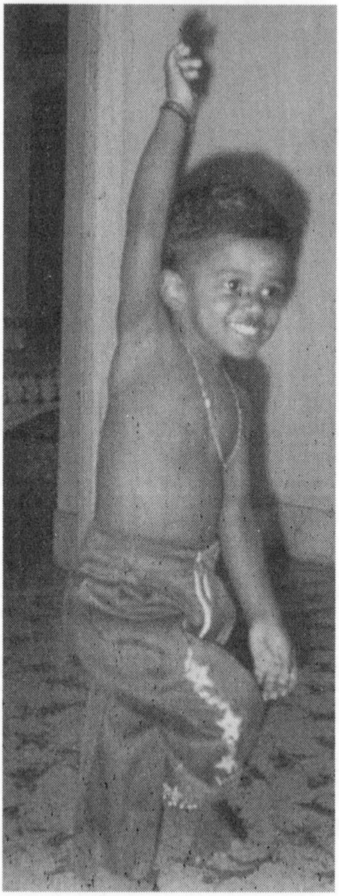

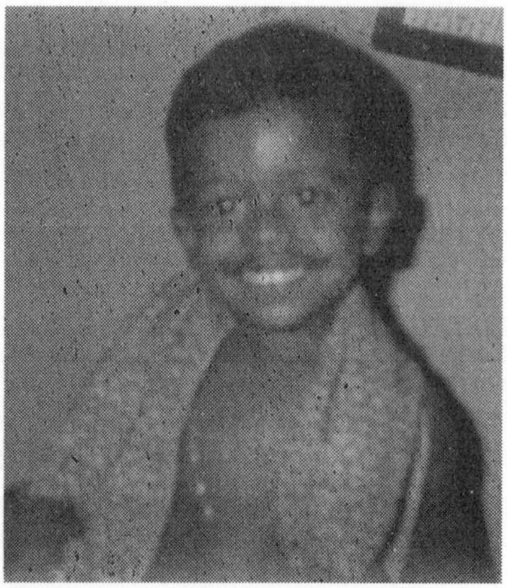

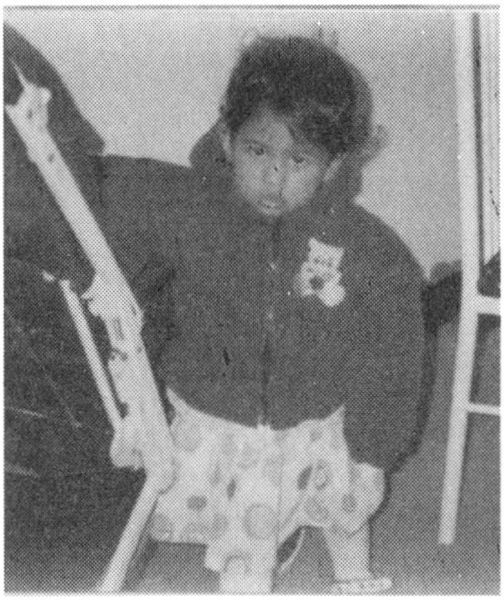

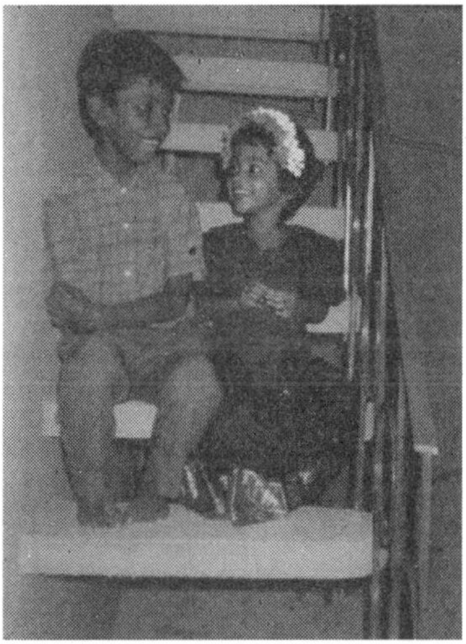

In a pre-primary school guidance in social development is given by the teacher. She teaches desirable techniques of approaching others. A child meets with success when using desirable techniques.

Children learn to take turns. The child learns the fundamentals of sharing at home. He continues to learn about sharing, taking turns and possessions at the pre-school.

Sharing also refers to communicating with other children and the adult in the pre-school. By communicating with each other children become more secure in group situations. At the age of four and above children in pre-school get interest, enhance the span of attention and readiness to participate in a group situation.

Activities to Promote Social Development and Adjustment in Pre-School

Child to child programme, where the older children take care of the younger ones, outdoor group play, lunch time where children are encouraged to serve others, wait for their turns to come, dramatization etc. will promote the social development in pre-school. The teacher can play a vital role in encouraging the children to help each other and share the property with other children. If a child has nothing to share she can identify something to share, even the toys.

Teacher can encourage children to participate in group activities where in children learn to adjust with others, develop self-confidence, over come fear of defeat, of being alone etc. Many researches have proved the effective role that a pre-school can play in socializing the child as well as adjusting to new environments and people very well.

7

Emotional Development

An emotion may be described as a stirred up state of the organism accompanied by certain physiological changes in the body and an impulse to act. Fear, anxiety, anger, digest, grief, jealousy and excitement are some of the common emotions expressed by human beings.

Emotions can be broadly classified into two. One is positive-integrative emotions and the other is negative-disintegrative emotion. Positive-integrative emotions are pleasant in nature. The individual feels happy at the expression of these emotions and the expression of these emotions is liked and welcomed by others. Such emotions as joy, love, affection, curiosity, and sympathy are included under this category. The negative-disintegrative emotions, on the other hand, give an unpleasant feeling to the individual who feels it and the expression of these is disliked by others. Emotions such as anger, jealousy, fear etc. are included under this category.

Common Emotional Patterns

The new born infant exhibits only a general excitement and no specific emotions. But as he grows, he shows different forms of emotional behaviour. Psychologists are of the opinion that the ability to respond emotionally is present even at the time of birth. This ability develops due maturation or biological growth process and learning.

Babyhood: An account of the various during unpleasant emotions expressed by child, Babyhood are as follows:

Anger: Common stimuli that gives rise to anger in babies are interference with attempted movements, thwarting of some wish, not letting them do what they want to do, and not letting them make themselves understood. Typically, the angry response takes the form of screaming, kicking the legs, waving the arms and hitting or kicking anything with in the reach of the child. During the second year, children may also jump up and down, throw themselves on the floor, and hold their breath.

During early childhood, the most common causes of anger are conflicts over play things, the thwarting of wishes, and vigorous attacks from another child. Children express anger through temper tantrums, characterized by crying, screaming, stamping, kicking, jumping up and down or striking.

Fear: The stimuli or causes most likely to arouse fear in babies are loud noises; strange persons, objects, and situation, dark rooms, high places, and animals. Any stimulus which occurs suddenly or unexpectedly or which is different from what the baby is accustomed to give rise to fear. The typical fear response in babyhood consists of an attempt to withdraw from the frightening stimulus, accompanied by whispering, crying, temporary holding of the breath, and checking the activity engaged in when the baby become frightened.

In early childhood, conditioning, imitation and memories of unpleasant experiences play important roles in arousing fears as do stories, pictures, radio, television programmes and movies with frightening elements. At first, a child's response to fear is panic, later responses become more specific and include rushing away and hiding, crying and avoiding frightening.

Grief: Young children are saddened by the loss of anything they love or that is important to them, whether it be a person, a pet, or an inanimate object, such as a toy. Typically express their grief by crying and by loosing interest in their normal creativities, including eating.

Anxiety: Tersild define anxiety as a painful uneasiness of mind concerning impending or anticipated ill. It is a mental condition which involves undefined fear, dead and a general feelings that all is not well. This anxiety pattern is clearly present in the child by the third year of life. An anxious child is unhappy, and is irritable. His mood swings he has restless sleep, gets angry quickly and has high sensitivity. These forms of behaviour lead to adjustment problems.

Anxiety generally centres around routines, parent-child and child-child relationship. Insecurity in children has been found to be the major cause for anxiety. Insecurity mainly arises from in consistency in social rules, conflicting authority and atmosphere of emotional tension. When parents are strict disciplinarians or when they behave inconsistently, children feel anxiety. Some times anxiety is constructive. It drives the child to work hard and reach perfection. But it is necessary that needless anxiety or worries that may persist into adulthood must be eliminated. A happy home atmosphere minimize the occurrence of anxiety among children.

Forms of Pleasant Emotions

Some of the common pleasant emotions found among children are as follows:

Curiosity: Curiosity is the interest in new things, stranger, incongruous or mysterious elements in a person's environment. It can also be said as the desire to know. The pre-primary school child is highly inquisitive or curious. His curiosity is endless. He is curious about his body, people and things. Mechanical devices, toys, novel situation changes like new ways of dressings of his parents, changes in his body like the eruption of teeth etc. also cause curiosity in the child's mind.

Curiosity can be found in babies from the third or fourth months onwards. It is expressed bodily at first. The baby tenses his body and shows a startled expression at first. Then he gets hold of the object and explores it by pulling, sucking and rattling it. As soon as he can talk; he begins to ask questions to satisfy his curiosity. The questioning age begins around the third year and reaches its peak around the sixth year. Four year old children are called as "walking question marks" as they go on asking questions. Curiosity helps in the widening of the child's awareness of his environment.

Elation: Elation denotes a condition of being in high spirits. These emotions are expressed in the form of smiling, chucking, and laughter. Stimuli that evoke laughter in pre-primary school children include surprise, incongruity, contrast situation and play situations. Achievement of success in an activity after a long-time, and trial is another important source of happiness or joy during early childhood.

Joy: Joy is stimulated by physical well-being. By the second or third month of life, babies react to being played with, being tickled and watching or listening to others. They express their pleasure or joy by smiling, laughing, and moving their arms and legs. When joy is intense, babies coo, gurgle, or even shout with glee, and all bodily movements are intensified.

Young children derive joy from such as a sense of physical well-being, incongruous situation, sudden or unexpected noises, playing punks on others and accomplishing what seem to them to be difficult tasks. They express their joy by smiling and laughing, clapping their hands, jumping up and down, or hugging the object or person that has made them happy.

Affection: Anyone who plays with babies, takes care of their bodily needs, or shows them affection will be a stimulus for their affection. Later, toys and the family pet may also become love objects for them. Typically, babies express their affection by hugging, patting, and kissing the love object or person.

During early childhood, young children learn to love the things – people, pets or objects – that give them pleasure. They express their affection verbally as they grow older but, while they are still young, they express it physically by hugging, patting, and kissing the object of their affection.

Erikson's Concept of Emotional Development

Erikson was a neo-Freudian whose theory is called the psycho-social theory of development.

According to Erikson every one has to pass through eight stages of development. The stages and the duration and the major characteristics of each stage are as follows:

1. *Stage I*: Birth to eighteen months. The child has to acquire a sense of basic trust while overcoming a sense of mistrust.
2. *Stage II*: Eighteen months to three years. The child during this stage has to acquire a sense of autonomy while combating a sense of doubt and shame.
3. *Stage III*: Three years to six years. The child has to acquire a sense of initiative and overcoming a sense of guilt.
4. *Stage IV*: Six to twelve years. The child has to acquire a sense of industry and to fend off a sense of inferiority.
5. *Stage V*: Twelve to eighteen years. The adolescent has to acquire a sense of identify while overcoming a sense of identify diffusion.
6. *Stage VI*: Eighteen to twenty four years. The young adult has to acquire a sense of solidarity and avoiding a sense of isolation.
7. *Stage VII*: Twenty four to fifty four years. The middle aged

adult has to acquire a sense of integrity and avoiding a sense of self absorption.

8. *Stage VIII*: Fifty four years to death. The adult has to acquire a sense of integrity and avoid a sense of despair.

Characteristics of Childhood Emotions

The emotions of the young child differ markedly from those of an adult. An analysis of characteristics, features of the child's emotions, contrasted with those of the adult, will make these differences apparent. These characteristics are the following:

Children's Emotions are brief

Typically the young child's emotions last only a few minutes and then end abruptly. Because the child expresses his emotions in overt actions, he "clear his system", and as a result, the emotion lasts for a relatively short time as contrasted with the long-drawn-out emotional reactions of the adult. As the child grows older, social restraints on the overt responses which formerly characterized his emotional reactions lead to "moods" or emotional states drawn out over a period of time, and expressed slowly rather than in short, abrupt outbursts.

When the child is with playmates of his own age, free from parental or other adult restraints, he expresses his emotions freely and quickly. In the presence of adults, however, the child begins to display moodiness around the fourth year, and this tendency reaches its peak during adolescence. The typical moods of childhood are "sulkiness" from restrained anger; "scariness", "jumpiness", and "timidity" from repressed fear; and happiness or "good humour" from controlled joy.

Children's Emotions are Intense

The young child's emotional outbursts are characterized by an intensity which is seldom observed in the emotional reactions of an adult. His emotional responses lack gradations or degree of intensity, with the result that his responses to a trivial situation will call forth an emotional reaction of as great intensity, as a situation of a more serious type. To adults, unfamiliar with childish behaviour, the intense emotional reactions of a little child to a petty annoyance are the source of great surprise and wonder. This is especially true in the case of fear, anger and joy, all of which are expressed in pronounced overt responses. A disturbed child has the same emotional development as a normal, well adjusted child, but in the disturbed child the negative emotions are more frequent and more intense than in the well-adjusted child.

Children's Emotions are transitory

The transitory character of a young child's emotions, which results in a rapid shift from laughter to tears, from anger to smiles, or form jealously to affection, is incomprehensible to many adults because it is so different from the way in which the typical adult expresses his feelings. The child's behaviour, which at one minute is characterized by an intense outburst of one emotion, suddenly shifts to an equally intense outburst of a totally different emotional reaction. Reactions from extreme shyness to extreme exuberance and boisterousness characteristics of pre-school children.

Children's Emotions appear frequently

Children's emotions occur more frequently, on the average, than do those of adult. The reason for this is that as the child grows older, he has greater ability to make adjustments to situations and emotional reactions than when he was younger and less experienced. Because he has learned that social disapproval or punishment often follows an emotional outburst, he tries to meet situations by reactions other than emotional ones. The result is gradual decrease in the frequency of emotional responses.

Children's Emotional responses are different

Observations of children of different ages show wide variability in their emotional responses. Among newborn infants, the patterns of response are similar. Gradually however, as the influences of learning and environment are felt, the behaviour accompanying the different emotions is individualized. One child in fear will run out of the room, another will hide behind his mother's skirt, while still another will stand on the ground and cry. The same is true for all other emotional patterns.

Emotions can be Detected by Symptoms of Behaviour

An adult is generally able to hide his feelings and emotions well and it is difficult for others to know just how he feels. Not so with children. Even though they may not show their emotional reactions directly in behaviour related to the way they feel, their emotions can be detected by tension, restlessness, day dreaming, nervous mannerisms as nail biting, thumb sucking, eye blinking, and rubbing the genitals, speech difficulties, lack of appetite, babyish behaviour, frequent crying, obstinacy, and hysterical outbursts. Boys generally show more symptoms of emotionality than girls.

Changes in Strength of Emotions

At certain ages, certain emotions are strong and then wane. Other emotions, formerly weak, later become strong. For example, little children show marked timidity in the presence of strangers or in strange place. Later, when they realize there is nothing to be afraid of, their timidity wanes. Similarly temper tantrums have been found to reach their peak before the child enters school, after which time they decrease not only in frequency but also in intensity.

Changes in Emotional Expressions

The little child wants what he wants when he wants it. He does not stop to consider whether this will be harmful to him or to others, nor does he consider whether the price he will have to pay is worthwhile. Unless he gets what he wants, he will become angry and fly into a fit of temper. Similarly, when frightened, he does not hesitate to run away and hide or to show his fear by crying. Even when happy, he does not wit to express it at a convenient time or place. He smiles or laughs even though this may appear to others to be a case of "gloating".

Factor Affecting the Emotional Development of Children

A number of factors contribute to emotional development. The factors that are common to all children are maturation and learning.

(*a*) *Maturation:* Emotional behaviour is possible only with the appropriate neural and endocrine development. It has been proved experimentally in animals that removal of cortical region of the brain made them extremely calm. Hence maturation of cortical region is very important for emotional development. Likewise, the development of adrenal glands in size has been found to affect emotional expression to a great extent. Muscular development is also an important prerequisite for visible physical expression of emotions.

(*b*) *Learning:* Generally children learn emotional behaviour through two methods conditioning and imitations.
In the method of conditioning children learn by association for example, pain due to injections creates fear for the doctor or the nurse because the child associates injection with the person who gives it.
Children imitate the emotional behaviour of people whom he has a chance to observe. Very often, emotional reactions, to specific situations develop by imitating others. For example, when someone in the family fears cockroach or lightning, the child develops fear towards cockroach and lightning through imitation.

(*c*) *Intelligence:* As intelligent children have mental age of older children they have emotions not of their age, but of an older age group. Fear, jealousy, curiosity, etc. will be at an advanced level. Likewise, a child with less intelligence has emotions that are characteristic of younger age. The child may be branded immature he exhibits emotions of lower age group.

(*d*) *Sex:* At all age girls show more fears than boys. Other feelings associated with girls are jealous and elation.

(*e*) *Socio-Economic Status:* Lower social class children have more fears than upper class children. Aggression is also found to be more among lower class children.

(*f*) *Physical Condition:* When the child is ill or tired or under stress he is easily irritated and expresses negative emotions than positive emotions.

(*g*) *Social Contacts:* Fear is said to decrease in a social situation of peers. A child who has more contacts with adults than with peers tends to have emotional characteristics of adults.

(*h*) *Ordinal Position:* First born will be more stable emotionally because of added years of experience. Also society expects that the older child has more control over his emotions than other children.

(*i*) *Personality:* Some children are by nature insecure, they fear more, some are aggressive by nature, some are always happy and friendly by nature.

Common Emotional Problems

Common emotional problems in children include bedwetting, thumb sucking, temper tantrum, nail biting, masturbation, sibling rivalry, irritation, etc. Emotional problems arise mainly when children feel insecure. The etiology for these problems is lack of love, attention and security feeling in children. Children make up for the lack of happiness and security by indulging in activities like the ones mentioned above.

Role of Pre-School in Guiding Emotion

The pre-school is in a position to prevent and guide emotional problems in children. Children grow secure and confident in a pre-school. According to Read (1966) Security refers to the feelings that come with having had many experiences of being accepted as we are rather than rejected and of feeling safe rather than threatened. Adequacy refers to the feelings which an individual has about himself that is his concept of the kind of the person he is.

The feelings of security and adequacy arise out of the way the child's basic needs are met, his experience with feedings and later with toileting, the kind of response he gets from other people and the satisfaction he finds in exploring the world out of these early experiences the child builds a feeling of trust to the world. Having learned that he can trust people he develops confidence in himself. The pre-school teacher knows this and she tries to build trust in himself, in her and in school, some of the ways in which she accomplishes them are as follows:

The teacher encourage children by loving words she never lets them down. The child finds acceptance from teacher. This greatly boosts his self concept. As we know children are influenced in their feelings by the attitudes of adults. The teachers protect them from acting in ways which will have damaging consequences. This helps him to avoid disappointments.

The experiences provided to the children are adapted to their readiness. This also helps to avoid disappointment, and builds trust.

From the children's speech and behaviour the teacher comes to know about both their positive, and negative feelings. The teacher does not condemn or blame him for the negative feelings are accepted in the pre-primary school.

It is important that the negative feelings are put into action. They must be trained off in ways that are not distractive. Children are helped to drain off feelings in acceptable channels like physical activity or through action songs or hand work. Children give vent to their negative feelings through vigorous physical activity like pounding or throwing a ball hand against some thing. Creative activities offer possibilities of expressing their feelings. Activities like finger painting using a punching pag, hammering board, running, digging, painting at the easel, working with clay and playing in water help a child to relax. Music is another channel for the experience of feelings. In the case of timid children the teacher makes them feel assured and secure by accepting even their bad behaviour. She tries to make the child to move with other children.

Thus we see that the whole programme of the pre-school as well as the equipment provided contribute to the feelings of security and adequacy of children. The peer group provides many change for the feelings of happiness and adequacy. The child comes to know that he is just like other children while in the company of peers. This gives him a sense of security.

Though these various means child's emotional development is guided in a pre-school.

8

Cognitive Development

Cognition is knowing. The term cognition is used to mean a kind of knowing that is more definite, more certain, and more lasting than immediate sense perception. Sometimes it is used to mean the parts of dimensions of knowing that can be distinguished from emotion. Sometimes it seems to include the entire breadth of mental life.

A typical psychological dictionary defines "Cognition as a general term covering all the various modes of knowing, perceiving, remembering, imagining, conceiving, reasoning". Cognition might be described as the process by which the brain registers and files all the information.

Piaget regards cognition as a form of biological adaptation – the organism's constant effort to bring about a harmonious interaction between his own schemata and the outer world. It is a "system of living and acting operations" that strives for equilibration, or a balancing between what the individual knows and what he perceives in the world.

Piaget's Theory of Cognitive Development

Most influential theory of cognitive development in recent years is proposed by Jean Piaget, a Swiss Psychologist. He has been studying the cognitive development of children for more than last fifty years. According to Piaget, there are four recognizable stages of cognitive development:

1. Sensorimotor Period (birth to 24 months)
2. Pre-operational-Representation Period (1¼ to 6 years)
3. Concrete Operational Period (7 to 11 years)
4. Cognitive Thought or Formal Operational Period (12 to 15 years)

Sensorimotor Stage

Piaget describes the cognitive process of infants as sensorimotor intelligence, for until an individual is about two years old, he concentrates on regulating his sensations and controlling his motor activity. There are six stages in the period of sensorimotor intelligence, the last of them ending around the child's second birthday. Cognitive development in the sensorimotor period is a gradual and continuous process, but the order of six stages is always the same. Each stage occurs in proper sequence and is a necessary preparation for the next. No child, however, is a "Pure" example of one stage or another, one aspect of the infant's behaviour normally advances faster than another.

Piaget used the terms assimilation and accommodation to describe the two processes that work towards equilibrium and gradually promote the infant from one step to the next. Assimilation results from the organism's tendency to use a structure in more than one way. The structure known as the sucking reflex, for example, is specifically adapted to the nipple, but the infant seeks to exercise it on anything he can get in his mouth. A blanket, a thumb, toys or a pacifier will serve as "nourishment" for his need to suck. And when he uses a blanket in this way, he assimilates it—makes it similar to other suckable objects.

As soon as certain actions prove successful, the infant begins to modify them to make them more effective. This modification of an action to improve the way it meets the environment is what Piaget terms accommodation. It is exemplified by the breast-fed infants learning to search for the nipple with increasing effectiveness.

Reflex Stage

The human infant is born with certain sensorimotor reflexes, such as orienting reactions to sound and light, crying and thrashing about in response to any loud noise, sudden bright light, or abrupt movement. But even at this earliest stage—roughlv from birth to one month of age – the baby does not function by reflex alone. The lifelong process of learning by experience begins almost immediately. One of his first accomplishment is to expand his sucking response. At birth, his lips begin to suck as soon as they are touched; two weeks later he sucks much more efficiently and practices sucking between feedings. His original instinct is generalized to the sucking of rattles and blanket corners.

This is not to say, however, that the infant cannot differentiate between the genuine article and imitations. Before the end of his third week he has usually caught on to the fact that while many soft substances provide relief from the trials of life, only one of these suckable objects results in the joys of a full stomach.

Primary Circular Reactions

During the second stage—from one month through four months of age—a gradual process of discrimination sets in. The infant begins to repeat simple activities, such as opening and closing his fists, purposefully rather than accidentally. Other actions are discontinued out of the sense of purpose; a little girl may, for instance, continue to suck the corner of the blanket but discard her rattle. Her perceptive explorations grow less haphazard, more goal oriented; she looks in order to see, touches in order to feel.

At this stage the infant begins to develop such reactions as bringing the hand to the mouth. By initiating these movements she is rewarded with a pleasurable result in terms of her own body. She then learns to obtain the result by repeating the patterns of movements, beginning a "Circular" process of reward, reinforcement, and repetition.

The infant also begins to anticipate future events. The first signs of curiosity begin to appear at this stage, as well as evidence of some interest in unexpected events. The child also shows some signs of expectancy by watching the spot where an object has disappeared.

Secondary Circular Reactions

The circular reaction of the previous stage revolved almost exclusively around the baby's own body, whereas those that make their appearance, in the third stage—from the fourth through the eighth month—involve the environment to an increasing extent as the baby learns to group.

This is the time with the child begins to evolve a concept of objects and to classify objects into groups. The secondary circular reactions, such as accidentally causing a rattle to sound and then trying to reproduce the result, show that the infant has learned that he and external objects are separate entities whose interaction he can bring about at will. For example, having found that it is fun to make the rattle sound, and doing so repeatedly, the infant will realize that he can produce the sound by shaking the rattle. Now there is no holding him, dizzy with the sense of power; he will perform this miracle over and over again, gurgling with joy. There is no longer anything accidental or tentative about this particular action; it is the deliberate performance of a specific act to bring about a specific result.

On the thirteenth day of his own son's fourth months, Piaget observed.

The infant can now perceive the difference between a slight movement of his own and a more vigorous one and he distinguishes between the loud and soft sounds of the rattle. He notes the relationship between sound and movement.

The infant's object concept the knowledge that an object exists even though he cannot perceive it at the moment is initially acquired by coordinating schemata with one another and realizing that there is a relationship between them. The schema of the seen rattle for example, is coordinated with that of the heard sound. Then, out of the building blocks of object concepts, he forms more and more schemata. As a result, he arrives at the first of four new abilities that Piaget recognized as specific to this stage. Because he can now conceive of objects, he can also anticipate where they will land when he drops them.

The second new ability is called interrupted prehension. When the baby loses an object while reaching for it, he will continue to make reaching movements with his hands. Then comes deferred circular reaction the spontaneous reception of an interrupted action. For instance, the infant is playing intently with the zipper. On his play with it the chiming of a clock distracts him. At an earlier stage he would have shifted his attention to the clock and forgotten the zipper; now his attention soon returns to the zipper, and he resumes playing with it. Lastly, the power of identification expands to the point where the infant is able to recognize a partly covered object of which he can see only an exposed side.

All these new abilities also indicate the development of a sense of object permanence and related to it a rudimentary form of general space perception. He becomes more interested in the relations of objects to each other and no longer relates every object exclusively to himself. Vaguely begins to understand that there is a big world full of objects and he is part of it but not the whole.

Coordination of Secondary Reactions and Schemata

At the fourth stage – from the eighth through the twelfth month—the infant first displays intention as the primary motivating agent for beginning an activity. In the earlier stages, some accidental result of his actions had given direction to his further activity; now he starts with an intended result clearly in mind. When confronted with an obstacle, he will not, as before, keep repeating a futile action. Instead he now activates the new faculty of originality – not, as yet, by discovering a totally novel solution, but by successfully applying an action previously used in a different context to the new situation confronting him. Through the process of generalized assimilation, an action turned under post circumstances is thus expanded to include new situations that are different, yet sufficiently similar to make the action appropriate in both cases.

During this stage there is also a great advance in the skill of imitation. The baby is now capable of making much more meaningful connections between the actions of a model, such as his mother, and corresponding actions of his own. In addition, he begins to imitate actions that he cannot see himself perform and that have not aroused his interest before – such as lip movements and vocal sound.

Any new action, such as smacking the lips or waving the hand – if at all within the baby's capabilities – now excites the age to imitate to a much greater than during preceding stages.

Imitation may at first be very approximate, but the baby's attention span has lengthened quite a bit by now, and she is often willing to practice with surprising patience and perseverance to master a new skill. In this as in other areas, she exhibits a growing sense of the organization of things with respect to herself as well as to her surroundings. She begins to be able to anticipate events that are not the result of her own actions, because she has become aware of the independence of objects from herself and of a certain systematic predictability in the way people and objects behave.

Tertiary Circular Reactions

The fifth stage – from the twelfth through the eighteenth month – has been called "the climax of the sensorimotor period." All the abilities learned in earlier stages are now expanded and applied to increasingly complex situations. The infant now becomes systematically adventurous in his explorations of the environment. He is much readier than formerly to try novel solutions to problems and to learn by trial and error. For the first time he shows curiosity about an object for its own sake and seems intent on learning everything he can about it. In this stage, his interest in novelty is an end in itself. Piaget observed that child, while playing with the soap dish, accidentally chopped it. The novelty of the situation immediately caught the child's interest and he attempted to repeat the event, dropping the soap dish several times in succession.

Experimentation with new means for achieving a goal is also characteristics of this stage. When child was one year and five days old, Piaget arranged the following problem for her : a pivoting box was placed on a table and stop the box, just out of the infant's reach, was a tray bottle.

At first the child attempted to inch the box, a manoeuver she had used successfully to obtain the handkerchief. Then, trial and error, she was able to accommodate her behaviour and discover a new method. By pushing the box, child was able to bring it closer. Her actions were directed both by the goal and by previous schemata that gave her an understanding of what was happening.

The Stage of Pre-Operational Representation

This stage covers the period of 1½ to 6 years. Piaget thinks that knowledge is not gained by mental perception of reality but upon modifying objects and events, or by actual operations. After sometime those operations become internal and one does not need to manipulate objects physically to understand them.

In the pre-operational stage the child begins to develop language, and is able to talk and form simple concepts. But he has very little understanding of operations. For example, if water contained in a tall narrow glass is poured into a small broad glass the child at a pre-operational stage will judge that there was more water in the narrow glass than when it is poured in the broad glass.

The Stage of Concrete Operations

This stage covers the period from 7 to 11 years, when children perform with the help of actual objects. Even when operations are performed by them internally, they refer to physical or concrete objects rather than to hypothetical events. Piaget illustrates the use of concrete operations as he observed how 8 year old child learnt what factor controls the oscillation of a pendulum. The child changes the length of the string and observes that the shorter distance from pendulum weight to the other and of the pendulum increases the frequency of oscillation. He also varies the quantity of weight and learns that it is not a factor affecting oscillation. During this stage, the child also learns to organize system of classification for the perceptions and concepts acquired by him.

The Stage of Cognitive Thought or Formal Operations

This stage includes period from 12 to 15 years. Now the youngster acquires the ability to think and reason beyond his own immediate world. He applies formal logic to solve his problems, and approaches them more systematically. He comes to acquire ideas of social justice and proper modes of social interaction.

In addition to the system of reducing consequences from a variety of alternative hypotheses, the child can assimilate and combine information from a variety of sources. Rather than evaluating single factor in solving a problem, as the concrete operational child does, the child at this stage is able to consider combinations of factors and simultaneous interactions of factors which will affect the solution.

It is in this flexibility, mental hypothesis testing and appreciation of the many possibilities in a situation, as well as in the awareness of the complexity of problems, that the adolescent differs from the concrete operational child.

The stage of formal operational and the flexible problem solving associated with it are not attained by all adults. This is attributable partly to cultural and educational factors and partly to general intellectual level. Subject who score below average on standard tests of intelligence do not attain formal operational thought. In contrast, very bright children have been found to perform as well or better than more adults. In addition, scientific training in such subject as physics, chemistry, or logic has been found to be associated with greater ability to use formal operations.

Characteristics and Achievement in Stages of Intellectual Development According to Piaget

Stage	*Approximate Age Range-Years*	*Major Characteristics and Achievements*
Sensorimotor Period	0-2	Infant differentiates himself from other objects: seeks stimulation and prolong interesting spectacles: attainment of objects permanence, primitive understanding of causality, time, and space, means-end relationships: beginnings of imitation of absent, complex non-human stimuli, imaginative play and symbolic thought.
Preoperational Period	2-6	Development of the symbolic function; symbolic use of language, intuitive problem solving: thinking characterized by irreversibility, centration, and egocentricity: beginnings of attainment of conservation of number and ability to think in classes and see relationships.
Period of Concrete operations	6 or 7 through 11 or 12	Conservation of mass, length, weight, and volume; reversibility decentration, ability to take role of others; logical thinking involving concrete operations of the immediate world, classification (Organizing objects into hierarchies of classes) and seriation (Organizing objects into ordered series, such as increasing height)
Period of formal operations	11 or 12 on	Flexibility, abstraction, mental hypotheses testing, and consideration of possible alternatives in complex and problem solving.

Implications

This theory implies that children should be provided a great deal of direct experience before they can be expected to cope with abstract ideas and concept. Piaget's theory also stresses the importance of readiness. We should not expect the children to work at the level of formal operations when the child is still at a pre-operational stage. Piaget is critical of a system of education in which there is so much emphasis on learning through books, and teacher's talks, and on evaluation by use of verbal tests.

Piaget's principles have been found particularly useful in working with children from poor disadvantaged families. He believes that perceptual-motor development or the ability to coordinate perceiving and manipulation is basic for conceptual development. This principle has been found useful in understanding reading difficulties of children from disadvantaged class, and also to faster reading readiness in them.

However, psychologists are critical and dissatisfied about research techniques used by Piaget. He has not given details of procedures used by him, or he has maintained photographic and other detailed recordings of children's behaviour particularly in his earlier studies. For the reason his principles such as communication with one self at the preverbal stage, are considered only tentative.

Some psychologists have questioned that stage of cognitive development suggested by Piaget may only be applicable to children in middle-class European homes and schools. Thus, his system may underestimate or even overestimate the age at which children can perform certain processes.

According to Piaget difficulty in school may result from lack of basic perceptual-motor experiences. But it may also happen because of other factors, such as low motivation of children from disadvantaged homes, or poor skill of teachers teaching them, or lack of adequate models from whom one can learn attitudes and skills.

The basic point in Piaget's theory is that biological development sets the pace for cognitive child. One of the principles in his theory states that ability to conserve quantity appears about the age of seven. Silver and Schneider were able to prove the validity of this principle. But Goldshonid was successful in teaching kindergarten children certain modes of conservation. Similarly, Piaget holds that problem solving ability emerges between 14 to 16 years of age. But Anderson could teach first-grades a number of complex problems varying one factor at a time but controlling the other factors constant.

This is to suggest that Piaget's principles can not be interpreted rigidly. Slow cognitive development may occur due to limitations set in the development of the brain, or because of the limited opportunity to learn. Piaget himself recognizes that children may develop rapidly or slowly within his own proposed theoretical framework.

COGNITIVE AND CONCEPT FORMATION

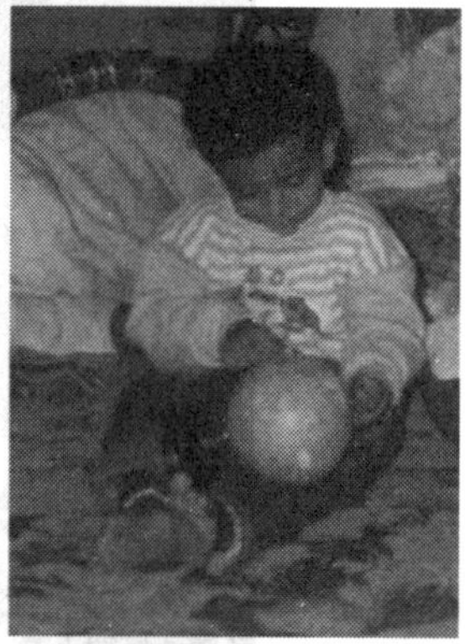

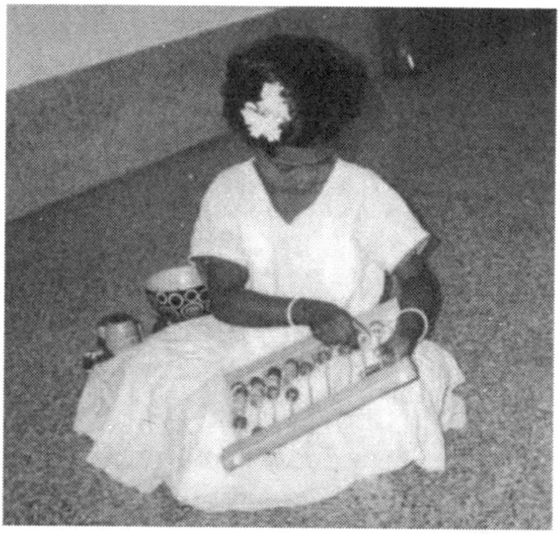

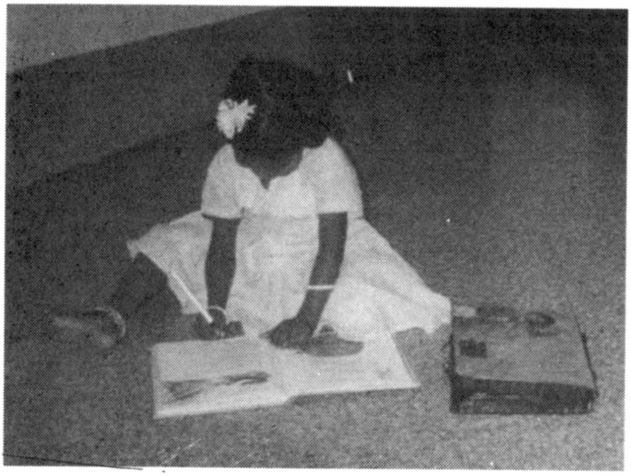

9

Concept Formation

The early childhood is the period when the child is very curious to know the existence and functioning of the various objects around him. He is fascinated by the rising and setting sun, the twinkling stars, the appearance of the moon in the sky and sometimes the floating clouds in the sky catch his attention and provoke him to ask a volley of questions. Furthermore, it is surprising to him to know that the fire is hot, the ice is cold and he is inquisitive to know the reasons for the same. Take for instance a peculiar situation when the child comes to understand that he has a home; his friend in the neighbourhood has also a home; the sparrow's nest is a home for him; the rat's home is like a hole, the lion's den is again a home and so on. Enquiring as he is during this stage of his age, he tries to find out the similarities and contrasts between various alike and differing situations. The child's inquisitiveness is due to the reason that at this stage of life he is forming some concepts of the things around him.

A concept is an abstract grouping of experience that helps to reduce their complexity. Some concepts are truly abstract, such as the concept of happiness, while other concepts define categories of objects or events which are themselves quite concrete. The concept "boll" encompasses a set of concrete instances that are likely to be seen in similar situations; consequently, this concept appears quite early in the young child's repertoire of abstractions.

Some of the important concepts that the child develops at this stage are classifiable as the concepts of science and mathematics and nature. For example, the concepts of time and season; living and non-living things; human body, etc., could be broadly put under the category the concept of science. The development of such concepts as those of shape, size and colour, numbers, volume would be classified as the concepts of mathematics.

Stages of Concept Development

Stages 1 and 2 (0 to 4 months)

Most researchers seem to agree with Piaget that the infant does not have the concept of object performance at this early stage. In a techniques used by Bower (1970), among others, objects are made to "Vanish" by sliding a screen between them and the body. The infant acts as if the object no longer exists, a sort of "out of sight, out of mind". More interesting is the fact that most infants will seem less surprised if the object is missing when the screen is moved away than if it is still there.

Stage 3 (4 to 8 months)

Infant at this stage seem to have the first glimmerings of object performance and will try to regain visual contact with an object that has disappeared from view.

Stage 4 (8 to 12 months)

At this stage children will begin to search regularly for objects which they have seen disappeared, first only if the object has just been seen a moment ago and then even after, periods of considerable delay.

Stage 5 (12 to 18 months)

At stage 5 child is able to recognize that he or she must search for missing objects where they were last seen and that this factor is more important than where the object was found before on previous trials. Even so, the concept is not yet complete because the child cannot yet infer invisible displacements.

Stage 6 (18 to 24 months)

The completion of the development of the concept of object performance occurs during this stage.

Meaning and Nature

With the development in learning and perception there is development in the child's concept of objects, events and relations. The concepts of forms, size, and space in a young child are abstractions which are built on his direct experiences with the real objects. According to J.B. Carrol "Concepts are properties of Organiemic experience" more particularly, they are the abstracted and often cognitively structured classes of 'mental' experience learned by organisms in the course of their life histories.

Concepts show a high degree of similarity, because of the continuity of our physical, biological and social environment. Through language learning many concepts acquire names, and language also makes possible the diffusion and sharing of concepts as classes of experience. Thus, throughout the world people have much the same concepts of sun, moon, day, night, man, animal walking, sitting, softness, hardness, etc. The child must be oriented to, and attend to the relevant stimuli in order to form a concept. The objective test of the formation of concept is the ability to respond correctly and reliably to new positive and negative instances of a concept.

A child who has learned a certain concept, *i.e.*, he can recognize certain experiences as being similar, may or may not be able to verbalize what attributes make them similar. But the fact that he consistently makes certain response to certain class of stimuli, indicates that he has formed a concept. To give an example, we observe that many small children are afraid of haircut because the barber's scissors look like those of a doctor whom he has already learnt to fear. This example also exemplifies the fact that concepts may include effective components. They include all the elements of experiences that may occur in common perceptual and cognitive elements as well as motivational and emotional elements. One child may have concept of dog which may reflect his positive delight and experience with the animal, whereas the other child's concept may reflect the fact that he had unpleasant experiences with the animal.

Necessary Conditions

One necessary condition for the formation of concept is that the person must have a series of experiences that are in one or more respects similar. Another necessary condition is that the series of experiences must be preceded or followed by experiences that constitute negative instances of the concept. Appropriate serving of positive and negative instances is very necessary to ensure adequate learning of this concept. For example in developing the concept of lion one must indicate the range of variations that could be found in real lions and in what way animals like tigers, panthers, leopards, etc. differ from lions.

Development of Concept of Objects

An infant acquires many concepts even before he learns a language. One kind of concept, that is acquired by an infant quite early, is the concept of objects which he experiences, for example a favourite toy, or a dress. The acceptance or rejection of a toy is the objective evidence of the attainment of a concept. The concept of even a particular object represents a certain degree of generality. A further stage of generality is reached when the child is able to recognize successive sample of something for example food. And a higher stage of generality is achieved when the child will accept and make a common response to any of a number of rather different stimuli, for example, for different types of food.

Direct experience allows the infant to attain concept of readiness, warmth, softness, heaviness, sweetness, loudness, pain, comfort, etc. In some cases such concepts may be rather undifferentiated as a thing which is a big, is generally heavy, and so the concept of weight and size a may not be able to form many adequate concepts. For example, child's concept of redness may cover a wide range of colour if he happens to live in a culture which pays little attention to the difference in "red", "orange", "pink" and other shades of red.

Piaget postulates that child's concepts develop from immediate simple relations of things experienced together to general abstractions. He also suggests that child's concept of size, weight and other physical attributes of objects do not contain the nation of "Conservation". This is only taught to him by his later experiences. The child's first concepts of distance are limited to his immediate environment. Places remote from his home have no meaning. Gradually, he learns to find his way if he leaves his house for play or for school. It is only when he is introduced in school to the use of the ruler that he comes to acquire definite concept of length. The child lives in the present and so at first concepts of "Yesterday" and "Tomorrow" are quite vague terms to him. By the age of three he has some understanding of these terms. By the age of seven he is able to name the days of the week, but can only name the months of the year when he is eight number concepts are also difficult to master.

The child has some understanding of bigness and littleness or moreness quite early, but the concept of number is formed later. At two years he can distinguish between one and more than one. Gradually he learns to count objects, and before entering the school he may count up to ten or twenty, but this is mere verbalization. Many abstractions used by the adults are beyond child's understanding. Pre-school children find it difficult to understand terms like "God" and "death". Child's concept of himself gradually increases with increase in self-awareness. By the age of three he learns to identify parts of his body, know whether he is a boy or a girl, and also his name. By four years he is likely to know much more about himself, and is much interested in his appearance.

Concepts in the course of a person's life become more complex, and more loaded with significant aspects. Concepts reside in particular individuals with particular histories of experiences, and they classify these experience in their own particular ways. For example, the concept of "Stone" of one person may not precisely be the concept of another person because the experiences with stone in two persons may be quite dissimilar. In the realm of science and technology and in the real of social sciences the concepts attained by different people will differ most. Concepts vary because of the ways in which cultures are organized. However, within a given community, there will be a high degree of communality in the concepts recognized and attained.

Development of Reasoning and Thinking

The reasoning process of children function much in the same way as that of adults. However, there are many differences in the problems faced by children and adults and their resources to solve their problems successfully. Most of the problems faced by children are related to their own immediate concern. Children also lack language ability to phrase their thoughts and conclusions like adults. They also lack relevant information and experience, as well as the capacity for concentration for a longer period. They are less responsive to social demands. They also frequently resort to trial and error in dealing with new problems.

Piaget has proposed that reasoning processes of young children are different from those of adults. He states that before the age of seven or eight years a child can not think using a general proposition, or cannot carry on a genuine argument with others. However, other researchers in this area do not support distinct stages in the development of children's thinking. If the child faces a problem related to his own fund of knowledge and experience, he gives evidence of using good logic within the limits of his understanding. In studies of concept of casual relations in children it was found that children at all ages gave answers is terms of physical or mechanical causes, rather than in terms of magic or mysterious forces. They gave logical and scientifically plausible answers at all age level. As they grow in age they were capable of giving adequate answers to a large number of problems. However, children's reasoning often appeared to be haire and inconsistent. A child may offer a logical and correct answer to some problems at one time to other problems about which he is not informed adequately.

The child gains some idea of cause and effect relationships early in life when he learns that certain acts are disapproved, and thus are "wrong" and the acts which are approved are "right". But if the parents are inconsistent in their approbation and disapproval, or if there is difference in the attitudes between parents, he feels greatly confused. It has been found the children even at the beginning school age have the capacity to generalize from particular examples, or to deduce from a given promise.

Between the ages of seven and eleven, the child is found to be engaged in logical thinking. He interprets natural phenomena in his own way; summer means vacation from school, rains mean to play with paper-boat and taste sweet mangoes. During later childhood he looks for cause and effect relationships about the problems he faces in his daily life. The elementary school child seeks much satisfaction from comparing his thoughts with those of other children of his age. However, the accuracy and richness of child's understanding and reasoning will depend upon the kind of stimulations he has received in his earlier years as well as on the level of his mental maturity.

Thinking is defined as mental manipulation of images or concepts. In thinking we manipulate ideas which emerge as a result of previous of sensory experiences. The act of apprehending or working is closely related to thinking. The thinking process includes perception, imagery concepts, use of language symbols, as well as the memory of past experiences. All thinking includes some aspects of problem solving.

The levels of thinking are; day dreaming, aesthetic appreciation, acquiring information, reflective thinking and creative thinking.

In day dreaming the world of reality is temporarily substituted by that of fantasy. Numerous ideas are formed but with little or no conscious control of their practical significance. Aesthetic appreciation involves appraisal of beauty in an emotionalized manner. The end result is emotionally satisfying state. In acquiring information the individual is engaged in mental activity directed towards seeking, assimilating and recalling new experiences. Reflective thinking usually refers to problem solving, the thinking activity originates by the need to find out the solution of some problem. Reflective thinking may involve inductive reasoning or deductive reasoning. In creative thinking mental activity is directed towards the formation of new ideas or concepts.

Development of Imagination

Children begin to engage in imagination in infancy and continue to do so to some extent throughout their life. Make believe plays an important role in the process of development. During infancy and later it serves as a means of organizing group activities when children grow older. It is through the power of imagination that the child is able to think beyond time and space.

The imaginary activities of pre-school children are to a large extent related to domestic theme or to their experiences of daily life such as house keeping, preparing food, washing clothes, caring for young ones, going in a motor car, or a train, etc. In their make-believe children are found to express many of their unfulfilled wishes such as more sweets to eat or new toys to play with. Children also unburdened their emotional problems in their make-believe play such as their jealousy towards younger sibling or their hatred for a very strict grandmother. Make-believe themes are very frequent in the play or early elementary school children.

But after that there is decrease in child's imaging as revealed through over activity; and it seems to become more private and little related with every day events. Then it includes more adventurous themes.

As the child grows older and comes to possess more abilities and powers, there is little need for him to indulge in make-believe acts. With increased knowledge and experience, he becomes more aware of the inconsistencies so inherent in a make-believe situation. However, older children vary in their tendency indulge in fantasies. It may also serve different purposes for different individuals. To one child make-believe may serve as a momentary form of relaxation, to another it may serve as a substitute for action and to another an excuse for his failure.

Imagination in young children is stirred by nursery rhymes and fairy tales that are told to them. Through their content and from visualizing the possibility of the impossible he drives much emotional satisfaction. Later, he becomes much interested in the exploits of heroes, and heroines in adventurous and mythological stories, and tries to identify himself with them. It is through such stories that he comes to learn that good just always prevail. Most boys prefer tales of adventure, and girls prefer romantic stories. Such emotion arousing stories provide them with excitement and also motivate them to enact dramatic roles. However, too great involvement in the world of fantasy cause to arouse unrealistic and unachievable ambitions, experience failure, and thereby retreat further into the world of fantasy. The most important thing for a child who is sufficiently mature is that he eventually comes to appreciate the relationship between world of fantasy and world of reality. So far as the child can appreciate consciously this relationship, his involvement in some make-believe activities will help to develop his imaginative powers and creative potentialities during adulthood.

CONCEPTS AND THE CUP

This absolutism and unawareness of relativity, while is it most obvious in these object-concept problems, seems to play in a number of other contexts. Consider the ordinary task of drinking out of a cup. Bruner has beautifully described the dreadful problem that cups present for young babies. At first the baby doesn't really comprehend the relationship between the angle of the cup and behaviour of the liquid it contains. He seems to imagine that liquid will come out of the cup more or less as a sold goat and simply turns the cup up when he gets it to his face. The inevitable result may be amusing enough for the baby, but is not very effective from the standpoint of drinking.

Before the age of one year, the baby has worked out the complex relationship between liquid level, gravity, and the edge of a cup. Babies of this age can drink smoothly and efficiently. They simply pickup the cup and tip it to the required angle. However, their absolution shows in another situation. Suppose we show a year-old baby some milk in a transparent container, pour the milk into a narrower, opaque container, and allow the baby to drink from that : Evidently babies think the milk will be at the same height in the narrower container, and so they tip it accordingly, again with the age inevitable result. Similarly, if the liquid is transferred to a wider opaque container, so that the level is lower, they are disappointed, because with they tip the glass, nothing comes into their mouth. They seem to imagine that liquid levels stay constant and are independent of the shape of the container the liquid is in.

Once again, this should remind us of the baby's inability to appreciate relationship between the container and the contained. Babies get over this problem around the age of fifteen months, and can scope when their milk or juice is transposed from a glass of one shape to another. There is an intermediate stage in which the baby must look at the liquid level to know where it is. By the age of fifteen months they don't need to look at it. If they are prevented from doing so, by a lid on the cup, they can still drink smoothly and efficiently without any difficulty at all.

Development of Moral Standards

A child's first idea of right and wrong is determined largely by the verdict of parents, and perhaps of other adults of his family. To a small child, parents are the ideal persons, and the child follows them almost blindly. If the child always remains within his family confines, there will perhaps be no moral conflict. He will follow the moral codes of his family members.

The trouble arises as soon as the child is allowed to mix with others outside his family. Perhaps the neighbours follow a different moral code. Very often the children with whom he plays at the street corner of his class-fellows in the school have a code different from the one followed by the child at home. Within a racial group there are marked sub-groups and each sub-group has its own moral code. Socio-economic distinctions create moral codes some what different for different sub-groups following conflicting standards, the child is bewildered. Thus, it appears that socialization has not only its limitations, but also its attendant dangers. The child feels the pull of his early upbringing, but sometimes finds himself justifying the codes of other groups.

Other forces are also at work. An athlete, a movie actor or a cook may catch the youthful fancy of the child. This danger increases with age. The child is concrete in his attitude. He would admire a person in flash and blood, someone whom he know personally. With increasing age, however, his range widens and the weakness for public characters, cinema stars and historical characters, may develop. Boys are more prone to the cult of hero worship than girls. Besides this sex difference there are individual differences caused by innate abilities. The lively extrovert type of boys prefer bravery and quickness. Introverts prefer poets and painters. Thus we find that we cannot judge the growth of moral standards simply in terms of growth and development.

In the first place, schools must have definite rules in unambiguous terms about what the pupils should or should not do in the class. But, in setting up codes of conduct, they should realize that these edicts loss their influence gradually. As children grow, they try to judge things for themselves. But if schooling starts early and continues, the force of habits acquired at an early age may pull them through in later life. Moreover, school standards of conduct should be based on good sense for then only are they likely to be followed by the adolescents.

Development of Aesthetic Standards

To develop aesthetic standards, children should be given opportunities to grow and to express themselves whether in music or in fine arts, in dancing or in modelling. In this period they should be faced with as few restrictions as possible. Even if their outputs is inadequate, they should not be criticized. This will develop their creative urge. Perhaps we can not expect too much from all. Artistic ability is the product of heredity, environment and early conditioning. Here we are depending solely on one of these factors, namely early conditioning.

In the second stage, creative work needs critical analysis, and no analysis is better than self-analysis. Self analysis is possible only when children know the standards to go by. For this purpose children should be given opportunities to come across standards of perfection. This should be attained gradually beginning with such standards of perfection. This should be attained gradually beginning with such standards as are easily accessible and moving on to those which are really high. This is possible if children are taken to art galleries where they can see the works of master painters, to music conferences to hear master musicians. Perhaps, children of artists and musicians excel others because they are provided opportunities at home for comparing their performances with those of their talented parents. It is at this stage that children will be able to find out their own inadequacies.

In the third and final phase, children should be allowed to go on with their creative work, but with the enrichment of standards. Their achievement needs critical examination and evaluation in a constructive manner. Only when all these processes are followed we can expect artistic talents to develop in children.

Perhaps a beginning should be made quite early, when the child is two or two and a half years old. Perhaps primary schools receiving children at five will not find it too late to develop the talents of their pupils to a certain degree. But the teachers should be patient enough to pursue all the three phase and should expect only a limited degree of success.

Time and Season

The concept of time is difficult for the pre-school child. Having had little past that he can remember, he has only a scanty basis for conceptualizing notions of past, present and future. Generally, children seem to exhibit a clear understanding of "Yesterday" and "Today" than of "Tomorrow".

The concept of time is closely related to the notions of motion and speed. Because the child has had little experience in dealing with distance and velocity, be tends to confuse time with space. A four year old boy is taken for two drives lasting about the same time but to different destinations and is told that on the second trip he went farther than on the first. He may then suppose that the second trip lasted longer.

If on a third trip the car stops frequently for gas or food, the boy may be convinced that this trip was the longest. Although there was no real differences in elapsed time. Here we can see that his concentration on stopping points is very important to his estimation of time, his inability to concentrate prevents him from taking certain elements into account, such as the speed of car.

Most pre-school children are incapable of adding successive intervals of time. Given that durations A, B and C are equal, for example, the child cannot deduce that A + B = B + C. Again it is the inability to concentrate on two aspects of a problem simultaneously that limits the child in his comprehension of this fundamental principle of logic. In their estimates of the passage of time, children seem to be more concerned with ending points than with starting points.

Various activities can be arranged in a way that the child is able to distinguish between play time, work time, snack time, rest time, stories and songs time, etc. He is also to be made aware of maintaining a proportion between the various timings. Furthermore, when he grows older that is. When he attains the age of 4½ years or more, he may be encouraged to arrange his schedules by rising early, brushing his teeth before the morning breakfast setting out some time for prayers after taking his bath, preparing to come to the school and so on.

Similarly, the child can be made to understand the concept of the various seasons and their sequential order by pointing out how they feel during summer season, rainy season and winter season. The concept of seasons can be conveyed to the child by associating their actual experiences of feeling warm or cold or wet with the actual seasonal periods during the course of the year and by recalling their experiences during the course of each day.

Space

As adults, we are very much concerned with spatial orientations; indeed, we use a great variety of words to describe relations in space. Up and down, left and right, under and over, here and there, in and out help us to achieve a clear conception of how things are situated in space.

A young child does not start with all these linguistic aids to help him understand space. He learns to deal with and name spatial phenomena as they affect his personality. The word left and right, for example, are meaningless to him until he is taught to raise his right hand or turn to the left.

Many aspects of time and space are closely interrelated. For example, the elements of starting and stopping—the beginning point and the end point are common to both phenomena. Many of the child's misconceptions about time have close counter parts in his efforts to deal with space. The tendency to concentrate, the irreversibility of thought processes, and the inability to concentrate on transformational states, all make it extremely difficult for children to make mature judgments concerning the measurement of space.

Quantity

Adult perception of quantity generally rests on two fundamental concepts: Conservation and one-to-one correspondence. These concepts are not usually used consciously, but they account for our ability to make sense of a world where it is often important to make accurate estimates of quantity under conditions that may be confusing or misleading.

In pre-school children these concepts are still poorly developed. The tests used by Piaget to investigate them often involved presenting children with two identical beakers filled with identical amounts of water, or asking children to examine or handle identical balls of clay. Then, as the child watched, the shape of the water or clay was changed; the water might be poured from a short, wide beaker into a tall, narrow one, or the clay might be molded into a narrow as usage shape. When the child consistently recognizes that the changes in form do not change the amount of water or clay involved, he has learned to conserve quantity.

At the age of about four, children are usually quite unable to conserve quantity. In the experiments with water, for example, the four year old will usually concentrate on the height of the water in the beaker, being unable to decentrate, he will not understand that the quantity of water has remained constant. By the age of five or six the ability to conserve has begun to develop, and it is well established by about age seven. It is interesting to notice that conservation of different properties develops at different ages. At the age six, Sara may have a sure grasp of conservation of quantity at the same time she will almost certainly not be able to conserve continuous weight or volume, because these concepts do not develop until several years later.

Concept of Volume

Another important mathematical concept that should be explained to the children is the concept of volume. The idea is not to teach the children the procedure to measure the volume of a container but simply to help them know what is meant by volume, what is the difference between area and volume and how to know whether the volume of vessel is less or more than that of another vessel. Here again the teacher can explain the concept through demonstration of the vessels of different sizes, containing water. She can discuss the shapes of the various vessels and containers and then show them the differences in volume by pouring water in them or form one to another etc. In certain cases, the exercise can be repeated by using sand, cereals, etc. in place of water.

Concept of Number

Another aspect of quantity is number, and this is where the concept of one-to-one correspondence is important. Given a number of objects, an adult can construct a second set with the same number simply by counting. If the given set contains six members, for example, we simply take six other objects to create the second set. Even if we were unable to count, however, are could still create a second set by matching up the new objects with the originals one by one.

As adults, we take it for granted that quantities are not altered by physical arrangement. Ten pennies remain ten pennies whether they are in a line, in a circle, or in a pocket. Neither this concept referred to as conservation of number nor that of one-to-one correspondence is at all obvious to the pre-school child, who is unable to compensate for the effect of density on length. Later in her development she may consider either length or density, but it is not until the end of the pre-operational stage that she can consider both factors simultaneously and then divorce these spatial elements from her conception of number. Pre-school children may attend to number rather than length, however, when the quantities involved are extremely small.

The ability to count does not necessarily indicate a mature concept of quantity. Children may count equal numbers and still deny numerical equality.

When the attention of the children is drawn to the number of seats required for whole group and for a smaller section of the group, number of pencils or fruits given to each child, then they get some understanding of concepts such as many, few, etc. Understanding of number relationship may also be fostered among the children through the provision of the following opportunities without stress to remember any numbers as such:

(*a*) Naming units of quantities.
(*b*) Associating symbols with quantities by means of cards.
(*c*) Naming and recognizing numerical symbols.
(*d*) Using money in buying things for example in a shopping project.
(*e*) Hearing that the day is divided into parts which occur always in regular sequence – morning, noon, afternoon and night.
(*f*) Knowing the name of days and months.

(*g*) Naming of one-to-one relationship through games and suitable activities.

The best way to elucidate the concept of numbers is through giving examples of the concept objects supplemented by number songs, play-way activities involving numbers and some stories giving ideas of numbers.

Relations

The ability to conceive of relations is one that begins to develop in infancy. The infant can discriminate between objects and to some degree, differentiate levels of intensity. For example, he perceives that one sound is louder than another or that one object is larger than another.

As we might expect, the pre-school child has difficulty in dealing with relation that involve more than two elements. If he is handed two bean bags, he may be able to say that the green one, for example, is heavier than the yellow one. He can make such absolute distinctions rather easily. But if we now give him a red bean bag that is even lighter than the yellow one, he may be unable to tell as which of the first two was the heavier. He centres on the immediate experience and becomes uncertain about the relationship he learned just a moment ago.

Piaget devised a number of experiments designed to test children's grasp of order among objects. One study involved the ordering of a series of different-sized sticks. The child was given ten sticks and told to arrange them in ascending order that is, to put the smallest stick first, the next smallest second, and so forth.

The youngest group tested (ages four to five) offered a variety of unsuccessful solutions to the problem. Some created an entirely random arrangement. Others began correctly and then continued at random. An interesting approach attempted by some children was to select any stick at random to start and then to line up the sticks in such a way that the top of each stick extended slightly above the top of the preceding stick, but without regard to the bottoms.

This solution-focusing on the tops of the sticks and ignoring the bottoms-exemplifies the inability of young children to centre on more than one aspect of a situation as the same time. Although five and six year olds were considerably more successful they too experienced much difficulty, proceeding in a manner that might best the characterized as trial and error. It is not until after the pre-school years that children consistently exhibit the ability to devise a logical plan of action in order to solve such problems.

Classification

One of the most important operation to develop during the pre-school years is that of classification. The ability to organize objects and ideas into useful categories is a fundamental prerequisite for nature reasoning.

Classes have four fundamental properties. First, classes are mutually exclusive. No figure, for example, can belong both to the class of circles and the class of squares. Second, a class can be determined by its intention that is, by the common characteristic shared by all its members. Third, a class can be determined by its extension that is, by the list of all its members. And fourth, intention must define extension; we should be able to name the members of a class if we know the characteristics that they have in common.

In order to test the pre-school child's ability to classify, experiments present the child with an assortment of objects and then request that he groups the ones that go together. Young children rarely complete this task in a consistent way.

As the pre-school years near their end, children begin to group objects successfully and to exhibit the ability to subdivide groups into consistent components as well; however, the five or six year old who accomplished this task may still fail to fully understand the true nature of classification. Some concepts, such as colour, are established early, but the development of mature conceptual capabilities is not complete until after the pre-school period.

Living and Non-living Things

It is easy for a child to distinguish between living and moving and non-living objects. But his mental horizon have to be broadened further by telling him what factors differentiate and what are the broader categories in which we usually place the living and non-living objects. Take the instance of a plant or a tree. It is non-moving but growing. It is to be classified as a living object but the dry twig has ceased to grow and hence it is a non-living object. A finer distinction between these objects would not be possible here. The pre-school teacher can give some knowledge in this area by dividing the objects in four categories:

(*i*) Living and non-moving *viz.*, plants;
(*ii*) Living and moving *viz.*, animals, birds, insects, human beings, reptiles;
(*iii*) Non-living and non-moving—minerals, rocks, etc;
(*iv*) Non-living and moving—cycles, trucks, aeroplanes, boats, trains, etc.

The teacher can utilize the field trips to draw the attention of the children regarding these distinctions. He can also tell about many such objects related to the indoor situations.

Concept of the Human Body

By the age of 3 years, a child knows the names of the parts of body and he also understand their physical functioning. It is possible to give some elementary knowledge of physiology to the little children. While talking of the teeth, the pre-school teacher should not stop merely by saying that one should clean the teeth but she should convince children of the advantages of keeping the teeth clean. Similarly, the usefulness of good habits like the regular habits of taking food, keeping neat, keeping a handkerchief, etc., showed one of the techniques is to demonstrate good habits through puppets. The teacher can arrange an ordinary puppet show by showing two puppets one with a handkerchief and the second without any. The second puppet sneezes and asks the first one to loan his handkerchief for blowing off the nose. Meanwhile a nurse (another puppet) appears on the scene. She prevents the first puppet from loaning the handkerchief to the second one and gives some general instructions for avoiding the infection. The arrangement of such activities has a measure of recreation and education both. The teacher can think of a number of activities on such lines and help the children in developing healthy habits.

Development of Colour Concept

Studies of colour concept have shown a steady increase in the ability to perceive and use colour correctly. Cook has investigated the development of colour concept and discovered that as the age of the child progresses there is an increased efficiency shown in colour, discrimination and colour naming. Colour discrimination comes earlier than the naming, thus indicating that the verbal symbols are learned later than the colour concept which developed earlier. Cook's results also indicate that children can discriminate the hues (red, green, yellow, etc.) more accurately than the differences in brightness or saturation.

Little children are attracted by colours and like to differentiate them. Standing in the open field, the children can see the blue sky, the green leaves, the red rose, the yellow saffron and so on. They can also be told that air is colours of vegetables and fruits may follow this. Then the children wear coloured clothes. They can be asked to match the colour of their clothes with the above said objects. From these concrete examples, the pre-school teacher can bring the children to activities by giving them coloured papers and scissors. They may be helped in matching the various colours and adjusting the good combination for their dolls or puppets or even for themselves.

Concept of Physical Causality

According to Piaget, there are three distinct stages in the development of this concept:

First Stage

All explanations are psychological, phenomenistic, finalistic and magical in nature. When asked the question as to why the clouds do not fall, the children at this stage would respond by saying that they do not fall because "They stick" or because "The God keeps them there".

Second Stage

The explanations are animistic and dynamic in nature. When children at this stage are asked the questions as to why the cloud do not fall, their reply will be "The sky keeps them up" or "Man keeps them there".

Third Stage

Explanation are more rational, and logical educations are used for explanations or explanations are spatical and mechanical in nature. Child passing through this stage will explain the clouds not falling by saying that "The wind pushes them" or that "They themselves hold there so that they do not fall."

Piaget studies the age levels of children for different stages of development of this concept. According to his findings the child covers the first stage by three years and enters the second stage which he masters by seven or eight years of age. After eight, the third stage sets in. But the child gives explanations comparable to those of adults by twelve years of age.

Role of Teachers in Promoting Concept Formation

The teacher's role and the atmosphere which she creates in the classroom are critical factors. The teacher is not the source of all knowledge. Her task is to establish an environment and encourage children to use it. The pre-school should plan certain learning experience which are relatively complete, and scientific relationship can be observed children will in this way have tools with which to approach what is unknown. A child can learn that there are many possible bases for categorizing fruits and vegetables those eaten raw and those eaten unripe, those with many seeds and those with one large seed and those with few seeds, round ones or long ones, different colours of skin, rough skins or smooth skins. They can realize that categories may be discrete or overlapping; some fruits are eaten only raw, others are eaten only after cooking, some may be eaten only raw, other are eaten only after cooking, some may be eaten either way. They become aware that objects look different on the inside from how they appear on the outside.

Many things should be available for children to investigate on their own. These things must be varied and stimulating—picture books, magnifying glass, plastic hose pipe for pouring water and sand, sieves, assorted buttons, rough and smooth objects, old mechanical toys to be taken apart, to mention only some—to be taken and handled freely by the children.

There should also be a definite place to which they are to be returned, so that there is order in the classroom and children can independently find the things that they want, can take responsibility themselves for maintaining orderliness. The teacher generally does not need to show the children what to do, but can let them experiment. When she sees a child who is stuck for a long time at one stage of any activity who keeps sorting buttons at random for three weeks, say may ask him a pointed question about the properties of the buttons: What colours is this button? Do you see any other of the same colour?

The teacher encourages every child to talk about what he sees, to try to say on what basis he has sorted the buttons to tell about buttons that he has at home or has seen in the shop, to describe the buttons on his shirt, to bring buttons from home to make a class collection.

Conceptualization requires language and language development furthers conceptualization. Once the child has the name of the shape 'square' he will expand the concept of square and start naming all the square objects that he sees.

The teacher must have a sound background of general knowledge and be interested in learning more. Her own enthusiasm and curiosity set an example for the children. She must be willing to say, "I don't know", and follow it up with, "Let's find out. How can we find out?" She must be aware of sources of information upon which she can drawn materials, books, people in the schools and community.

The teacher needs facts, but she also needs to realize how facts are related to each other. These relationship can be on many levels.

We may plant seeds and note the requirements for their growth. These are the facts of plant life. We may then compare the needs of a plant with the needs of a person, thus developing a concept of the commonness of all living things. Watching the plants, we may note the way they change as they grow. This can be compared to a human or other animal. We may cook the bhaji we have grown and watch it change in another way, from different causes, when the leaves become limp and water appears. Thus the concept of change broadens to include physical change as well as biological change. In this way facts are seen as related elements within a unified world. Only in this way can information be given meaning, can a structure of knowledge be created, can an individual proceed to independent search and learning. This can be done very simply, if the teacher herself is aware and thoughtful, just by a simple sentence at the right moment, by a comparison or suggested observation, that starts the children thinking along these lines. In this way the teacher can facilitate and speed the child's understanding, and many times can point the way to a comprehension that might otherwise never occur.

10

Language Development

Language is the ability to communicate with others. It includes every means of communication in which thoughts and feelings are symbolized so as to convey meaning including such widely different forms of communication as written, spoken, sign facial expression, gesture pantonima etc. Speech is one of the forms of language. The child's adjustment is influenced by his language development and his language in turn by his environmental factors. The normal language development is very necessary to make a child well adjusted in the society and teacher has to help a lot in it.

Language development is said to be sound shaping development. A growth process processing from the vague, indistinct to a properly shaped, clear, direct and a controlled form. This is a type of behaviour which helps the child to form the concept of the world around him to transform from an ego-centric to a social being to make assumptions for him to set up conventions; to guide and control him, to inform him, to instil in him the thoughts, the feelings, the attitude and make him feel secure and insecure through the words which he uses and hears. The children who learn to communicate will make better social adjustment with others as compared to a child who is retarded in its language growth.

Language is a system used by a society for classifying, preserving and transmitting its knowledge, skills, beliefs and values to all its members. It is in the bosom of the society that language is formed, and it has existed from the first day when man experienced the need for communicating with one another. Language is thus the social fact par excellence the result of social contact. It has become one of the strongest bonds uniting societies and it owes its development to the existence of the social groups.

Psychologically, the original linguistic act consists in giving to a sign a systematic value. Human language no less natural than that of animals but it is a degree higher in that man has given to signs and symbols objective values and is able to modify and improve indefinitely by convention. Since the animal language is not determined by convention, it does not admit either of change or of progress. Human language is enriched by adding new words, and forms of sentences from other language, whereas the animal cries of the ancient day and of today are the same. No change is found in their cry. Thus, human language is unique.

Language serves to assist memory and facilitate thought to communicate meaning and when necessary to conceal it and to express feeling. Language provides symbols for thinking and also socialized thought through interaction with other people.

The child needs language for survival just as he needs food. The information she receives from the significant people the adults may be regarded as raw material for her future dealings with the world. Language is also a tool, the child can use in recalling her communicated experiences, manipulating concepts and projecting possible patterns of behaviour in her thoughts and actions. Most of the more complex psychological processes that are differentiated during development depend upon the use of symbols of one sort or another. Thus, growing skills in symbolization and the manipulation of symbols results in greater development of self by increasing the number and complexity of the meanings that constitute it. At the same time, it places at the disposal of the individual effective means for evaluating situations and events, defining her goals and plans of action.

Functions of Language for the Child

The purpose that language serves are many and varied. The purposes have been grouped under the following five major headings:

Language as a Means to Make Wants and Needs Know

The child at first tries to convey and satisfy his needs just by some signs and symbols. When he realizes that there are many situations which are not satisfied by these means he starts using language to express his needs and feelings precisely.

Language as a Means for Expression of Emotions

During infancy laughing, cooling, and crying are the chief means of expressing pleasure and displeasure. This he starts expressing his feelings directly, physically *i.e.*, by wordless actions. During the pre-school years an important shift is occurring, the child is becoming much less direct, less physical, much more symbolic in his expression of emotions. Instead of hitting he starts using hitting words.

Language as a Device for Gaining Information

Asking questions and getting answers is an important activity in this period. He learns about the world around him by asking questions.

Language as a Means to Social Interactions

Pre-school children are highly motivated to engage in social behaviour. The pre-school child that he has to depend on others for many things. Therefore, it is necessary to expand his skill in communicating with others. Indeed language is the basic adhesive that binds on society together. Through language it is easy to assign roles, and it is the basic organization. Through language we can come to some agreement with others.

Language as an Aid to Personal Identifications

The desire to be recognized by others is strong in each one of us. Through language one may be able to tell what he is and what he might be and gets personal identification.

Stages in Learning to Talk

Early Sounds

The first sound produced by the child is an incidental accompaniment to the rapid expulsion of air from the lungs. The first of these is usually the birth cry. The neonates first sound does not express either his feelings or to solve some problems. He makes them by accident.

Speech requires the maturation and co-operation of many organs, such as larynx, lips, tongue and throat muscles.

Infant Babbling

Gradually the reflex crying, which occurs as a result of emotional stimuli, merges into what is called the "babble stage". The sound that child produces at this time is a stimuli for their continuation and he makes the sound as a form of play. This gives the child pleasure. Babbling begins in the 3rd or 4th month and gradually merges into the saying of words at about 15 months.

Babbling is the period for practicing vocalizations because he produces variety of sounds. So it should be encouraged. Adults interpret this meaningless babbles as the uttering or meaningful words.

This kind of incomprehensible utterance, reaches a peak between 1¼ and 1¾ years of age and then tends to give plan to meaningful expressions. When the child is 2½ years old about 93 per cent of his speech is comprehensible, and when he is 4 years old, practically all is understandable. These babblings of infants provide the foundation for later meaningful speech.

The Learning of Words

The sounds that a child produces may be spontaneous, or by some objective elements in the environment or by some other persons. If there is a uniform sound when a specific adjustment is made, this sound becomes a part of that situation. There is considerable evidence that ability to speak words lags behind the ability to comprehend them. The child does not build his vocabulary from his own first sounds, but learns to imitate and uses the words used by others.

The progress begun by infants was continued in somewhat the same direction in pre-school children.

Growth of vocabulary is an important phase of child development. This growth is primarily an increase in the number of words that are familiar to the child, but it involves, as well, the learning of discriminations of meaning, the specific emotional tone of each, and the manipulations of words as a phase of intellectual procedures. Verbalization may originally be a form of self expression, it becomes a form of social influence; a means of controlling the behaviour of others.

Pre-school children often talk to themselves to explain what they are doing. Their talking and thinking go on simultaneously; they talk so that they will know what they think. Children's knowledge of words varies in quality as well as in quantity. The meanings they attach to some words have grown out of first hand experience, and vivid and precise; their understanding of other words is vague of incorrect.

Beginning with single words mostly nouns and verbs, and single word sentence, pre-school children's speech develops to complete sentences of 6 to 8 words. During the same period, their output of incomprehensible speech and incomplete sentences decreases. Active vocabulary increases rapidly. The rate of acquisition of words during pre-school period is said to be around 500 to 600 per year. The vocabulary increase may cease if he does not hear good speech.

At three years a child may use 11,000 or 12,000 words, a four year old may use 15,000 words a day. Child's pronunciation also improves markedly at this period. His sentence structure increases in complexity. Till 4½ he uses a small proportion of complex and compound sentences, by 5 and 6 the proportion rises.

Pre-school child uses languages for narration more extensively than toddlerdom. Phantasy and wishful thinking are often mixed with reality, when he narrates. At four the child can narrate events and tell stories. He gains the ability to express his feelings and tell stories. He gains the ability to express his feelings and thoughts through language more and more. On the average, 10 to 15 percent of their conversation consists of questions. Almost all questions concern immediate environment, and sometimes about the things which he doesn't know like God, heaven etc. Their questions should be answered with simplicity and honesty so that the urge to ask questions is preserved. It will help them develop their intelligence and creativity.

Children ask questions for many reasons.

1. To satisfy their natural curiosity of an inquiring mind.
2. To get information or reassurance.
3. To get attention.
4. To solve a problem.
5. To test their own judgment.
6. To be sociable.

Schedule of Speech Development

1. Vocalized spontaneously—babbles.
2. Definitely attunes to vocal stimulation by turning head toward or watching person vocalizing.

3. Uses syllables consisting of consonant and vowel in spontaneous vocal activity.
4. Vocalizes in response to being talked to.
5. Shows comprehension by some specific and consistent response to verbal stimulation, waving "bye-bye" on demand etc.
6. Uses vocal symbol to express meaning.
7. Uses final consonant in syllables.
8. Imitates sound in pitch or inflection.
9. Uses five symbols to express meaning.
10. Uses ten symbols to express meaning.
11. Combines two words or symbols to express meaning, such as "bye-bye", or "here dady".
12. Uses six conventional words accurately. Pronunciation need not be perfect, but words must be intelligible to one unfamiliar with child.
13. Uses agent-action or action-object structure, such as "ride car" or "hurt baby".
14. Definitely uses noun-verb or verb-object structure. Must give more than one instance.
15. Substitutes, more than once, a pronoun for other persons' name.
16. Uses prepositions more than once. Usually appears as the substitution of such a phrase as "go to town" or "ride in car" for "ride car".
17. Qualifies noun with adjective.
18. Qualifies verb with adverb.
19. Uses auxiliary in verbs.
20. Uses regular plural in nouns more than once.

Language Skills

Infancy covers the period from birth to 19 months, and toddlerdom extends from 16 months to two and a half year. During these stages, the child's language makes considerable strides. The rate and pattern of growth, however, are not the same for all children. Most babies begin to use a few words when they are around a year old.

From two months onwards most infants seem to experiment with the vocal mechanism. By four months, most of them have mastered the basic use of the vocal apparatus. They blow bubbles, chuckle, coo and make various other sounds constantly using the larynx and breath control. By four months, the child has a command of most of the vowel and a few consonant sounds.

At the sixth or seventh month the baby can make most of the vowel and consonant sounds and many of the diphthongs—and syllables includes in the adult speech. Child's vocabulary at ten months consists of one word, at twelve months it is three, and at fifteen it goes up to nineteen.

The toddler makes a varied use of language. The first activities use of usually to name people, things and action. He picks up names, such as, dog, cat, baby etc.

Further advance in the development of language is made when around the end of the second year he uses narrative language. Thus from feeling and action, he proceeds into the new realm of the exchange of facts.

Language development during the pre-school year between three and six years attains greater complexity and is used for many ends. During this final the child learns to communicate his complex feelings and motivation to others, and uses language to solve problems which he formerly solved by physical means. Instead of trial and error attempts on a physical plane, the child surveys all possible solutions to the problem in terms of language. He remembers, generalizes and reproduces former experiences through words and applies them in the context of the present situation. Language becomes the means of understanding his environment, or securing further information about the world, of people and events and of acquiring other intellectual skills, such as reasoning, number concepts, time concepts, etc., language is influenced by the social environment, and in turn exerts its influence on the environment, thus becoming a part of social living.

During the pre-school years the child's pronunciation improves markedly, though the individual differences remain. The pre-school child's sentence structure increases in complexity, upto the age of four and a half year he uses a small proportion of complex and compound sentences. But by five or six years, their proportions rise and every form of sentence structure appears in the child's speech.

Now the child uses language for narration more extensively than in toddlerdom. At 3 years the narrative is much longer than during the previous stage of development. Phantasy and wishful thinking are often mingled with reality in the children's narratives. At 4 years a child has marked ability to narrate events and tell stories. Around this age, children begin to use language for the expression of complex thought and reasoning.

Sometimes at three, children go through a phase of revelling in the use of bad language. They do not understand what they are saying, but do realize that these words shock adults. A year or so later, children are apt to use 'dirty' words even more. They love to indulge in 'toilet talk' and have a full understanding of its meaning. A wise thing for teachers and parents to do would be neither to be shocked, nor to listen to the 'dirty' talk without comment, but to tell the child firmly that people do not like to listen to such talk, and that he should not talk so.

At 3 and 4 years, children go through the question asking stage. The child's questions may serve many motives other than curiosity. Sometimes the questions are asked for establishing social contact or receiving attention or gaining reassurance, solace or help. Some questions spring from worry, fear or uneasiness. Children often repeat the question even after it has been answered. Such repetitions may be for purpose of getting attention, but it may also indicate that the child is puzzled or disturbed.

The most perplexing questions are those that concern, God, death and sex.

Death's idea is difficult for the pre-school child to grasp, children between 3 to 5 years do think of death as final. They tend to interpret it as 'absence' for a longer or shorter time. It is better to explain that in death there is cessation of breathing, feeling and moving, hence when death is mentioned, he reacts as though his own death is being discussed. Since he dreads separation from his parents and has a keen desire to live and be with his father and mother, mention of death may perturb him greatly. However this is no cause for avoiding answers regarding death. Spock says that by four or five years most children make some kinds of adjustment to the idea of death partly by suppression and partly by denial.

A typical question regarding sex is 'where the baby come from'? Such questions deserve an honest and a simple answer. An answer such as, "The baby grew from a tiny egg in a bag in the mother's tummy" usually satisfied the child's initial curiosity.

Factors Influencing Language Development

Physical condition has an important influence on the development of language. Severe and prolonged illness during the first two years can retard the development of speech.

There is considerable evidence in the literature to show that there is marked relationship between the socio-economic status of the family and child's linguistic development; children of higher socio-economic group. Social contacts and relationships of the child have an important influence on speech development.

Much of the child's language development takes place through imitation of the language patterns of adults, and the opportunity to hear and to use words, hence, it is decidedly influenced by cultural environmental factors. Following are the significant factors, influencing language development:

1. Degree of maturity sets the limit to language growth and language stimulation. The study by Strayer shows that early training in language does not facilitate language growth and no special stimulation can transcend the limits set by child's level of maturity.
2. Level of intelligence also determines language development. Many studies reveal that children of superior intelligence talk early and are advanced in every phase of language development.
3. Sense and prolonged illness during the early years can also retard language and development. Hurlock also shows the negative influence of poor physical condition on the development of language.
4. Family members exert considerable influence on language development of the child. Parents speech and interest in language reading and conversation influences child's language habits. Travel and other stimulating activities provided by the home also motivate children to learn and to use new words. Another factor in the family questions as "When is your next birthday? When do you get up"? "When do you have your meal?" When they are five years old they can tell how old they are, when they go to bed, the name of the day, etc. By the age of six they can state the grade on which they read. By

seven years they can tell the time, the season and the month, the name of the month, and the name of the year.

Role of Pre-school Programme in Language Development

The child develops skill in the language arts by participating in various experiences and activities. One activity can contribute to growth in several of the arts and, for that reason, activities have not been labelled as appropriate for reading, speaking, listening or writing. Using information pertaining to development and experience of the children in the class, the teacher can select and adapt the activity most appropriate for them, like story telling, using poetry, sharing, dramatizing, etc.

Initial Preparation

The teacher should prepare the child initially learn language. This she can do by (*i*) teaching good and attractive rhymes and action songs to the children. (*ii*) by encouraging them to take part in dramas and puppet plays. The teacher should relate stories, rhymes, lullabies, action songs, etc., in a very interesting way, with actions, expressions and gestures. For example, if she is telling a story she should bring out different characters in the story.

Conversation

Teacher should encourage the children to talk freely. Whenever she has time she should try to listen to the experiences of the children. She should make the timid and shy children feel that they are important and create confidence in them and she should pay attention to every individual child.

Story Telling

Young children today enjoy a good story just as children always have. Although the content of the story may vary from generation to generation, the use of story telling to entertain, to teach and to develop appreciation of literature continues to be an important art. Primarily story telling is an activity that offers opportunities for developing skills in the language arts. Specifically, the child may learn to listen and have experience in speaking while talking about the story or telling original stories. The child may learn to keep in mind a sequence of ideas, increase vocabulary, and enlarge the background of experience.

Use of Books

Not by accident does a child develop a love for books, a feeling that books can be friends and companions, an awareness of the fun and enjoyment that can come from books, an appreciation of good literature, the knowledge that books can be sources of information, and an interest in caring for books. All these attitudes, which it is hoped the young child will develop, evolve as the child has many pleasurable experiences with books both at home and at school.

Opportunities for the children to listen to and enjoy stories, read and tell, to handle, use, and love books can help them to learn that reading can be fun and to become interested in learning to read. In selecting books, the contents, illustrations, and physical make up are important items to be considered.

Poetry

Experiences with poetry can be happy, and spontaneous one for children. They enjoy the sounds around them, create sounds laugh at on usual combinations of words, sense the rhythm of running, skipping and speaking. The spontaneous language of children is often poetic in nature. Poetry, if well selected and correctly used, can help the child to listen carefully, to learn new words and ways of expressing one's feelings; to develop increased auditory awareness or acuity; to improve the quality of one's own voice; and to feel secure in the group as one participates in saying poetry with the group. Poetry can bring laughter and happiness to the child.

Dramatization

Dramatization can offer many activities through which creativity in oral language may be encouraged. Dramatization may include dramatic play, creative dramatics, and using puppets. While there is no clear-distinction, each does have a unique characteristic.

Sharing Time and Group Discussion/Free Conversations

Sharing may also refer so communicating between children or between teacher and child. As this informal communicating and sharing continues the child uses more words to express her thoughts. As children become more secure in a group situation, they want and need to talk together, and time in the school day for planning and sharing may be designed. The time for beginning such a group activity, however, will depend on the children involved – their interests, attention span, and readiness to participate in a group situation. Sharing time implies communication. Objects may be shown and talked about, but plans, incidents, and news may be discussed too by the teacher as well as by the children.

Discussion time, however, with teacher and children, is usually problem-centered. Plans may be made for a trip or a special project for the morning. The choice of activities may be discussed. This type of sharing time and discussion can be rich in opportunities for developing skills in the language arts.

Puppet Play

Teacher can make good puppets and she can show a puppet play to the children. She can ask the children to show a puppet play themselves. It will increase their vocabulary as well as pronunciation.

Doll's Corner

Doll's corner also helps the children in their language development. 3-4 children can play in a doll's corner and they act out all sorts of household environment they like adults and behave in a similar manner.

Drawing and Painting

Children are interested in drawing, painting, etc. Teacher can tell them that she is going to draw a very funny figures on the board. She can draw one cypher and add a semi-circle to it and it will become A.

She can tell the children that this figure is known as (A).

All these things will help in the development of language of the child.

The Role of Teachers in Language Development

Teacher should use simple and correct language. She should be careful not to use incorrect language as the child picks up a good deal of language from her. She should not talk fast with the children as it will be a strain for them to learn and they would not be able to get the correct pronunciation. The teacher should speak slowly and with intonation that will clarify the meaning of words. This would add interest and variety.

The child can not think in abstract terms. So the teacher should start with what is concrete. Let the child observe a thing and then associate meaning with it. In this way the child will pick up language more quickly.

Teacher should introduce new words to the children through stories, rhymes, dramas, action songs, rhythmical exercises and games etc. and she should repeat these words again and again so the child is able to remember it.

Teacher should provide group activities to the children so that they can chatter among themselves *e.g.*, she can make 3-4 children sit at one table.

Teacher should provide them with story books, picture books, etc. She should take them for excursions, to the Zoo, places of historical interest, Railway station, gardens, etc., and tell the name of new things. It will increase children's vocabulary.

If the child uses baby speech; does not do the same due to love, affection and enjoyment. Use the correct language and the child will pick up correct language gradually.

Last but not the least teacher should be very affectionate, etc., loving and sympathetic towards children while teaching language to them because children will love her and follow her.

Preventing Speech Disorders

Since children are in the process of learning to speak their native tongue during their entire pre-school period, any apparent speech defect they may have is only evidence of incomplete learning. When such a defect is marked, however, the child should be examined by a physician. If there is no underlying physical defect the child should be helped by the teacher to furnish him with a clear pattern of speech and help him with difficult speech sounds.

Many children stutter or have stammer speech at some period during their pre-school experiences. Realising the nature of the stuttering and stammering defects and the conditions usually associated with them, the nursery teacher should make every effort to help the children in whom these tendencies occur. She should watch carefully to see if the children in the nursery group are subjected to any over expectations or other pressure which can be reduced or removed, or if they need more loving attention.

When a nursery teacher has a child whose speech is retarded, she should work with him as she would with a younger child helping him to learn simple words used by other children in his age group. It will take the child time to work through each of the earlier phase of language development, so the teacher must be patient as well as loving as she observes his gradual mastery of speech.

It is well known that, sense of loving builds up confidence and enhances the speech development in pre-school children. Piaget, in studying language development in children, carefully limited his study to the language children use with other children, rather than the language they use with adults. The process of assimilating experience is speeded up tremendously when the child communicates with other persons who answer his questions, help him to name things accurately, and show him how to use—language in thinking so the nursery group and kindergarten should provide an opportunity for the children to talk freely not only with other children, but also with adults.

By being both a good listener and a conversationalist, the adult encourages—children to explore desirable ways to thinking. By smiling in appreciation, she rewards the child who remembers and expresses a pertinent idea whenever she extends the conversation, she increases the probability that the child will express more pertinent memories.

In all listening-talking situations between children and adults, the adults should keep in mind the importance of building the child's self-confidence especially by making the situation a pleasant and rewarding one for him.

In addition to all these, teachers can also introduce certain items in following manner.

The child can not think in abstract terms so the teacher should start with what is concrete. Let the child observe a thing and then associate meaning with it.

Teacher should introduce new words to the children through stories, rhymes, action songs, rhythmical exercises and games etc., and she should repeat these words again and again so the child is able to remember it.

Teacher should provide group activities to the children so that they can chatter among themselves.

Teacher should provide them with story books, picture books etc. She should take them for excursion, to the zoo, railway station, gardens etc., and tell them names of new things. It will increase children vocabulary.

If the child uses baby speech, don't encourage him due to love, affection but use the correct language and the child will pick up the correct language gradually.

We can teach language to the child through play way method. Play is the medium of expression for them. So the teacher can teach language to the children through play.

Linguistic learning has its beginnings in the earliest days of a child's life. The child's own speech which has its roots in his earliest expressive utterance is the sound pattern which he employs to satisfy his needs. From these patterns linguistic development which have long been habitual with him he moves in directions determined by his needs, emotions and purposes. His language development moves forward because of the daily interchange of his behaviour with those around him. Conventional words and their meanings have an impact on him and has a result what emerges is a transition to the mother-tongue. In the course of learning to use words he comes to recognize that words may be names of things.

11

Habit-formation in Children

An act becomes a habit through repetition. Habits may lead to a well ordered disciplined, fruitful and fulfilled life, or make a person misfit with lack of determination, blaming others for his failures. It may also make a person mediocre. Habits save time and energy by motivating action unconsciously, automatically, simply and easily. Habits save thought and are very valuable, but habits should be controlled rather than allow them to control us.

Habit formation is easy in early childhood and systematic training could go a long way in the development of the personality of the child. The three basic principles of habit formation are simplicity, regularity and consistency. Since the child spends his formative period of life in the pre-primary school, it becomes the responsibility of the pre-primary school teacher to guide and direct the child in the development of proper formation of habits.

Habit training occupies a very important place in pre-primary school curriculum. The teacher should adopt techniques with slow movement, adjusting with the pace of development of the child. Forcing the child to learn for which he is not ready, should be avoided. The teacher should avoid the training when she is angry or when the child feels frustrated. To achieve success, teacher should be gentle and patient. Children who are simple and temperate in their habits grow up pure, strong and true.

Pre-primary school children should be guided in the formation of good habits in matters of eating, sleeping, urination and bladder control, bowel, control, cleanliness, sex education, social adjustment and discipline.

Eating Habits

A healthy child will have healthy appetite. The problem with children is, that either they do not eat or they do not eat enough. They mess their food, themselves, and the surroundings, while eating children have no sense of time, too in the pre-primary school, the teacher should announce that meal time is approaching so that they could get ready themselves. The most important criteria is, offering some food to children when they are hungry. It must be remembered that appetite varies from one child to another and even for the same child from day to day depending upon his mood, activity and health. Every child knows how hungry he is and eat as much as he needs. So the quantity that a child should take should be left to him to decide.

The Techniques the Teacher can Follow for Making Eating Procedure Easier:

1. Offer them warm food but not extreme hot or cold.
2. They like mild flavour more than those with sharp and pungent taste.
3. Children like liquids and semi-liquids better than hard food and those that stick and require a lot of tongue work.
4. They like food that they can pickup and manipulate with their fingers.
5. New food must be introduced gradually and in small quantity, and when the children are hungry.
6. While preparing food for children nutritional value should be kept in mind.
7. Cater to the aesthetic appeal.
8. Attention should be given while preparing food for children. It should not be over or undercooked, burnt or too hot.
9. Offer the food with a pleasant attitude to the children.
10. Provide food for the development of the teeth. It should be easy to chew and provide chances for mastication.

Encourage children to eat with hands, it aids neuromuscular development. Good eating habits can be created in children by demonstration than verbal instructions. The pre-primary school teacher should eat with the children sitting with them and set an example by not talking while eating, grabbing the food, or talking while her mouth is full or eating with a sloppy manner. Environment is also important in forming good eating habits. Children should be allowed to play with kitchen pots and pans and help in preparation of food. They should be given training in arranging, serving and cleaning after eating.

Sleeping Habit

Sleep is an indispensable as food for the growing child. Nothing can better promote a child's readiness for responding well to the demands of his environment than regular and sufficient sleep. During growing period adequate rest, relaxation is required to avoid fatigue and nervous exhaustion later. Every child will sleep as much as he needs. Unlike adults children cannot fight sleep and show obvious signs when they need rest. A child may yawn, his eyes begin to look tired, he is more irritable and excitable, and all these are the signals for his sleep.

In pre-primary school curriculum sleeping and rest hour should be included and this should follow a period of teaching physical activity.

Points to be kept in Mind while Making Arrangement for Sleeping and Resting:

1. Each child should be provided with sufficient space for sleep. The material provided for sleeping should not be too hard or too soft.
2. There should be a room where the children are put to sleep. It should be provided with good ventilation with plenty of fresh air.
3. While putting children to sleep the garments worn by the children should be made loose.
4. Sleeping atmosphere should be created by making the room dark and by silence.
5. Before making the child sleep he should be sent to the toilet and make him settle for sleep.
6. Sing a lullaby or a rhyme or tell a story in order to make the child to have pleasant association for sleep.
7. While putting the children to sleep visible distractive toys should not be around. In the case of a disturbed child he should be allowed to sleep with his toy which he is clinging to and later on remove it.

Toilet Habits

Good and proper toilet habit helps the child to control involuntary reflexes, as it is a co-ordinated activity and require time to learn it. During the period of learning sometimes the child is successful and sometime not, but there will be gradual improvement. Urination and bowel movement help elimination of waste products from the body.

Opportunities and facilities should be provided by creating an atmosphere for the child to develop a wholesome attitude towards elimination. Getting angry with child and shaming him before others or punishing him, if he has little or no control in his bowel movements, make the matters worse.

The pre-primary school teacher should encourage them to use bathroom. She can keep a watch on such children and send them to the bathroom at regular intervals.

They can be taught to give some indication as to when they want to use the bathroom and teacher should attend to them promptly. If this method is followed children will learn the toilet habit effortlessly and easily.

CLEANLINESS

Tidiness

To live in peace with neighbours and to get on efficiently certain degree of tidiness is essential. Systematic training in early childhood helps a lot. To achieve this virtue the children should be tactfully guided in using things, putting away things in the proper place before using the others. This rule will help the children while taking meals and resting. Destructiveness is a characteristic mood shows itself frequently in children, and it is easily aroused. This is why toys should be made so as not to break easily. The children may be guided to respect propriety, appreciate the value of things. If the children see the teacher caring for their toys and looking after them properly they will learn to imitate her.

Washing

Washing indicates cleanliness and this should be indicated to the children in the early years of life. To children, washing is an enjoyable experience, for they love to play with water. The pre-primary school teacher should guide, and help in washing. The pre-primary school may be provided with low basin, tap, mug, bucket, napkins, mirror and a rack for the purpose.

Clothing and Dressing

In the matter of clothing, the pre-primary school has little control and unless otherwise uniforms are provided by them. However the pre-primary school teacher can guide the parents on the following points:

1. Children should be given a choice for their colour preference. The size and construction should be proper. The clothes are not ill-fitting to the child and cause discomfort, *e.g.* Wearing tight or short loose and long dresses. Ill-fitting clothes hinders movements of the children.
2. As children should be encouraged to use footwear the parents should be guided in the purchase. The footwear should not be too large or too small and tight.

Sex Education

Handling of sex organs which is so common among young children should be considered normal. This should not cause alarm and worry to the mother or to the pre-primary school teacher. Its appearance in young children is only an expression of perfectly natural curiosity, a passing phase if not emphasized and his attention drawn. The mother or the teacher who discovers the child handling his genital is usually taken aback and they feel difficult to control their emotions. They forget the fact that to the child one part of his body is as indifferent or interesting as another. He has no knowledge of sex, or sex consciousness of the adult.

In the case of young child handling his sex organs, no mention of the matter should be made, but his attention should be diverted. With other children activity should be watched with a view to providing outlets for all the impulses to action that appear. The real need is to keep the child's attention away from the undesired habit. If care is taken to keep the child occupied until he is tired to fall asleep and put to bed; occasion for falling back on self stimulation will seldom arise.

Don't make the child sit too long on the toilet, keep all parts clean and free from irritation, and avoid tight clothing.

A happy child who is active, and interested all day long with work and play material and companion of his own age, who gets good food and enough rest, and who is given much attention which he prefers, will not be much interested in his own body as a source of pleasure.

Social Adjustment

The child's awareness of himself as a being distinct from others and his realization of their separate identity makes him conscious of his contact and association with others. How successfully the child will adjust to the social group will depend largely upon how closely he conforms to the approved pattern of behaviour of the group. No child can hope to fit into a social group and be accepted by the members of the group unless he is willing to learn, conform to the patterns of the group. The child who learns to conform to socially approved pattern of the behaviour, is accepted by the group. Through group interaction he learns to adjust to others and thus become socially well-adjusted individual.

During pre-primary school period child's companions are usually the adults at home, brothers and sisters, or a few children from the immediate neighbourhood. When he enters the pre-primary school, however, his group and companions widen, and he has an opportunity to select playmates from a larger group. He selects one or two the group whom he wants to sit beside or play with. They may be of the same sex or opposite sex. When the child becomes more selective in choosing his friends, factors of age, intelligence, and good sportsmanship is more important, though the sex of the child is less important. If the child is not able to select his companion for play there are four courses of action open to him:

1. He must modify his behaviour to fit into that of the available companions.
2. He has to develop imaginary companions who will play with him as he wishes.
3. He may have to fall back on the companionship of his parent and siblings.
4. He may have to develop solitary interest and play alone.

But in pre-primary schools the child is exposed to group play and where he could avoid the above-mentioned courses of actions which is not satisfactory for the development of the personality of the child.

In any group of children, there will be no equality. One child usually stands out as a recognized leader. To be a leader the child must be able to adapt his behaviour to the needs of the group, must elicit positive reaction from the group, must demonstrate his willingness and ability to carry cooperative task, through their cooperation. Child leader is characteristically superior to the other members of the group in size, intelligence and generally in age. The child leader is usually accepted by ascendant behaviour, along with social responsiveness, a tendency to resist, adult control and expression of rivalry, competitive attitude, and self-confidence.

Discipline

Discipline means a "process of training and learning that fosters growth and development". It consists primarily of habit formation and thus involves four essential principles:

1. The child must act in a desirable manner and eliminate undesirable behaviour.
2. He must associate satisfaction with desirable and dissatisfaction with undesirable acts.
3. He must make the desirable act. So automatically it will be repeated of its own accord without any supervision.
4. He must learn to substitute desirable for undesirable behaviour.

The child needs discipline if he is to be a happy and well adjusted individual. When he shows that is expected of him, he has the steady influence of values and attitudes that remain relatively unchanged. Discipline helps him to direct his energies into approved channels, thus make him to behave in an approved manner.

There are certain needs that discipline fills for a child and thus adds to his happiness and adjustments:

1. Discipline gives the child a feeling of security to know where his boundaries limit, and freedom are, he needs to know how far he can go and what he may or may not do.

2. He needs to live according to certain standards in order to have less feeling of guilt. From time, he is bound to do some wrong things and feel guilty. However, too much feeling of guilt makes him unhappy and poorly adjusted.
3. When a child does the right thing, it makes it possible for adults to praise him. Praise is equivalent to love as the child interprets it, while scolding and disapproval are interpreted as lack of love and as rejection. The child needs love to develop successfully.
4. Discipline serves as an ego-bolstering-motivation to the child to accomplish what is required of him.
5. Discipline helps the child to develop a conscience, the "internalized voice" that directs him to do this or that pressures from adult. Over a period of time, become the pattern for the internalized voice of conscience to guide that child in making choices of his own.

Adult can help the child to learn to behave in a socially approved manner so that he will eventually learn to discipline himself.

Pre-primary school teacher can help the child in this manner so that the children can learn easily by:

(*a*) setting an example of willing acceptance of discipline.
(*b*) proper timing of discipline to avoid trying to have the child do something before he is capable of understanding the reason for it.
(*c*) helping the child to understand the purpose and benefit of self-discipline, which can be done by explaining the rules to the child and by praising him for following them.

Ways of Disciplining the Child

1. When pressure is applied, the child must be reassured that he is loved. He must be reassured that the pressure applied to the act, not to him.
2. Those in control must stand together and be consistent in their discipline to give the child a feeling of security.
3. The child must be passed to behave in certain ways by praising

him for acceptable behaviour and by withholding privileges for unacceptable behaviour.

4. Teacher must give the child an example of well-disciplined lives.
5. Teacher must help the child to understand why certain arrangements are required.
6. The right time must be chosen for introducing rules and regulations.

12

Behaviour Problems of Children

Almost every child develops certain kinds of behaviours which are annoying or embarrassing to the adults to handle. Adults frequently label such behaviour as "problem behaviour." Behaviour problem is a deviation from the accepted behaviour pattern of behaviour on the part of individual in a society. There are many factors which are responsible for the problem behaviour of the child in the family for instance:

1. Parents' attitudes
2. Overprotection
3. Rejection
4. Parents' imbalanced relationship
5. Poverty
6. Lack of parental love.

In school:

1. Relationship with teacher, and
2. Classmates and playmates.

There are so many types of behaviour problems such as stealing, thumb sucking, day-dreaming, temper-tantrum, bed-wettings, masturbation, nail biting etc.

Masturbation

The very word "masturbation" make some people feel like blushing.

The fact is masturbation will not injure people's bodies or make them unable to marry. It will not cause them to "go crazy". It is not something perverted or to be looked upon with shock or horror. It is not the masturbation itself which is serious or harmful but the worry and anxiety it causes to both parents and children. Masturbation is not a cause of other problems but it can be a symptom that other things are wrong in the child's life. When it is excessive it is signal of emotional distress.

Masturbation can be defined as artificial excitation of sex organs for the purpose of deriving pleasurable sensation. The excitation is brought about by the person himself or herself or by another person. When masturbation occurs in infants and small children they attach little, important to sex unlike we grown up understand it, and has no moral value. In little children, it should be completely ignored and nothing should be done to fix the child's interest on it, unnecessary feeling of shame, seen secrecy, and mystery should not be created in the child's mind regarding this activity.

Causes of Masturbation

Guilt, fear and anxiety are the basis for the child's worries. They are the underlying causes of many behaviour problems of childhood and many lead to unwholesome, unhappy, attitudes in adult life. Other problems such as nightmares, temper-tantrums, aggressive behaviour and habits such as bedwetting, thumb-sucking are the outcomes of these too. Therefore, if a child's parents punish him for masturbating they may only increase his problems. Disapproval, scolding or punishment intensify the child's guilt and fearful feelings. It may happen that the more he is forced to think about masturbation, the hinder it is for him to refrain. A vicious circle is set up. The more he masturbates the more he worries; and then the worry causes still more masturbation.

Local irritation due to skin disease in genital or penal region and this leads to the discovery of pleasurable sensation. Close fitting and uncomfortable clothing may have similar effect. Lack of parental love, broken homes, unkind treatment of the parents and teachers, many results in finding out some other source of pleasure. Mutual masturbation often occurs in children's institutions like 'remand house'.

How to Handle?

Threat and punishment should be avoided. Parents and teachers must be made to understood it is only phase in child's development and not a disease. Faulty notions about the ill-effect, after-effect of the habits have to be corrected.

The child should be thoroughly examined physically for any skin disease in genital or penal region. Too fitting clothes should not be worn. Avoid words, attitudes or actions that might make the child afraid or ashamed. Give praise and affection at special time such as when he is going to bed, or has been disappointed or has had trouble with other children. Give him satisfactory answers to his questions of sex.

In most of the cases we have seen the root causes of the problems in children are almost the same. In some cases the parents are the ones who need more help than the children. A child who comes to the earth is innocent. Whatever he turns to be depends largely on what we provide him with, as parents teachers and friends. The responsibility and blame are ours and not theirs. So let us be awake, be careful, and conspicuous, a lot could be solved.

Enuresis

Involuntary passage of urine by children usually more than 3 years is called enuresis. Bladder control in 10 per cent of children is attained in about the twelfth month; in about 30 per cent of children by about the eighteenth month; in about 65-80 per cent of children by about the twenty-fourth month, and by about the thirty-sixth month the average child is dry at night. Enuresis could be due to organic reasons also. But they are called as urinary incontinence. Age distribution varies from the 6 to the 16th year, peak of the incidents being between 9-11 years. The reasons may be any of the following. : (1) Physiological and anatomical (weak kidney, weak bladder, etc.). (2) Nutritional (diet rich in fluid). (3) Endocrinal part of certain mental disorders substitute for masturbatory habits, etc.

Training and Parental Control

Enuresis may occur in retarded children but all neurotics are not retarded. Due to the maternal over-protection the child may take time to become dry. Mother's inclination to keep the child in dependence is again another reason. No inheritance of enuresis is inevidence. But there seems to be a tradition in the families. In certain families, it is accepted as a matter of fact which they have to undergo.

Lack of opportunity of training. Cold winter nights, bathrooms being away from place of living, etc., may be the cause.

Following illness they become enuratic. The desire to retain the attention shown to them during illness make them enuretic. Gerard notes the following as causative factors; Regressive response in which the arrival of new siblings make children enuretic. Revenge response in which realization is the prominent motive towards their mothers who are nagging and who punish the child often. Enuretic responses in which children wet their bed due to unconscious fear of persons of opposite sex.

Effects of enuresis on the children themselves: Enuresis gives rise to additional difficulties in children. Attitude of people around make them tense, and sometimes accounts for disturbed sleep. Then refuse to go to school because they are afraid of incontinence during school hours. The peers also tease which creates the feelings of inferiority in them. Weak kidney and bladder make the child feel that he is different and inferior to other children. Punitive measures of elders create tension in children. These above attitudes add to the already existing insecurity, sensitiveness, apprehension and general unhappiness of these children.

How to handle?

Psychological way of tackling the situation lies in :

(1) Removal of punishment, (2) Stopping the fluid food at least sometime before going to bed. If the children report to be thirsty a bit of ice or fruit may be given, (3) Waking the child at approximate time of urination and training them in bathroom practice, (4) Encouraging the child to become dry by providing some incentive measures, *e.g.*, the star chart, fixing up stars for those nights in which the child was dry. This helps children with limited intelligence but not too limited. Wherever the case appears to be more complicated and where enuresis is one of the many symptoms the child manifests, psychotherapy may be helpful.

Thumb-Sucking

Thumb-sucking is the earliest form of habitual manipulation which is rarely seen even in infants that are just born. It is reflex involving the touch of the lips aided by foetal posture. It is acquired habit during the first year of life. Any fingers may be sucked. It is usually the thumb and, hence, the term thumb-sucking is used. While children suck the finger of one hand, the other hand engages itself in other movements which are accessory movements. Some children do it all the time and some others prefer to do it just before going to sleep.

Hunger, embarrassment, shame, fatigue, boredom, unpleasant experience may result in this habit. In the first few weeks of life the habit is always associated with hunger; after which the habit recedes. After this time, the habit occurs before and/or after feeding. From the fourth month onwards usually the habit continues throughout the day. Sometimes the habit aids in relieving pain of the teeth that are to erupt after weeks. Thumb-sucking results because of forced toileting. Insufficient lip movements or incompleteness of the sucking phase of the feeding results in this habit. They may be due to any of the following reasons: (1) Spontaneous withdrawal from rapidly flowing bottle, (2) Forced withdrawal, (3) Feeding schedule either long intervals or short feeding time may provoke thumb-sucking, (4) Incomplete satisfaction of feeding is maintained through thumb-sucking and the child usually falls asleep, (5) Emotional deprivation like placing the bottle on unpreferred food is also another unpleasant feeding situation which results in thumb-sucking. Freud points to the erogenous nature of lips. Continually reinforced during the act of sucking which may develop at later ages in oral activities like smoking, drinking and over-talk activeness. Parental concern and cultural attitudes backed up by the scars created by dentists regarding misshaping of teeth and jaw, and the danger of germs getting into and spreading infectious diseases, contribute to the over concern of parents. The act of finger sucking by itself is the over concern of parents. The act of finger sucking by itself is not a serious effect on personality. But the seriousness results from restraint and cohesiveness to which the child is subjected. Some mothers smear quinine or soap-nut powder on the fingers of the child by which, probably, the child develops a liking for such materials.

Guilt feelings, fear, sneakiness, sensitivity about appearance may result out of thumb-sucking.

How to handle?

No therapeutic measures need to be taken if the habit is within 2 to

3 years of life of the child. In other places it should be directed to parental attitudes. Anxieties based on belief of danger to appearance, susceptibility to disease must be eradicated. Though it is not harmful to personality very much, the habit needs correction. Close watching and admonitions should be abstained from the child's attention can be kept away from the habit by giving him a job to do or toys to play with. If the child sleeps with the thumb in the mouth, the thumb may be gently removed. Mother-child relationship involving hostility should be corrected. In older children the habit is a manifestation of general, emotional and social immaturity. Life situations and conflicts, etc., should be understood and tackled.

Nail-Biting

This is the most widespread habit which involves biting manipulation. This is seen in a number of children and also in a few adults. Age, intelligence, etc., do not seem to have any correlation with the habit. This is "an everyday problem of every child". Thumb-sucking is indulged in a set of satisfaction but nail-biting is an expression of tensionness by anticipation of a difficult test or parental punishment or any other excitement, *e.g.*, during an interview, at the start point children do not bite their nails but when questions involving difficulty are put to them they start biting the nails. Thumb-suckers are relatively calm and placid, but nail-biters are usually hyperactive and fidgety. Viets points out that there is a frequency of tense situations in which all the children in the class were nail-biters, the cause of which was found in the severely punishing type of teacher. Nail-biting is a combination of tension and combined with the pattern of behaviour of the older members of the family. The intensity of the habit varies with the degree of tension, threats, punishments. Mechanical appliances, pepper over the nails have the same effect as in thumb-sucking except in few cases. Causes for tension and for the origin of maintenance of it must be traced and treated. Appeal to pride (*e.g.*,) "nice finger you have", etc., are helpful. Appeal through sermon has little effect. Manicuring, especially if the parents also do it, is helpful in certain number of cases. Occupying the child with intrigue toys and associating them with older children may be helpful. Nail-biting usually is a difficult problem in childhood to treat.

Lying and Stealing

Willing falsification of facts is not known to children of 3 or 4 years until it is introduced into his reactive equilibrium, either directly or indirectly from outside. Misstatements may be found in children. *Criteria for lying*—Knowledge of untruth and goal of gaining some advantages or of avoking unpleasantness. In the beginning period of acquisition of speech, lying is absent. Imperfection of the linguistic tools of children sometimes gives impressions to lying. For instance, before acquiring the concept of man every man is "daddy" for the child. And if the child says "no" on the mother's finding that the milk has been spilled, it does not necessarily mean the child says he did not spill. It may mean "please, Mummy, don't punish me" or "don't get angry with me." Insufficient discrimination between a fact and a fancy, as in situations to make believe things in the environment, may give the impression that the child is lying. Wrong interpretation and immature elaboration of things seen and heard may give impression of lying.

Types of Lies—(1) Simple reversal of truth, saying "no" for "yes". (2) exaggeration. Teacher's small praises, father's strength, influence income, etc., are exaggerated by the children. (3) Fabrications. Incidents like fire which has not occurred, experience of a good trip which has not been made are instances of fabrication. *Wrong accusation*: When the child itself spills the milk it may accuse the cat or the maid servant as having spilled it. Lies may be uttered by the children in three different varieties of situations: (1) In self-defence to avoid punishment. (2) Imitation of adult behaviour. When the unwelcome visitor steps into the house the father might send a sick leave letter through the child. By these habits from the environment the child learns to tell lies. (3) To receive attention and admiration. Wanting to be in the limelight and a desire to outdo others may be the causes for lying. Monotonous environments lead to breaking, boastfulness, etc. The child may say that somebody is dead or he might tell a lie saying that he went to the circus or on a trip, etc., etc.

How to Handle?

(1) Fear of punishment should be avoided. (2) Children should not be made to confess through promises of for giving and later punished. As far as possible parents and adults in the immediate environment of the

child should not deviate from truth at least in the presence of their children. If you have to tell a lie in his presence, explain to the child the necessity of telling a lie. Breaking monotony at home by at least occasionally taking him to a picture, or occasionally celebrating some small events at home, help children.

Stealing

Stealing for long like lying had been considered as a moral issue which calls for some kind of a punishment. Now it is realized that it is psychological problem which needs to be attended to. Stealing may be of many kinds: (1) Casual stealing. Yielding to occasional temptations. (2) Selective stealing. Stealing objects which will be of use for oneself. (3) Solitary and group stealing, engaging in the act of stealing by oneself alone or being in a group to commit theft. Larceny, stealing things that are easily accessible. Like in lying, in stealing knowledge of wrong doing and comprehension of conventional meaning of property should be present.

Stealing may be taken to under varieties of situations:

1. *Desire for possessions.* While waiting in the store when the mother purchases a thing, the child takes away some thing which may be designated as stealing. Parental inability or refusal to buy and the ownership of similar articles desired by the children being possessed by other children evokes greater temptations. The child may visit shops and lock at the show-windows and finally steal a bicycle.
2. *Loose social standards at home.* A social and anti-social attitudes at home encourage the child to steal. If the father is an alcoholic, and the mother rendered to small thefts, the siblings themselves being committed to jails, the children also render to steal. More incidences of stealing in children in slum areas is probably due to the social influence of the environment. Intellectual inadequacy plus lack of training do not result in adequate social habits and hence stealing results.

How to Handle?

From the beginning the child must be made to understand that he should hand over anything which he takes from others. At the same time parents should also be able to get things which he likes most or else at least convince the child.

So, in short, the pre-school age is a continuous period of learning of trial and error, or exploration and discovery. The responsibility of guiding the child's activity during this period into constructive channel lies with the pre-school teacher. It would be easy to do so, if she could understand the fundamental principles involved in the training of young child.

13

Children with Special Needs

Meaning of Exceptional Children

It is not an easy task to define an exceptional child. The problems become more difficult the exceptional or deviated child is studied by various disciplines like psychology, sociology, physiology, Medicine and Education and each discipline studies the exceptional child from a different children from educational point of view.

In the words of Samuel A. Kulu, "An exceptional child is that child who deviates from the average or normal child in mental, physical, or social characteristics to such an extent that he requires a modification of school practices or special educational service in order to develop to his maximum capacity." This definition says that an educationally exceptional child is one who requires a modification in the education programme to meet his specific needs. The usual classroom activities cannot help him much.

Classification of Exceptional Children

Exceptional Children

- Mentally challenged
  1. Gifted
  2. Backward
  3. Retarded
- Physically challenged
  1. Orthopaedically handicapped
  2. Visually impaired
  3. Hearing impaired
  4. Speech impaired
- Socially and emotionally challenged
  1. Delinquents
  2. Problem Children

GIFTED CHILDREN

Meaning

James Drevel defines gifted children as "Children possessing high intellectual ability, generally or in a particular field."

According to R.J. Having Hurst, "Gifted children are those individuals, from kindergarten through high school age, who show unusual promise in some socially useful area and whose talent might be stimulated." Generally, the individual, having I.Q., range more than 140, is termed as a gifted children.

Identification of Gifted Children

It is necessary to identify the gifted children of the school. For this parents, teachers, psychologists and social workers must co-operate in the work. There are several methods for identifying gifted children. Some major procedures are :

(*a*) Intelligence tests
(*b*) Achievement tests
(*c*) Cumulative Record Cards
(*d*) Teacher's observation.

Characteristics of Gifted Children

Although there are individual differences among gifted children, still there are certain common characteristics. Different psychological studies have revealed some of the following characteristics of gifted children:

(*a*) *Physique and Health:* Generally gifted children are slightly physically superior. They recognize the value of sleep, play and good food habits.
(*b*) *School Achievement:* Most gifted children like school and usually they are high achievers.
(*c*) *Reading Development:* They can read quickly, safely and better.
(*d*) *Interests:* Giftedness is characterized by enthusiasm and gifted children are interested in activity. This usually persists in the face of difficulty appears to them worthwhile.

(*e*) *Social and Emotional Development:* They possess a high organizing capacity which influence their emotional development. They generally, are emotionally stable but become aggressive and challenge the authority on situation that are unreasonable.

(*f*) *Character and Personality:* A majority of gifted children show superiority in character and personality. They excel rapidly in learning and remembering, the ability to analyze, reasoning, reproducing activities already learnt etc. They have the power of sustained attention.

Educational Provisions for Gifted Children

It is the duty and responsibility of the school to provide educational materials and situations in accordance with the individual needs and abilities of the individual, so that the individual will grow to the fullest extent. The gifted children needs special attention and care. Some of the steps that the school can undertake may be summarized as follows:

(*a*) *Proper Assessment of Individual's ability should be made:* This should be done by using different tools and techniques of assessment to know the exact position of the individual in the group.

(*b*) *Proper Environment is Necessary:* The school should provide an environment that help positively towards the development of the gifted children.

(*c*) *Special Talents are to be Identified:* The students having special talents and aptitudes are to be identified as soon as possible.

(*d*) *Continuous Educational Provisions*: The special educational provisions for the gifted child be continuous as the child passes from one stage to the other.

(*e*) *Proper facilities and materials are to be provided:* Gifted children need some advanced learning materials. So, facilities and provisions should be made for that.

(*f*) *Competent School Staff if necessary:* School should be equipped with efficient teachers, psychologists, guidance workers, curriculum planners and administrators.

(*g*) *Individual attention should be given:* The gifted children need individual attention and instruction.

(*h*) *Homogeneous grouping:* It is better to divide the students into groups of homogeneous ability so that it will be easier to provide educational materials and situations to each group.

(*i*) *Special methods of teaching and activities:* Teaching should be imparted through methods like Dalton plan, Winetika plan, Project method, Assignment method etc., special library and club activities should be provided to the gifted children.

(*j*) *Aoceleration:* It is defined as progress through an educational programme faster at an age younger than convention. This can be done by admitting the child into the school earlier by promoting the child to the next higher class in the middle of the session etc.

(*k*) *Enrichment:* Enriched curriculum and instructional materials should be provided to the gifted children. This can be done either in special classes or in the regular classroom where the gifted children are encouraged to pursue the subject beyond the regular requirements. The enrichment programme may include independent study, club activities, project work etc. It also may include :

— Special assignment (within or outside the syllabus).
— Work on independent projects.
— Preparing reports and participation in panel discussion.
— Independent library reading.
— Visits to the places for getting first hand information.
— Construction of models, aid-material and improvised apparatus etc.
— Participation in the organization of curricular activities.
— Experimentation and independent research.

In this way, the learning experiences should be so enriched that the gifted children find something new and challenging for them.

THE BACKWARD CHILD

Definition and Meaning of the term Backward Child

According to Barton Hall, Backwardness is general, is applied to cases where their educational attainment falls below the level of their natural abilities.

According to Burt, Backward child is one who in mid-school carrier is unable to do the work of the class next below that which is normal for his age.

Characteristics of a Backward Child

According to Jock Couch and Robert Dehaern some of the major characteristics of a backward child are as follows:

- He is a slow learner.
- His I.Q., is between 90 to 100.
- He is unable to think abstractly or to handle symbolic model.
- He is unable to understand and carry through directions for assignments.
- He lacks 'Common Sense'.
- He is unable to understand complex game rules.
- He is slow in all areas – academic, social, emotional, physical.
- He breaks rules of conduct of games and is often unaware of it.
- He is unable to work independently.
- He is really confused.
- He has a short span of interest and attention.
- He is behind normal grade achievement in school.

Kinds of Backwardness

Backwardness is supposed to be of two kinds—General backwardness and Specific backwardness

General backwardness

This is, in fact an all round backwardness. The child suffering from such backwardness is found to be weak in all the subjects of the school curriculum.

Specific backwardness

This refers to child suffering from such backwardness lacks behind in one or two specific subjects only, when in other he shows satisfactory or even extraordinary progress.

Causes of Backwardness

According to Kuppuswamy "educational backwardness is the result of multiple causation." These causes may be discussed under the following heads :

A. Individual limitations of the Child

1. Subnormal physical development.
2. Physical deformities.
3. Physical diseases.
4. Low general intelligence.

B. Family limitations

1. Poverty of the family.
2. Size of the family.
3. Family conflicts.
4. Uneducated parents.
5. Bad habits of the parents.
6. Extreme attitude of the parents.

C. School limitations

1. Absence from the school.
2. Lack of facilities in the school.
3. Poor school atmosphere.
4. Indifferent attitude of teachers

Educational Provisions for Backward Children

The school should have some special provision for backward children. Some of the major provisions are as follows :

Special group formation

Backward children owing to their low intelligence (I.Q. 90-100) do not benefit much from normal teaching. So, they should be grouped into special classes. They should be taught as a slower rate than the average children and should be given more concrete and practical curriculum.

Individual Teaching

They need individual attention of the teacher and so individualized instruction should be provided to them.

Special environment

The school environment and activities may be slightly modified in accordance with the interest and ability of the backward children.

Size of the class

Size of the class should be small so that there will be better possibility for individual attention.

Teacher

The teacher should be understanding and sympathetic. He should have sufficient patience to deal with such children.

Curriculum

The curriculum should be light and attractive. It must be helpful for the future employment of the children. It should be work oriented.

Method of Teaching

The backward children need more practice, repetition, drill and review. New instructional materials should be introduced in small and easy does.

MENTAL RETARDATION

Mental retardation means impaired or incomplete mental development. Grossman (1973) defines mental retardation as significantly subaverage general intellectual functioning existing concurrently with deficits in adaptive behaviour and manifested during the developmental period.

Symptoms of mental retardation

— Inability to acquire the necessary motor skills.
— Low mental growth.
— Brain structure not normal.
— Not able to understand life situations.
— Low life span.
— Poor social adjustment.
— Signs of bodily disorders.
— Inability to concentrate.
— Lack of the control over fulfilment of needs.
— Ugly body structure.

Classification of Mentally Retarded Children

On the basis of Binet Simon Intelligence Scale the following categories of persons have been classified on the basis of their I.Qs. :

I.Q.	*Category*
140 and above	Genius
120 to 140	Very Superior
110 to 120	Superior
90 to 110	Normal or Average
80 to 90	Dull
70 to 80	Borderline
Below 70	Feeble-minded
50 to 60	Moron
20 to 50	Imbecile
Below 20	Idiot

Classification on the basis of acquired skills

American Psychiatric Association has classified the mentally retarded into the following five groups :

Profound Mental Retardation

Such persons can't learn anything as their I.Q. is generally below

20.Their physical structure appears to be very ugly, and the whole face appears to be not only fearful but repulsive also such persons have hysterical fits also at time.

Severe Mental Retardation

Such persons usually look very dull and their I.Qs. range between 20 and 40. Their motor and speech development are very much marred. They cannot be trained to take care of themselves.

Moderate Mental Retardation

Persons of moderate mental retardation have I.Qs. between 40 to 50. Such persons behave like children of about 8 or 9 years of age. Some of such persons are trainable. But on the whole their behaviour is just like that of young children.

Mild Mental Retardation

Persons under this category have I.Qs. within the range of 50 and 65. Most of the persons with mental retardation generally fall under this category. Persons under this group behave like children of about 10 years of age, even when they become adult or old. They have week memory and they can't decide things for themselves.

Borderline Mental Retardation

Persons under this group have I.Qs. within 65 and 80. By appearance, persons of this category do not look retardation but due to their very slow speed of learning language, mathematics and various motor skills, they are regarded as borderline cases. In many situations of life their behaviour appears to be quite normal. They do not look abnormal as regards their body structures.

Clinical Categorization of Mental Retardation–Cretinism

It is a kind of mental retardation which occurs due to hormonal imbalance which may exist while he would be baby is in its mother's womb or it may also happen after birth due to malfunctioning of thyroid glands which results in inadequacy of thyroxin.

Factors leading to Cretinism

Because of this hormonal imbalance the individual may remain of short stature throughout his whole life and the various parts of his body also become unsymmetrical. The I.Q. of such a person roughly ranges between 30 and 70. If the quantity of iodine in the mother's blood is not sufficient the child may become a victim of cretinism. Certain diseases like whooping cough, diphtheria and small pox etc. may also develop due to the features of cretinism in the child.

Symptoms

- — A victim of cretinism has a misshapen and unsymmetrical body.
- — His or her head may be very small or big in comparison to other parts of his body.
- — The hands may be unusually longer than what they should be in proportion to other parts of the body.
- — The belly may be bulging out and hips abnormally projecting out.
- — The spinal cord is curved. So the person can't stand straight.
- — His or her skin may be thick and dry.

Treatment

Synthetic injection with the element of iodine had also been prepared.

Hydrocephalus or Hydrocephaly

It is an abnormal accumulation of fluid inside the cranium.

Symptoms and Causal Factors

In the tendency of hydrocephalus the size of head appears to be twice of the entire body. The facial features of such a child may not be queer. Because of the accumulation of fluid in the brain encephalitis and meningitis may also occurring the individual at times.

Treatment

Surgery is generally the only treatment considered as useful in cases of hydrocephalus.

MONGOLISM

A person of Mongolism type may have an I.Q. between 55 and 75.

The name mongoloid is applied because a Mongoloid person bears a certain superficial resemblance to the Mongoloid race, with the slanting eyes and depressed bridge of the broad, flat nose. The head is small in size with all measurements significantly below the average of normal children. The head is broad and short, with the thumb and little finger much shorter than the others which are often practically equal in length.

A typical Mongoloid learns to walk and say a few words and can perform very new simple routine tasks. He is usually placid unless irritated or disturbed.

The causes for Mongolism are unknown. It is believed to the result of some endocrine deficiency and pituitary deficiency.

MICROCEPHALY

Microcephaly is a pathological condition characterized by exceptional smallness of the head and brain of a human being.

Factors Leading to Microcephaly

It is generally attributed to some deviation in the combination of chromosomes. Intrauterine infections of pregnant women and their irradiation may also cause microcephaly.

Symptoms

Since the head and brain of a victim of microcephaly are very small, the mental retardation of such a person is very severe. The I.Q. of a microcephalic person ranges between 25 and 55.

Treatment

Microcephaly is a severe type of mental retardation. Therefore no such patient has ever been cured.

Phenylketonuria (P.K.U.)

P.K.U. is a kind of mental retardation in which the physical and mental development of a child is blocked due to metabolic disturbances. It is not a very common disease.

Factors leading to P.K.U.

P.K.U. develops due to lack of enzymes. Enzymes, work with amino acid known as phenylalanine in the process of digestion. Lack of enzyme increases the quantity of phenylalanine. As a result the whole metabolism of the child is disturbed. This situation affects the functions of the brain adversely.

Symptoms

Under the effect of P.K.U. a child of even a few months may start vomiting at times and he has fit also. The eyes and complexion of the skin appear yellowish. The function of the skill spinal cord is disturbed and the development of motor skill is blocked.

Treatment

The P.K.U. case of the child should be diagnosed at the earliest. If his P.K.U. malady is confirmed, the quantity of phenylalanine in the diet should be very meagre.

Measures for Prevention of Mental Retardation

Proper Nutrition

I.Q. attention should be paid to the balanced diet of the expectant mother and of the baby after birth.

Regular Medical Examination

If some abnormality is observed medical examination and necessary treatment must never be delayed.

The Health of Expectant Mother

The expectant mother should be given all the necessary care in order to prevent and untoward happening. From time-to-time the position of the baby in the womb should be ascertained for adopting certain measures if necessary.

Services of Obstetrician

Obstetrician will be of great help for preventing any undesirable features at the time of delivery. Many babies become mentally retarded due to brain injuries suffered at the time of birth.

Research Programme

Through certain researches deviations in the combination of chromosomes should be identified. Persons likely to produce abnormal children should be either sterilized or advised to use contraceptive methods as advertised by the family planning programme.

Education of the Mentally Retarded

The mentally retarded need special schools and institutions for their care where they are divided according to their mental level. It is not possible to have a mentally retarded at normal school, the programmes and curriculum of which will be too taking to him.

The educable and trainable children could be allowed to come as dayschloras while the totally dependent children need custodial care. The programme should be occupation oriented, to train them for a job which will them independent in future like book binding, basket making, mat weaving, dying and such simple jobs. Boys learn shop work, carpentry and the like while girls learn sewing, cooking and other household tasks.

TEACHING THE SLOW LEARNERS IN PRE-SCHOOL

During the pre-school years *i.e.*, between 2½ and 5 there should be some systematic stimulation programme the slow learners. A good pre-school atmosphere will help the child develop confidence and be ready for formal learning. There should be complete freedom for the child to move around, manipulate and experiment with objects around. Opportunities should be provided for developing observation and listening skills so that he could develop the capacity for discrimination. There should also be encouragement for doing their own work and for taking up simple responsibilities in the school. There should be direct contact with objects so that the slow learner gets concrete concepts of the objects. The slow learners should never be forced to do anything at this level.

Readiness activities for reading, writing and arithmetic should be given to the children which will encourage them for furthering their interests for formal learning. There should be activities for visual readiness, auditory readiness and motor readiness. The children should be taught to have proper visual perception and discrimination. Hearing deficiencies could be reduced if proper training is given to discriminate between different sounds. In learning to read and write a child has to acquire the habit of moving the eyes from left to right along the line to fix at certain points, to look at the words and then to move to the beginning of the next line. Proper eye-hand co-ordination should be enriched at this stage of educational system.

Physically Challenged

Crippled or the Orthopaedically Handicapped

The crippled child in the orthopeadic sense is a child that has a defect which causes a deformity or interference with normal function of the bones, muscles or joints. His condition may be congenital or may be due to disease or accident. It may be aggravated by disease, by neglect or by ignorance.

Some of the types of handicapped are—the poliomyelites or the infantile paralysis, congenital anomalies, traumatic crippling, tuberculosis of the bones, tumors and other minor conditions causing crippling.

Poliomyelites

It is a disease which attacks the children mostly. It is caused by a virus which is contagious. The virus may be transmitted directly from person to person and sometimes by carriers who do not have the disease themselves. In its early stages, it is characterized by the upper respiratory and gastro-intestinal symptoms. Some cases progress to the involvement of the central nervous system with non-paralytic and paralytic effects. The muscles which are controlled by the affected nervous atrophy end in crippling. Fortunately the vaccine discovered by Dr. Salk is available. Which when inoculated gives the resistance against polio.

Congenital Anomalies

Children may be born with same congenital anomalies. The absence of one or more limps and congenital dislocation of joints, cleft palate, clubfoot and clubhand are some examples.

Traumatic Crippling

This includes

(*a*) Amputation of one or more limps because of accidents, injuries of infection.
(*b*) Traffic Accidents.
(*c*) Serious Burns.
(*d*) Sprains from falls or from abnormal postures in play or in lifting may force various joints such as shoulders, elbows, wrists, hips, knees and ankles out of normal portions.

Tumors

Tumors are abnormal masses with no physiological function but produce excessive swelling and disruption of the normal life process. Tumors may develop on the bones or on any other part of the body. Cysts are collections of morbid matter which gather in various natural cavities including those in the bones.

Education and welfare services of the Orthopaedically Handicapped

The education of the handicapped must aim at the harmonious development of head, heart and hands. It should be its crutch to enable him to face the world as a self-supporting and competent member.

The curriculum in schools should not be different from that of normal children but may need special emphasis. It should be flexible and include individual instruction allowing for children helping each other children should be encouraged to develop interest in some hobbies. The creative urge may find satisfactory way of expression in some of art such as drawing, painting, music, writing, needle work or some kind of craft.

Welfare Services

In India a few institutions cater to the handicapped. The aims and objectives of these Institutions include assessment of the physical abilities and mental capacities of the patients and provision of treatment physiotherapy and occupational thrapy on the basis of the assessment. Training in day-to-day activities and occupational therapy make the children fully independent.

VISUALLY IMPAIRED

Definition

The blind visually impaired are those who suffer from either of the following conditions.

(*a*) Total absence of sight.
(*b*) Visual acuity not exceeding 6/60 or 20/200. Snellen in better eye with correcting lense.
(*c*) Serious limitation in the field of vision generally at an angle of 20 degrees :

Partially sighted persons are those who can see only big objects with the help of powerful lenses during day time or against light.

Causes for Blindness

The committee on statistics for Blind has classified the causes of blindness into two categories.

1. Causes resulting from the affect eye-ball, cornea, crystalline lens, retina, optic nerve, nerve pathway, cortical visual, vitreous. In these areas there may be congenital defective structure because of accidents or diseases causing destruction.
2. Causes resulting from infectious disease such as syphilis, accidental injury, poisonings neoplasm or numerous growth, parental influence and others including German measles, meningitis birth injuries, general diseases, fever, diphtheria and vitamin A deficiency in children which lead to Keratomalacia.

Major Visual Disease

Disorders of the Protective Structures

For example Trachoma is a serious form of conjunctivitis or pink eye where affects the cornea, conjunctiva and eye lid.

Refractive Errors

(*a*) *Myopia or near sightedness*: Light rays are bent and focused infront of the retina, because the eye-ball is too long or the lens are too thick and curred.
The person easily sees objects which are near but can't see objects at a far distance.
Treatment: Eye glasses with concave lens.

(b) *Hyperopia (far-sightedness)*: Light rays are bent and focused behind the retina because the eyeball is too short or the lens too thick and flat. Light rays do bend enough to focus properly on the retina.
Person can see objects better at a far distance than close up.
Treatment: Eye glasses with lens.

Astigmatism

- Results from an irregularity in or a defective curvature of the cornea or the lens.
- Blurred vision and sharp focus impossible due to the diffusion of light rays on the retina.

Prevention: Eye glasses/Contact lens.

Presbyopia

Lens of ability to focus sharply on objects close by. Usually found in older people and due to the normal aging process.

Amblyopial/Lazyeye

Reduction of visual acuity in one or both eyes. Use of only one eye for seeing or alternation of eyes focusing on objects.

Causes

Faulty alignment of the eyes due to muscular inadequacies or imbalance the one eye is turned inward or outward in relation to the other.

Treatment

Glasses, Surgery, Patching, eye exercise, strabismiss crossed eyes/ squint

- — the eyes fail to focus on the some object at sometime.
- — caused by faulty muscle coordination.
- — usually one eye turns inward toward nose and the other eye focuses on the object.

Heterophoria

- — Deviation on of the eye of not apparent.
- — Visual fusion is impaired or two images (an image from each eye) is fused into a single image.
- — Caused by faulty muscle balance.

Nystagmus

Quick jerky movements of eyes related to albinism or brain injury. Disorders in the receptive structure of the visual system:

Retrolents Fibroplasia

Detached retina caused by the subjecting of premature infants to excessive amount of oxygen.

Retinitis Pigmentosa

Deterioration and atrophy of the retina due to heredity.

Opticatrophy

Atrophy of the nerve fibres connecting the retina to the brain.

Cataracts: (Leading to blindness in the adult population)

— The lens becomes opaque due to a growth of cataract film.
— Visual acuity is lost.
— Causes are heredity, drugs, injury and disease.

Treatment

Removal of the cataract through surgery, glasses are then prescribed.

Glaucoma

Drainage of aqueous fluid is obstructed thereby causing damage to the eyes from a build-up of fluids.

Treatment

Surgery in severe cases, eye drops and oral medication to control building up of fluid.

Albinism

— Absence of pigments in hair, skin, and choroid.
— Refractive errors.
— Loss of same visual acuity.
— Nystamus.
— Photophobia, excessive sensitivity to light.
— Cause is heredity.

EDUCATIONAL PROGRAMME

Two type of schools are available for the education of blind children. They are:

(*i*) Special School or inclusire.
(*ii*) Integrated Schooling.

The integrated/unchist school is best or a special class in public school is preferable to a special school because the more contact the blind child has with the outside world, the better adjusted he will be organization of day classes for blind children includes three methods:

The Co-operative Plan

The child is enrolled in a special room and is assigned to the regular classroom for a portion of the school day. The teacher of the co-operation with the regular classroom teacher plans the educational programme for the blind.

The Resource Room or Integrated Plan

The child is enrolled in the regular school and has the services not only of his regular teacher but also of a fulltime qualified teacher of blind children, in addition, he can use the facilities of a resource room.

Intinerant Teacher Programme

The child is sent to a regular school with seeing children and the regular teacher obtains advice and special instruction and materials from an itinerant teacher of the blind employed by a large school unit or by a state education agency.

Curriculum: It includes,

— Adaptations of the general curriculum,
— Some additional or specialized content, and
— Specialized materials and equipment.

The material include :

— *Braille Materials:* Braille slates and stylus, Braille typewriter.
— *Audio aids:* Talking book reproducer, record players, tape recorder.
— *Arithmetic aids:* Arithmetic board and abacus Tape measurer, rulers watches, slide ruler, compasses, protractors and calculator.
— Composed and relief maps, Braille maps, jigsaw puzzles, and relief globes.

Rehabilitation Services

The blind children are given training in crafts such as chair caning, weaving, candle making, basket making, metal cutting, tailoring, embroidery, painting, knitting and toy making. Technical training, in light engineering, assembling and packing is also given for these children.

HEARING IMPAIRED

Deafness hearing impairment to the condition of individuals whose hearing is disabled and is expressed in terms of speech or other sounds calibrated for frequency and intensity (Lilly, 1979).

Classification

1. *The Deaf*: Those in whom the sense of hearing is non-functional for the ordinary purpose of life. This general group is made up to two distinct classes based entirely on the time the loss of hearing occurred. These include :
   (*a*) The congenitally deaf—Who were born deaf.
   (*b*) The adventitiously deaf—Those who were born with normal hearing but in whom the sense of hearing becomes non-functional later through illness and accident.
2. *The Hard of Hearing*: Those in whom the sense of hearing, although defective in functional with or without a hearing aid.

Types of Hearing Defects

Because of the complicated structure and functioning of the ear, defects in hearing may occur in many different basically these defects are of three main types:

1. A conductive hearing loss is one which reduces the intensity of sound reaching the nerve ear, where the auditory nerve begins.
2. A sensory—neural or perceptive hearing loss is caused by defects of the inner ear or of the auditory nerve transmitting the impulse to the brain.
3. In central deafness—the peripheral or receiving mechanism

of hearing is functioning properly but still the individual does not hear owing to some injury or abnormality of the central nervous system.

Causes of Deafness

1. Defect or disorder of any position of the ear.
2. Heredity or congenital formations of pinna.
3. Infections of the ear.
4. Inflammation of the various parts of the ear.
5. Birth injury.
6. Rubella or German measles of the mother during pregnancy.
7. Children putting small objects such as pencil, seeds etc., in the ear blocking the air passage.
8. Congenital defects of the ear.
9. Usteonylitis and otitis media affecting the bones in the middle ear.
10. Brain impairments affecting the auditory nerve.
11. Hard slapping of the ear or some other accidents.
12. Loud noise, sudden explosion and continuous loud sound.
13. Malnutrition.
14. Small pox and meningitis of the child.

SPEECH IMPAIRMENT

Van Riper (1972) has defined defective speech as speech which interferes with communication, brings negative attention to the speaker and causes social, emotional problems for the speaker.

Types of Speech Disorders

Articulation disorders—Refers to defective, inconsistent or incorrect speech and sounds.

Categories or Types

(*a*) *Omissions*—Sounds are not produced *e.g.*, 'at' for 'cat'
(*b*) *Substitutions*—Person recognizes appropriate sound but uses wrong one *e.g.*, 'yeth' for 'yes'

(*c*) *Distorions*—Attempt to approximate correct sound is distorted *e.g.*, 's' in 'say' articulated like 'z'
(*d*) *Additions*—Improper addition of sound to a word *e.g.*, 'on'—un the table.

Causes

1. *Functional Causes*

(*a*) Poor or inconsistent teaching methods by parents to stimulate speech.
(*b*) Poor speech models at home, in the neighbourhood or at school.
(*c*) Emotional problems.

2. *Organic Causes*

Dysarthria (disorder due to brain or nerve damage)

3. *Other Factors*

(*a*) Significant hearing loss.
(*b*) Oral facial abnormalities.
(*c*) Poor co-ordination of speech muscular organs.
(*d*) High and narrow palate that leaves little room for tongue to move.

Treatment and Management of Articulation Disorders

(*a*) Identify both the error and the standard sound to be used.
(*b*) Change the incorrect utterance until the correct sound is produced through a process of successive approximations to the final goal.
(*c*) Strengthen the new speech around through practice and reinforcement until it is used automatically in a variety of contexts.

Disorders of Rhythm or Speechflow–Stuttering

It is a condition in which normal flow rhythm of speech are disturbed by oscillations, fixaliens, repetitions or prolongations of sounds, syllables, words or phrases.

Causes

(*a*) *Constitutional differences*—Breakdown in fluency under emotional stress.
(*b*) *Cerebral dominance*—Lack of control by either cerebral hemisphere.
(*c*) *Dysphemia*—Neuromuscular condition characterized by nerve impulses that are poorly timed in coordinating speech musculatures.
(*d*) *Epileptic Condition*—A series of small seizures which interrupt speech.
(*e*) Brain damage or basic heredity problems.

Treatment and Management

(*a*) Play therapy, creative dramatis and parent and group counselling.
(*b*) Psychoanalysis.
(*c*) Behaviour modification and operant conditioning techniques.

Voice or Phonation Disorders

These disorders involve marked deviations from generally accepted local standards in voice quality, pitch, intensity and flexibility.

Types

1. *Vocal Quality Disorders*

A. Hyper nasality—for example, excessive nasal omission during speech.

Causes

(*a*) Paralyzed soft palate.
(*b*) Congenitally soft palate.
(*c*) Perforation in palate.

B. Hyponasatily or denasality—failure to produce adequate nasal sounds.

Causes

(*a*) Extreme deviation in amount of tissue in the oral nasal areas.
(*b*) Swollen adenoids or swollen oral nasal tissues from cold or allergies.

2. *Pitch Disorders*

It is a condition in which the pitch level is too high or too low.

Causes

Glandular difficulties preventing normal growth of the larynx.

3. *Intensity Disorders*

(*a*) This include condition in which the speech is too loud or too soft.
(*b*) Loss of voice (aphonia)

Causes

(*a*) Laryngities.
(*b*) Severe organic conditions in the oral area such a paralysis of growth.
(*c*) Hearing disorder.

Flexibility

It involves conditions such as:

(*a*) Stereotyped infections—*e.g.*, the voice drops in pitch and loudness after every pause.
(*b*) Monotone—lack of variations in vocal pitch and loudness.

Causes

(*a*) Emotional conflict in the environment.

(*b*) Lack of physical energy due to sickness or fatigue.
(*c*) Inability to hear normal variation in pitch and loudness.

Therapy

(*a*) Train the client to hear and distinguish vocal variations in himself and in others.
(*b*) Find an acceptable voice in person's repertoice and establish it until it is consistently exhibited.

Types of Language Disorders

Definition

Speech and language disorders are intimately inter-related. Language could be defined as an organized system of linguistic symbols (words) used by human beings to communicate.

Language disorders (dysphasia) are usually meant to apply to all disorders of symbolic formulation on expression.

Delayed Verbal Communication

The child does not acquire speech or the oral expression of language at the predicted 'normal' time or with a standard degree of accuracy.

This condition can be present even when the child's articulation and general speech production are quite normal for a child of his age.

Causes

Organic

— Hearing loss associated with a congenital or acquired physically based problem.
— Brain damage.
— Gross glandular irregularities.

Functional

— Poor teaching or child rearing procedures to stimulate verbal communication.

— Emotional problems.
— Negativism toward communication models.
— Environmental deprivation such as the child not being spoken to at home or not being encouraged to label things etc.

Therapy

Use of parallel talk with a therapist or with the parents will help a child to verbalise his thoughts.

Aphasia

The partial or total failure to develop use of language for oral communication.

Types

(*a*) *Sensory or receptive aphasia*—the person seems not to understand spoken languages.
(*b*) *Motor or expressive aphasia*—the person seems to be unable to speak properly.
(*c*) *Conceptual aphasia*—the person has difficulty in formulating generalizations or classifications or both.
(*d*) *Global or mixed aphasia*—all language forms are affected.

Causes

Due to brain dysfunction or damage.

Therapy

Parallel talking is often used in with the child and therapist tell what he is doing in simple words and phrase.

Multiple Speech and Language Disorder

Cleftpalate Speech

Cleftpalate or cleft lip or the both are created when the two halves of the bony upper gun ridge or the two halves of the hard and soft palates fail to grow together and unite in a normal fashion by the third months of prenatal development.

Types of Cleftpalate

(*a*) Cleft of the propagate that is the upper lip and alveolar process.
  (*i*) Partial Cleft (incomplete)
  (*ii*) Total Cleft (complete)
(*b*) Clefts of the palate both hard and soft palates.
  (*i*) Partial Cleft.
  (*ii*) Total Cleft.

Causes

— Hereditary cause certain forms of clefts.
— Factors in the prenatal environment may causes crafts.
(*a*) Malnutrition in the pregnant mother.
(*b*) Certain drugs such as cortisone or other types of thratogenic agents.
(*c*) Fetal anokia or other forms of maternal fetal trauma.
(*d*) Mechanical injuries.
(*e*) X-ray or other types of radiation.

EDUCATION OF THE AUDITORILY HANDICAPPED

The education of the auditorily handicapped must begin at an early age. If not the handicapped child may lose interest in learning and settle into a complete dependency.

The children who are hard of hearing need help in learning to use the eyes in receiving speech to supplement their defective ears. They must be introduced in the art of speech reading and lip reading.

Thus the educational programme for the hard-of hearing children consists of:

1. Training in the use of hearing aids,
2. Auditory Training,
3. Lip reading, and
4. Speech correction.

These children should be taught either in a school for the partially deaf of seated in the front rows of the classroom in the ordinary schools.

Educational Programme for the deaf includes two methods :

1. Oralism

Communication through speech and lip reading without the use of signs and gestures.

2. Manualism

Achieves communication by conventional gestures of the hands or arms to express thoughts.

The deaf children should be educated in special institutions or residential school. The school for the deaf include the following aspects in the curriculum.

- Speech development,
- Speech reading and auditory training,
- Language development,
- Reading, and
- Other school subjects.

Areas of Activity

The areas of activity are as follows:

- Speech therapy by a qualified whole time speech therapist and Audiologist.
- Class Education—Integration of Vocational Education with moral and physical training.
- Rehabilitation of the children after completion of education and follow-up programmes.
- Cultural and extra-curricular activities.
- Counselling service for all formal teacher-client relations, training and rehabilitation.

Rehabilitation Service

Besides formal education, the children are given training in skills like light engineering, weaving, fine crafts, knitting, stitching, embroidery etc. to enable them to earn their livelihood in due course of time. The girls are given training which makes them fit for domestic duties and other skillful jobs, for absorption in industries or for starting personal enterprises.

SOCIALLY AND EMOTIONALLY CHALLANGED

Juvenile Delinquencies

Juvenile delinquent or young delinquent is a child or youth (minor in age) who deviate seriously from the norms of his culture or society and commits such acts, that, if committed by an adult would be punishable as crimes :

Etiology of Juvenile Delinquency

The following factors may be responsible for development of juvenile delinquency:

1. Impact of bad company.
2. Broken family.
3. Evil influences of various films and television scenes.
4. Uncertain discipline.
5. Children, rejected by parents and society.
6. Strains and stresses of difficult life situations.
7. Unhealthy ways of life of parents.
8. Parent's longer absence from home.
9. Mother dominance.
10. Neurotic delinquent.
11. Psychotic delinquent.
12. Mentally retarded delinquent.
13. Organic delinquent.
14. Sociopathic delinquent.
15. The delinquent of a such cultural group.

Symptoms of Juvenile Delinquent

Psychotic and Neurotic Delinquents

A psychotic adolescent delinquent may be generally so aggressive in native.

A neurotic adolescent may be neatly and smartly dressed and go on roaming the streets as if he is the lord of all that he surveys.

They feel a popular romance in satisfying their sexual desire in any manner possible for them.

Drug Addicted

Some adolescents get addicted to the use of intoxicant drugs and even liquors. Such adolescents get into the company of some adults who may incite them to steal money or obtain it through some other immoral ways. Due to use of intoxicants such adolescents look impulsive and at times at greatly elated while under intoxication.

Remedy-Prevention and Treatment of Delinquency

The solution of this problem requires, essentially, two dimensional attack.

Preventive Measure

Initially it will involve improvement of the social or environmental conditions which thwart the satisfaction of the basic needs of the individual and thus will help in prevention of delinquency.

Curative Measure

It is the rehabilitation and reformatory front which involves special arrangement for the rehabilitation and education of delinquents by the Government or Voluntary Organizations.

1. Preventive Measures (Improvement of Social and Environmental Conditions)

Following suggestion can work well in this direction:

Parental Education

Parents should know something about the psychology of delinquency so that they can treat and handle their children properly and provide them proper environment for the satisfaction of their basic needs and urges. It requires parental education. Help from the guidance services, clinics and other voluntary social services, can be taken for this purpose.

To Save the Child from the Bad Company and Anti-social Environment

Parents, family members and the school authorities should have a close watch on the activities and social environment of the children and take proper care so that he should not fall in bad company. Attempts should be made to save children from their clutches and children should get proper education for keeping themselves away from such elements.

Providing Substitute for the Defective Environment

Sometimes it is difficult to bring change in the defective family environment or bad influence of the neighbourhood and peer group are uncontrollable. In such cases children should be removed from their original environment and placed whether in the foster homes or well managed reformatories and special schools so that they may be provided with healthy environment for their proper emotional and social adjustment.

To Rectify the School Education and School Environment

School environment should be made health and congenial.

Curative Measures

The problem of juvenile delinquency in all circumstances should not be regarded as a panel problem. Delinquency requires reforms in the shape of rehabilitation and re-education and therefore, special local provisions should be made to deal with the juvenile delinquents. In the progressive communities of the world, the legal dealings with the juvenile delinquents.

ACTIVITIES

1. Select a child from a pre-school and observe the different developmental talks.
2. Write the case study of the child observed.
3. Read the lesson carefully.
4. Identify from a given question paper which type of tests are given much importance.
5. Observe the physical development of children in the pre-school and identify the differences.
6. Suggest activities that will promote physical development of children.
7. Identify the motor activities of pre-school children.
8. Prepare the programme to promote motor development of children.
9. Prepare a set of low cost equipment that will promote large and finer muscle co-ordination of children.
10. Observe the children of various age levels and identify their social behaviours.
11. Plan activities that will promote social development among pre-schoolers.
12. Identify the child who is not social, find out the causes and suggest remedial programmes.
13. Observe the emotional expression of pre-school age children.
14. Classify the expressed emotions in terms of characteristics of childhood emotions.
15. Find out the frequency of pleasant and unpleasant emotions expressed.
16. Observe the development of concepts in children.
17. Prepare teaching and learning materials to teach concepts.
18. Observe the children of various age groups and identify the characteristics of each age with regard to their Cognitive behaviour.
19. Develop activities to promote Cognitive development among pre-schoolers.
20. Observe Pre-school programme and find out where and how does the theory of Cognitive development is practices.
21. Observe the language of pre-school children in different situations.

(*a*) Count the number of works spoken in 5 minutes time.
(*b*) Find out the vocabulary of 5 years olds.

22. Prepare list of activities that will promote language of pre-schoolers.
23. Write a story and a song using the child's vocabulary.
24. Identify speech defects in children.
25. Find out the children with problems is eating, toileting and sleeping.
26. Prepare a guideline for parents to following habit formation of children.
27. Identify children with behaviour problems.
28. Visit their homes and identify the causes and the methods they follow in handling these problems.
29. Write the steps that you have followed in solving a particular behaviour problem of children in your pre-school.
30. Visit a school for exceptional children and observe the behaviour of children and the type of education given to them.
31. Identify the causes of exception among children.
32. Find out the exceptional children in your class and suggest the methods of educating them.

14

Health and Nutrition of Pre-schoolers

The pre-school children are vulnerable. They are affected readily where the diet is poor in quality and quantity and infectious diseases and infestations are widespread. The rate of growth and development of pre-school children depend to a large measure on the adequacy of the diet consumed by them. Frequent attacks of infectious diseases further increase the requirements of various nutrients.

The pre-school growth rate is not as rapid as in infancy. This group comprises 15 per cent of the total population. Among these, 2/3 is malnourished and a group of 1/3 is well-nourished. Moreover, this group is commonly affected by deficiency diseases like vitamin A deficiency and anemia. Apart from these, the most nutritional problems persisting among pre-school children are Kwashiorkor and Marasmus. Now you can see the physiological changes taking place during pre-school period.

Growth

During infancy, the increased weight is 7 kg. whereas the weight increment is 2.5 kg to 3 kg for the age group of 1-2 year child. Now, you can see the normal weight increment for the pre-school child.

Age group Yr.	*Weight Increase kg.*
2-3	1-2/Year
3-4	1½-2/Year
3-5	1-9/Year

This type of weight increment in children shows that they are under the category of normal.

When you watch on Height of the children, it seems to be,

Age Group Yr.	*Height Increase cm.*
0-1	25 cm/Year
1-2	10 cm/Year
2-3	7-9 cm/Year
3-5	5-6 cm/Year

This is the height increment to measure a normal child.

Water Content

During pre-school period, slimming occurs. This is because, their growth pattern is more longitudinal than horizontal. Some of the changes like the legs become longer, increased muscle mass, more adipose tissue formation, reduction in body protein and increase in mineral content. When we look on adipose, it is found more adipose in girls than boys. These criterias are studied by anthropometrically and found whether the child is normal or malnourished.

When interpreting the data, the height and weight utilized together, so that it could obtain a reliable information. For example, if the height of the child is on 75th percentile and weight of the child is on 25th percentile indicates that the child is malnourished. On the other hand, if the height lies on 25th percentile and weight on 75th percentile indicates that the child is obese.

To find out whether the child is growing well or not, the following clinical symptoms can be taken as a good indicators. There are:

1. *Sense of well being*: Alertness, interest in the activities, always be happy.
2. *Vitality*: Vitality includes the endurance during activity with recovery from fatigue, looks rested, does not fall asleep in the school and well sleep in the night.
3. *Weight*: In proportion to height, age and body frame.
4. *Posture*: Erect arms and legs, chest out and abdomen pulled in.
5. *Teeth*: Straight without grady, well shaped jaws.
6. *Gums*: Firm, pink and no signs of bleeding.

7. *Skin*: Smooth, slightly moist, healthy glow, shinigness, reddish pink mucous membrane.
8. *Eye*: Bright, clear and no circle of fatigue.
9. *Hair*: Lustrous, healthy scalp.
10. *Muscles*: Well developed and firm.
11. *Nervous Control*: Good attention for particular act, not irritable and restless, get along with others.
12. *Gastro intestinal tract*: Good appetite, normal absorption and excretion.

All these points discussed would help us to identify a normal healthy child.

When we come in to nutrition, the pre-school children may have the following problems. They are :

1. Feeding Problem : since their appetite is lower, feeding become problematic.
2. Some of the children develop dislike towards milk and milk products.
3. They prefer raw vegetables rather cooked ones.
4. They like crisp and spongy foods. They do not like sticky, gummy, slimy foods.
5. Fruit is very appreciable among pre-school children and they like it in any form like, fruit salad, fruit juices, etc.
6. They like plain foods. So, it is advisable to avoid spices and condiments in their preparation.
7. Items like sweets and sour preparation are not appreciated.
8. Since they are more active at this period, giving the food at regular interval is a must.

Feeding behaviour of a child is influenced by:

1. Family's ecosystem, and
2. Child's ecosystem.

1. The family's ecosystem includes the income, the availability of foods, knowledge of nutrition, stability of family environment, quality of housing, composition of the family members, society in which they live, their traditions and customs, etc.

2. Based on family's ecosystem, child's ecosystem will develop. Moreover, they are also influenced by school, peer groups, the books, and the teachers.

Based on all these factors, we should develop a proper feeding habits. Points to be remembered while serving meal:

The mother should develop eating habits like eating foods at regular interval and eat foods regularly. The food should be served in pleasant environment.

The child should sit comfortably for eating.

Bowls, tumblers, plates should be the separate one which suits the interest of the child.

The child should be seated with adults, thus help the child to develop good food habits.

The food should be more attractive, colourful, and non-monotonous. The food should be crisp enough and soft.

When introduced the food to the child, it should be introduced with little amount. If the child shows favourite on, serve a little more amount.

Interest on specific foods should be avoided.

Allow the child to have the food with the peer group.

Adults must be careful while showing aversions to some food. If the child is with them, it may lead the child to develop same aversion to the food. So, adults must avoid such habits when they are with their pre-schoolers.

Let us pass on towards the problem commonly seen in pre-school children, known as malnutrition. The causative factors are divided chiefly under four heads. They are :

I. Low income or poor economic status,
II. Ignorance or lack of nutritional knowledge,
III. Infections and Infestations, and
IV. Other factors.

Low Income or Poor Economic Status

Especially in India, 75 per cent of our population comes under rural areas. In these areas, per capita income is very low. In turn it affects their purchasing power.

Poor economic status is also due to (*a*) lack of subsidiary occupation; (*b*) Poor awareness on applying new technology on agriculture, their main occupation; and (*c*) Joint family system. In joint family system the head of the family should take up all the burden and he is in a position to look after the whole family members. Here also, the available is shared by all, thereby individual attention is lacking. Apart from that, imitation of rich people's life style also resist their attention on food and its importance. Too many children in one family also leads to poor social economic status.

Ignorance or Lack of Nutritional Knowledge

Mass illiteracy among women is a contributing factor to malnutrition.

Illiteracy leads the mother to:

1. do not have knowledge of nutritious food.
2. do not know proper cooking methods.
3. do not know the importance of breast feeding.
4. too much or unhygienic dilution of artificial milk.
5. do not have the awareness of weaning foods.
6. supply inadequate in quantity as well as quality of supplementary foods.
7. do not have knowledge in giving the type of food in particular diseases.

Infections and Infestations

Infection is mainly due to micro-organisms. Infestation is mainly of worm infestations like hookworm infestation, roundworm infestation. This is mainly due to poor hygienic practices and environmental sanitation. The following factors will compile the reasons for poor hygiene and infestation. They are:

- Lack of covering foods.
- Lack of storage facilities.
- Moving dirty places, without sleeper.
- No provision for segregating the viral infected patient.
- In such condition, it is transmitted easily to other person, *e.g.*, whooping cough.
- Poor ventilation.

— Poor medical facilities.
— Eating too much of sweets.

Other Factors

— Inadequate food supply.
— Low birth weight.

Ecology of Malnutrition

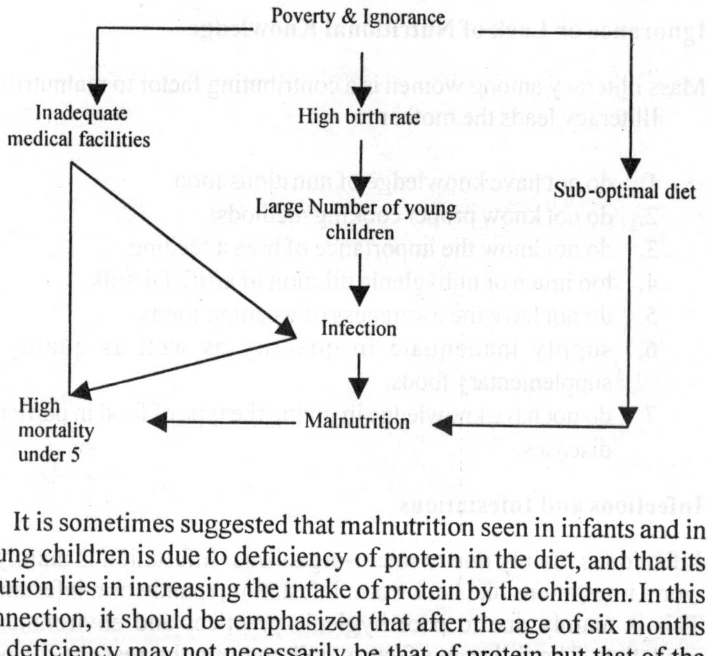

It is sometimes suggested that malnutrition seen in infants and in young children is due to deficiency of protein in the diet, and that its solution lies in increasing the intake of protein by the children. In this connection, it should be emphasized that after the age of six months the deficiency may not necessarily be that of protein but that of the total quantity of food eaten by the child. As a result, the diet may be deficient in calories as well as in proteins. Under these circumstances if the deficiency of only protein is made good and not that of calories, then the protein ingested would be utilized to a considerable extent as a source of energy and not for growth and building-up of tissues.

A number of surveys relating to diets of children of the pre-school age (1 to 5 years) carried out in recent years at various places in the country showed that the diets of more than 90 per cent of the children of poor economic group were deficient in calories while the deficiency of protein was seen only in 30 per cent of the children. Even in the latter cases, the protein deficiency would not have occurred if the existing diets had been consumed in amounts adequate to meet their energy needs. The first priority in combating malnutrition in our children would therefore, seem to lie in providing children enough food to satisfy their energy needs and not in distribution of protein concentrates and other protein processed foods.

Mid-Morning Snacks

Wheat—Murukku

Ingredients	No. of Servings : 2-4.
Wheat flour	— 100 g.
Chilli powder	— as required.
Salt	— as required.
Water	— as required.
Oil	— as required.

Method

1. Steam the flour for 10-20 minutes and serve it.
2. Add chilli powder, salt and mix it well.
3. Add water little by little and make a dough.
4. Put the dough in the murukku mould and fry it in hot oil, when it turns golden brown, remove it.

It serves 355.0 kcal, and 12.1 gm of protein and cost about 0.75 paise.

Wheat—Pulse Laddu

Ingredients	No. of Servings : 2-3.
Wheat Flour	— 100 gm.
Dal Flour	— 50 gm.
(Powdered) Jaggery	— 75 gm.
Vanaspati	— 10 gm.

Method

1. Roast, wheat flour and Dal flour separately till it turns golden brown.
2. Mix the roasted flour.
3. Add powdered jaggery and mix them well.

4. Melt vanaspati, pour the hot vanaspati in the flour and make Laddu.

Cost : 0.60 paise. Calorie : 879.75 k Calorie protein : 24 gm.

Arase or Anarese or Adirsam

Ingredients

No. of Servings : 2-4.

Jowar flour	— 100 gm.
Jaggery	— 100 gm.
Cardamom	— 2
Sesame Seeds	— 10 gm.
Water	— 100 ml.
Ghee or Oil	as required

Method

1. Make a syrup with jaggery and while it is boiling, add cardamom.
2. Sprinkle jowar flour over it.
3. Remove from fire and make this into a soft dough.
4. Divide the dough into small balls and sprinkle with sesame seeds. Flatten the balls.
5. Fry preferably in ghee or refined oil.

Cost: Rs. 1.60 Calorie: 719 kcal. Protein: 35.7 gm.

Kadubu

Ingredients

No. of Servings : 2

Jowar flour	— 100 gm.
Cumin seed	— 1½ tsp.
Salt (as per taste)	— 1½-2 tsp.
Coconut Scrapings	— 2 tsp.

Method

1. Mix the dry ingredients first and make dough by sprinkling water.
2. Knead it well and make a soft dough.
3. Make balls and roll them out into any shape you like.
4. Place these on a plantain leaf.
5. Steam these in a steamer at least for 20 minutes.

Cost : 0.60 paise. Calorie : 349 kcal. Protein : 10.4 gm.

Moong Burfi

Ingredients	No. of Servings : 2-4
Whole moong	— 100 gm.
Thickened milk	— 100 gm.
Ghee oil	— 100 gm.
Sugar	— 200 gm.
Chopped dry fruits, cardamom seeds. (If needed)	

Method

1. Clean moong and grind into coarse flour.
2. Put ghee oil in a vessel and fry this flour on low heat.
3. When ghee separates add thickened milk and fry for five minutes.
4. Take off from the fire and add chopped dry fruits, cardamom, ground sugar and set on a plate. After it sets cut pieces out of it and decorate on a plate.
   Cost: Rs. 2.80 Calorie: 2443 kcal. Protein: 44.0 gm.

Modagam

Ingredients	No. of Servings : 3-4
Steamed Maida	— 100 gm.
Boiled Water	— 100 gm.
For Filling	
Coconut Scrapings	— 50 gm.
Jaggery	— 75 gm.

Method

1. Add slowly the steamed maida to the boiling water and make dough.
2. Heat tawa and add jaggery and allow it to mellow.
3. Add coconut scrapings to the melted jaggery, when it starts harden take off from fire.
4. Make the dough into small balls and shape it as you like. Fill the filling inside and close it.
5. Keep this modagam in a greased idli plate for steaming.
   Cost: 0.75 paise. Calorie: 834.7 kcal Protein: 13.2 gm.

Groundnut Biscuit

Ingredients No. of Serving : 1

Roasted groundnut flour	— 25 gm.
Roasted wheat flour	— 25 gm.
Soda	— a little.
Curd	— as required
Sugar	— 20 gm.
Salt	— as needed.

Method

1. Mix all ingredients and add a little water to make dough.
2. Roll it out like chapati and cut as you like.
3. Fry it in the oil.

Cost : 0.40 paise Calorie: 336.9 kcal. Protein: 10.4 gm.

Cheedai

Ingredients No. of Serving : 1

Whole wheat flour	— 25 gm.
Maida	— 25 gm.
Chilli powder	— as needed
Salt	— for taste
Asafoetida powder if desired.	

Method

1. Make dough in the flour by adding water. Also add all the other ingredients while mixing.
2. Make small say tiny balls out of dough and press it out in the juicy filter/Coffee filter.
3. Fry it in hot oil, till it turns golden brown.

Cost: 0.40 paise Calorie: 172 kcal. Protein: 5.7 gm.

Laddu

Ingredients No. of Servings : 2

Ragi	— 25 gm.
Green Gram	— 25 gm.
Groundnut	— 10 gm.
Jaggery	— 20 gm.

Method

1. Roast ragi, green gramdal and groundnut separately and powder it.
2. Make syrup in a vessel with jaggery and a little water.
3. Pour this syrup to the powdered flour and make laddu.
   Cost: 0.50 paise   Calorie: 298 kcal.   Protein: 10.6 gm.

Burfi

Ingredients	No. of Servings : 1–2
Rice flakes	— 25 gm.
Roasted groundnut	— 20 gm.
Jaggery	— 30 gm.

Method

1. Roast rice flakes and add it to roasted, powdered groundnut.
2. Make syrup with jaggery and water.
3. Add rice flakes, powdered groundnut, mix to syrup and pour it on a plate.
4. Immediately cut it out.
   Cost: 0.50 paise   Calorie : 301.9 kcal.   Protein : 10.6 gm.

Mid-day Meals

1. Tomato Rice

Ingredients	No. of Serving : 1
Rice	— 25 gm.
Tomato	— 1 No.
Onion	— as required
Green chillies	— as required
Garam masala	— as required
Curry leaves	— as required
Salt	— as required
Water	— as required

Method

1. Cook the rice.
2. Chop the Onions, Tomatoes, Green chillies and Curry leaves.

3. Season chopped Onions, Curry leaves, Green chillies, Tomatoes and masala powder and Salt.
4. Add rice and stir well.

2. Curd Rice

Ingredients	No. of Serving : 1
Rice	— 25 gm.
Curd	— 50 ml.

Coriander leaves for decoration, salt for taste.

Method

1. Cook rice.
2. Add curd and stir well.
3. Garnish with coriander leaves, curry leaves. If possible do garnish with small pieced mangoes.

3. Dal Rice

Ingredients	No. of Serving : 1
Rice	— 25 gm.
Redgram dal	— 20 gm.
Tomatoes	— 1 No.
Chilli	— One.
Turmeric	— a little.
Salt	— for taste.

Method

1. Cook rice and dal in the same vessel. While cooking add turmeric powder and chopped tomatoes and chillies.

4. Vegetable Biryani

Ingredients	No. of Serving : 1
Rice	— 25 gm.
Carrot	— 10 gm.
Beetroot	— 10 gm.
Peas	— 10 gm.
Onions	— 2 No.
Tomatoes	— 1 No.
Chillies	— 2 No.
Salt	— as per taste.
Oil	— as required
Masala Powder	— as required.

Method

1. Cook rice, peas, separately.
2. Scrap or cut into small pieces the carrot and beetroot.
3. Chop the onions, tomatoes and chillies.
4. Season oil, redgramdal, chopped onions chillies, tomatoes, curry leaves and masala powder.
5. Add scraped/cut carrot, beetroot and salt. Allow to cook.
6. Add cooked rice and peas and stir well. Remove it from fire.

5. Mint Bhath

Ingredients	No. of Serving : 1
Rice	— 25 gm.
Mint	— 20 gm.
Onions	— 2 No.
Tomatoes	— 2 No.
Chilli	— 1 No.
Curry leaves	— as required.
Masala powder	— 1 tsp.
Salt	— as per taste.
Oil	— for seasoning.

Method

1. Cook rice.
2. Clean mint with water.
3. Chop onions, tomatoes, chillies and curry leaves.
4. Season oil, chopped ingredients. Add masala powder and salt.
5. Add cleaned mint and allow to cook.
6. Add cooked rice and stir well.

Variations

Any greens can be used in the place of mint then it is called "green bhath".

6. Lime Bhath

Ingredients	No. of Serving : 1
Rice	— 25 gm.
Lime Juice	— 10 ml.
Mustard	— 2 gm.
Blackgram dal	— 2 gm.
Cumin seed	— 2 gm.
Salt	— to taste
Oil	— For seasoning.

Method

1. Cook rice and keep aside.
2. Season oil, mustard, blackgram dal and cumin seed.
3. Add lime juice and salt, allow to cook for a few minutes.
4. Add cooked rice and stir well.
5. Serve hot.

7. Fried Rice

Ingredients	No. of Serving : 1
Rice	— 25 gm.
Peas	— 10 gm.
Carrot	— 1 small size
Potato	— 1 small size
Beans	— 2 No. (small size)
Beetroot	— 10 gm.
Onion	— 1 big
Capsicum	— 2 No.
Oil	— for seasoning.

Method

1. Cook rice and keep it aside.
2. Cook the vegetable and keep it aside.
3. Fry the onions and capsicum (chopped).
4. To this add cooked rice and cooked vegetables. Fry them for 15 minutes.

8. Nast-Gurih

Ingredients	No. of Serving : 1
Rice	— 25 gm.
Coconut Milk	— 40 ml.
Water	— 15 ml.
Peel of Lemon	— 5 gm.
Salt	— to taste.

Method

1. Wash rice well and keep aside.

2. In a thick saucepan, heat together all other ingredients.
3. Add rice, when it starts boiling.
4. Boil rapidly for about 5 minutes at lower heat. Cover and simmer gently till it gets done.

9. Coconut Rice

Ingredients	No. of Serving: 1
Rice	— 25 gm.
Coconut scrapings	— 20 gm.
Onions	— 10 gm.
Chilli	— 2 No.
Curry leaves	— a few.
Salt	— to taste.
Oil	— for frying.

Method

1. Cook rice and keep aside.
2. Chop Onions, Chillies and Curry leaves.
3. Season oil, mustard, redgram dal, Chopped onions, Chillies and curry leaves.
4. Add Coconut Scrapings and allow a few minutes to fry.
5. Add cooked rice and salt, stir well.

10. Vegetable Pulav with Pakoda

Ingredients	No. of Serving : 1
Rice	— 25 gm.
Cloves	— 1
Cinnamon	— 1 gm.
Cumin Seed	— 1/2 tsp.
Red Chilli Powder	— 1/2 tsp.
Garam Masala Powder	— a little.
For Pakoda	
Moong dal	— 15 gm.
Oil	— for frying.

Method for Pakoda

1. Soak dal overnight and grind to a very fine paste.
2. Immediately fry the pakodas in hot oil without adding any salt or any masala.

For the Pulav

1. Wash and cook rice for 1/2 an hour.
2. Add all the ingredients except garam masala in required amount of water.
3. Add fried pakodas. A little extra water is required to cook this. Pulav and the pakodas absorb some water.
4. Cover and cook on a slow fire.
5. Lastly add garam masala powder and shake. So the pakodas do not break. Remove from heat.

NUTRITIONAL REQUIREMENTS OF PRE-SCHOOL CHILDREN

Energy

The body needs energy to maintain body temperatures, for metabolic purposes, to support growth for physical activity.

In the absence of any data on energy intake of normally growing healthy Indian children, the committee recommended adoption energy allowances recommended by FAO/WHO in 1973 with necessary adjustments for the body weights of healthy, well nourished Indian children. For this purpose the committee recommended, the use of body weights of healthy children, who had no constraints of any nature and who could express their full genetic potential for growth.

Based on the growth of undernourished and underweight children on supplementation, the committee suggested that providing energy on the basis of ideal weight for age would be beneficial. The fears about the possible over-estimation of energy deficiency in a community using, these recommended figures were however, expressed.

Age Group Children	*Body Weight*	*Energy allowances Kcal*
1-3 years	12.03	1220
4-6 years	18.87	1720

Proteins

Dietary protein is necessary not only to provide amino acid but also nitrogen for the synthesising of body proteins and other biologically important nitrogenous constituents, all of which are turned over continuously in the body.

There are two basic approaches to determination of protein requirements. The first is based upon the factorial method, wherein endogenous losses are measured and the second is based upon the actual estimation of the lowest amount of nitrogen intake necessary to maintain nitrogen equilibrium. This observation has in fact, been taken into consideration by the FAO/WHO. Expert Group and data obtained from nitrogen balance studies have formed the basis of their recommendations.

Recent public data indicated that obligatory loss of urinary N in children per basal calorie is lower than that seen in adults, and available evidence suggests that the total endogenous loss may be over 2 mg/N/kg body weight. Using this figure and a relative protein value of 65, protein allowances have been calculated.

Age Group Children	*Body Weight Kg.*	*Protein g/day*	*Allowance g/kg/day*
1-3 years	12.03	22	1.83
4-6 years	18.87	29	1.56

Calcium

Calcium requirements of children can be calculated on the basis of the amount of calcium accretion during the period of growth. This can be computed for knowing the calcium content of the infant at birth and of an adult. In the absence of definite data on calcium requirements of Indian children at various age groups and in the absence of data on the extent of absorption of calcium from diets at different time points of growth, the committee recommended that dietary allowances of 0.5 gm suggested earlier may be used.

Age Group	*mg/day*
1-9 years	400-500

Iron

Iron is an important constituent of hemoglòbin, myoglobin and several enzymes. The human body contains between 3 and 4g of iron of which about 75 per cent is present as circulating iron and the rest as storage iron, consumption of diets which do not provide enough iron leads at first to a progressive depletion of storage iron and only later do levels of hemoglobin fall, leading to anemia.

Losses of iron in infants and children are not precisely known and amounts needed to replace these losses and therefore, difficult to determine. During growth, for an increase in each kg in body weight 30 mg iron is required and since the increase in body weight during childhood is 2 kg/year on an average, then daily requirements of iron for growth will be 0.2 mg.

Vitamins

Vitamins are essential for the maintenance of normal health. Although needed in very small amounts, they play an important role in the metabolism of several nutrients. Clinical manifestations due to vitamin deficiencies have long been recognized. There are considerable interactions between various nutrients in addition, vitamins and hormones interact closely. Although some of the vitamins are synthesized by the intestinal minoflora, the extent to which they are available to the loss is uncertain. Vitamin requirements, therefore have to meet through dietary sources.

Vitamin A

In the absence of direct evidence, recommended intakes for infants and children are calculated on the basis of vitamin A intake through breast milk for infants and extrapolated values of children.

The incidence of vitamin A deficiency signs are high and serum vitamin A levels are largely low among Indian children whose dietary intake is less than 100 kg. In a group of children receiving food supplements which provided total of a 300 mg. or vitamin A, per day over a period of 6 months, serum vitamin A levels were found to be around 30 kg and clinical signs of vitamin A deficiency were rarely seen.

Age Group Children	*Vitamin A. mg. of retinol*
1-3 years	250
4-6 years	300

Vitamin C

Although most species of animals can synthesise vitamin C, man can not do so and therefore, needs to get his vitamin C through diet. The functions of vitamin C include its role in the synthesis of collagen, wound healing, amino acid and carbohydrate metabolism and synthesis of some hormones. It also has an influence on the metabolism of iron. It has been claimed that the ingestion of large amount of ascorbic acid beneficially influence common colds.

The ICMR Committee, felt the requirements should be based on observations made in well nourished population and therefore, recommended daily intake of 20 mg vitamin C for infants and 40 mg for children.

Thiamine

Thiamine pyrophosphate functions as a coenzyme for carboxylase which is intimately involved in carbohydrate metabolism; as a result, it has long been recognized that requirements of this are related to energy intake particularly to energy derived from carbohydrates. The oxidative phosphorylation of pyruvic acid is dependent upon thiamine, in the absence of adequate thiamines, tissue levels of pyruvate increase. Thiamine is also needed for the activity of engymetransketolase and the activity of this enzyme in red blood cells falls in thiamine inadequacy; an observation which has in recent years been used to evaluate human thiamine requirement.

There are no studies on thiamine requirements of children. As the earlier committee had done, it was recommended that allowances for thiamine for children be made on the basis of 0.5mg similar to that for adults.

Riboflavin

Riboflavin is a part of flavo protein which are intimately connected with biological oxidations. It plays an important role in maintaining the integrity of mucocutaneous structures.

Among rich sources of riboflavin are flesh foods, legumes, green leafy vegetables and groundnuts. Although heatstable, riboflavin is destroyed when exposed to light. Cooking losses of riboflavin in Indian preparations are considerable ranging from 15 to 100 per cent depending upon the food and the type of cooking. It has, however, been found that the loss of riboflavin from commonly used legumes during cooking is negligible. A mean figure of 20 per cent loss for the whole diet as consumed may be considered while recommending allowances.

There are no data on intakes of riboflavin by normal Indian children. It was, therefore suggested that allowances for children be computed on the basis of 0.6 mg per 1000 k cal.

Recommended Dietary intakes of Nutrients.

Nutrients	*Children 1-2 years*	*4-6 years*
Calorie (kcal)	1220	1720
Proteins (gm)	22.0	29.4
Calcium (gm)	0.4-0.5	0.4-0.5
Iron (mgm)	20.25	20.25
Vitamin A Retinol (mg)	250	300
B Carotene (mg)	1000	1200
Thiamine	0.5	0.9
Riboflavin	0.7	1.0
Vitamin C	40.0	40.0

Balanced Diets for Pre-school Children

Food Stuff	*1-3 years*		*4-6 years*	
	Veg (g)	*Non-Veg(g)*	*Veg (g)*	*Non-Veg(g)*
Cereals	150	150	200	200
Pulses	50	40	60	50
Green leafy Vegetables	50	50	75	75
Other Vegetables Roots & tubers	30	30	50	50
Fruits	50	50	50	50
Milk	300	200	250	200
Fats & Oils	20	20	25	25
Meat & Fish, Eggs	—	30	—	30
Sugar and Jaggery	30	30	40	40

Health Education for Pre-school Children

Health education should aim at achieving the optimum health for all by giving not only information about good health but also by bringing about attitudinal change in their food habits and other health habits. Health education to children in pre-school is not only to aim at information thrust but to bring out a behavioural change.

Health Education as a means of social change.

Health consciousness
Health knowledge
Self-awareness
Attitude Change
Decision-Making
Behaviour Change
Social Change

Role of Pre-school in Health Education

The pre-school programme begins with a health check-up by the teacher. Children are susceptible to communicable diseases. They easily get affected. Hence, the teacher is conscious that the children when they reach the school are free from any disease. She also sees that children do not have long nails to avoid accumulation of dirt. Simultaneously she also talks to the children the need for cutting the nails and keeping it clean.

Children are taught to clean their hands and legs after their outdoor free play. This becomes a regular activity in the pre-school. Thus, the children are aware that whenever they play outside they should wash their hands and legs.

During the lunch time also before and after they eat they are made to wash their hands which in turn continues even at home. The child not only gets the knowledge of being clean but practices it in everyday life.

In pre-schools, it is emphasized that they get nutritious diet and taught through free conversation, story telling, rhymes and games the need for eating greens, vegetables, milk, pulses etc. In fact, this knowledge and habit of eating bring in children transformation in their life.

The children are also taught to keep their surrounding clean and tidy. They themselves pick up the papers flying around them and learn to use the dustbin.

Almost all the child welfare programmes including the national programme emphasise good health, immunization, nutritious food through health education both to parents and children.

Thus, the pre-school can play a vital role in promoting good health habits among the pre-school children.

15

Deficiency Diseases among Pre-schoolers

Unlike the young ones of other species, the human in fact is entirely dependent for his food and care on others. The period from birth to six months is a period of very rapid growth and therefore of high nutritional requirements percent of body weight. As in the case of the adults the active and healthy child needs food for energy. In addition, extra nourishment is required to provide for the continuous increase in the size of every part of his body. If the infant and toddler are not provided, with the nourishment they need, the development of malnutrition of one type or another is inevitable, depending on which of the nutrients are lacking in it.

So, the infants and the pre-school children are extremely vulnerable. They succumb readily when the diet is poor in quality and quantity and infectious diseases and infestations are widespread. The rate of growth and development of infants and pre-school children depend to a large measure on the adequacy of the diet consumed by them. A brief account of the deficiency diseases found among the pre-school children are given below :

Protein-Calorie Malnutrition

A majority of infants and pre-school children in the developing countries consume inadequate diets and suffer from signs and symptoms of dietary deficiencies. One of the most important signs of malnutrition in infancy is a stationary or falling body-weight due to growth failure.

The infant grows well as the flow of breast milk is adequate during the first six months of life but shows a rapid fall in weight during the second semester, the flow of breast milk becomes inadequate and the supplementary foods do not provide adequate quantities of proteins, vitamins and minerals.

Protein-Calorie Malnutrition can be defined as a range of pathological conditions arising from simultaneous deficiency of protein and calories and commonly associated with infections. This PCM is particularly in the age group of at risk e.g., 1-5 years.

There are several factors which contribute significantly to protein-calorie malnutrition. These are especially significant in the feeding of children and they include :

1. Prolonged nursing at the breast and late introduction of supplementary foods.
2. Inappropriate choice of and insufficient amount of supplementary foods.
3. Sudden weaning, transition from breast milk to adult diet.
4. Unhygienic feeding habits which predispose a child to diarrhoea.
5. The practice of drastic and medication and withstanding of foods in an attempt to cure diarrhoea.

The manifestations of protein-calorie malnutrition range from nutritional marasmus to Kwashiorkor. These two conditions are defined as follows:

Nutritional Marasmus

A condition characterized by muscle wasting, loss of subcutaneous and very low body weight, resulting from lack of calories for a considerable period together with storage of protein and other nutrients. It occurs mainly in infant and children below 5 years. Factors other then lack of enough food. *e.g.* Infection often plays a part in causation.

Kwashiorkor

A severe clinical syndrome, the main causes of which is deficiency of amino acids needed for protein synthesis with deficiency of calories as a usual contributory factors. Some or all of the following signs are present, arrested growth, oedema, muscle wasting, dermatitis, hair changes, enlarged liver, diarrhoea, mental apathy and misery. The syndrome occurs most frequently in children aged one to three years during or after weaning.

Treatment

If the child is very seriously ill, the child should be admitted in the hospital and should be fed with high protein fluid diet such as skimmed milk. The child should be treated for infection. If the child is less severely ill, the child may be treated at home and the child should be given high protein supplements, either of animal protein or plant protein. A judicious combination of vegetable protein foods such as cereals, pulses and oil cakes proves to be very effective in combating protein-calorie malnutrition.

Prevention

Breast feeding is essential and should be prolonged as far as possible. Nutrition education should be given to mothers to choose the right type of supplements and to start the supplements in correct time, and to give supplements in correct amounts. It is necessary to develop and to make as much use as possible of any locally available protein food, both animal and vegetable. Mothers also should be educated on how to rear the child.

Vitamin 'A' Deficiency

The tragedy of malnutrition is not so much that it is responsible for high mortality but that it cripples and permanently damages the growing generation. Of the many crippling effects, probably the most devastating effect is on vision. It is believed that the most common cause of preventable blindness is malnutrition due to deficiency of Vitamin 'A' in the diet.

Night blindness, the inability to see in dim light, is an early indication of Vitamin 'A' deficiency. The more serious stage known as Xerophthalmia means dryness of the eye, in which lesions predominate. This progresses to Kerotomalasia or liquefaction of the cornea, a stage of abnormal recell formation which may lead to total blindness.

Treatment and Prevention

When the treatment with large doses of vitamin 'A' in the form of fish liver oil or skimmed milk is given, eyes can be saved even when the process of distraction has already begun. The efficacy and availability of treatment must be an increasingly important factor in preventing blindness.

Vitamin 'A' can be obtained in the ready made state from such costly foods as fish liver oil, batha, eggs, liver etc. Alternatively any green leafy vegetables contain carotene which can be converted into Vitamin 'A' in the body. An average daily intake of about 50 grams of green leafy vegetables which may not cost more than few paisa will be able to provide the required amount of Vitamin 'A' to the child. An intake of about 100 gm green leafy vegetables daily will supply an adequate amount of Vitamin 'A' to the pregnant women. With a good store of Vitamin 'A' at birth, the infant's diet after about six months can include, green leafy vegetable properly cooked and mashed.

Studies carried out by the NIN at Hyderabad have demonstrated the value in children of a massive oral dose of Vitamin 'A' once in six months in preventing blindness. Based on these studies, the Government of India, have now taken up a countrywide programme of administering the dose to all pre-school children.

Vitamin 'B' Complex Deficiency

Beri-Beri

The deficiency disease caused by Vitamin 'B', or thiamin is known as beri-beri. Usually these are classified as:

1. *Wet—'beri-beri'*: A wet condition in which some oedema is present and heart failure often occurs.
2. *Dry beri-beri*: A chronic disease characterized by peripheral nerve lesions affecting different muscular systems but usually leading to paralysis of lower limbs.
3. *Infantile beri-beri*: Like wet beri-beri and dangerous condition, with varying clinical manifestations not closely resembling those of the disease in adults and often leads to death.

Treatment and Prevention

An administration of 10-50 mgs of thiamine hydrochloride per day or by injection for several weeks or dried yeast tablets 5.30 mgs thrice a day for several weeks till the deficiency signs disappear will treat the disease in children. This can be prevented by replacing the milled raw rice with parboiled hand pounded rice and whole wheat flour which supply thiamin in sufficient amounts.

Riboflavin Deficiency

Soreness of the angles of the mouth (Angular Stomatitis), degeneration of the Lips at the line of closure, called cheilosis, and in the tongue called glossitis.

Treatment

The fissures usually varishes quickly when a good source of riboflavin such as milk is given. Good sources of the vitamin are milk and milk products, egg and liver, green leafy vegetables and pulses.

Nicotin (or) Niacin Deficiency

Lack of vitamin in the diet causes a disease known as Pellagra. The main symptoms are symmetrical dermatitis, diarrhoea and often mental changes.

A good varied diet containing plenty of animal proteins such as milk and meat is universally regarded as an essential part of treatment. Groundnuts make a valuable contribution in the prevention of pellagra.

Vitamin 'C' Deficiency and its Treatment

Ascorbic acid is the most sensitive of all vitamin to heat and its destruction in foods by prolonged heat in cooking lead to the appearance of 'scurvy'. The inclusion of a few ounces of fresh fruits and leafy vegetables in a diet meets the requirements of Vitamin 'C'. Special attention should be given to artificially fed infants.

Vitamin 'D' and Calcium Deficiency

Rickets is primarily a disease of children in the first two years of life. This is a disease of calcium and phosphorous metabolism which occurs when infants and children receive insufficient Vitamin 'D'. This is characterized by protruding forehead, pigeon chest, depressed ribs, protruding abdomen, bow legs, knock knees, flat feet and bending of the ribs.

Treatment

Exposure to sunlight during which Vitamin 'D' is formed in the skin by the action of ultraviolet light which transforms ergosterol a precursor present in plant cells into Vitamin 'D'.

Iron Deficiency

Prolonged low intake of iron leads to anemia in pre-school children, pregnant and lactating mothers. When the hemoglobin level is below 11 gms/100 ml of venous blood in children aged 6 months to 6 years, it will lead to Anemia. For the formation of normal blood in the bone marrow, sufficiency of various nutrients is needed especially iron, folic acid. Vitamin B_{12} and protein. The most important nutrient in this contents is iron which is an essential component of hemoglobin. Hook-worm infestation is known to be an important cause of iron loss among children.

Treatment

The inclusion of about 100 gms of green leafy vegetables in the diet daily will help to supply the iron requirements adequately. Today anemia is treated by the administration of folic acid. Pregnancy anemia can be successfully prevented by routine administration of tablets containing iron and folic acid to all antenatal mothers at least during the last 100 days of pregnancy. Treatment with folic acid is combined with the provision of iron and Vitamin B_{12} and supplemented by blood transfusion when the degree of anemia is severe.

16

Common Ailments and Their Prevention

Malnutrition could make children more susceptible to infectious diseases and also alter the course and outcome of the resulting illnesses has long been in the history of medicine and public health. Some diseases are very common among the pre-school children. They are Diphtheria, Pertussis, Tetanus, Polio, Measles, Tuberculosis, Diarrhoea etc. Among these the first six are known as '6 Killer Diseases'. A brief account of causes for these diseases and its prevention are discussed below:

Diphtheria

Diphtheria is a deadful disease. It is a highly contagious disease caused by the Diphtheria bacillus. Children between the age of 1 to 10 are especially susceptible. The germs are usually carried by infected secretions from the nose or throat of a person who harbour these germs. The symptoms in the early case of diphtheria include mild sore-throat, and elevation of body temperature, and difficulty in breathing and swallowing. The diphtheria bacillus invades the membranes of the upper air passages. It may obstruct the passage of air and cause death by asphyxiation.

Pertussis

This is caused by a specific germs called '*Bordettella Pertussis*'. The first stage of whooping cough begins a week or two after exposure. During the first week the symptoms are safe as that of ordinary cold. After two weeks coughing becomes spasmodic and the typical whoop is heard. The patient's face becomes red and even bluish and the veins stand out on his head and neck as he struggles for breath. By this time he becomes nauseated and may vomit. This disease lasts for three to six weeks. Children who are affected may lose weight and become severely undernourished.

Tetanus

This is a life threatening disease which is caused by a germ called Clostridium Tetani. These germs are found abundantly in soil or dust with horse manure. When there is a cut or open wound the germs penetrate into the body, grow and produce their toxin. Symptoms usually appear within five to ten days after the injury. A stiffness of the muscles of the face occurs when the patient attempts to open or close his mouth. Stiffness spread to other muscles of his body.

Polio

Polios strikes most children causing deformities. 80 per cent of such children are within two years of age. Polio affects the brain, the spine, nerves and nervous system of the body. It also makes the muscles weak and ineffective. This is caused by a virus, which is transmitted through contaminated food and water, and affects the limbs of the child when resistance is low, the symptoms of polio are high fever, headache, severe cold and diarrhoea. When this disease strikes it affects the nerves and related areas, and paralyzes the hands or legs or both.

Measles

Mild fever is seen for the first one weak. Then red rashes are seen throughout the body. If the child is healthy it will vanish within one week. Otherwise it will result in death also.

Tuberculosis

Tuberculosis is an infectious disease which is caused by Tubercle Bacillus. It affects in all the age group especially the malnutrition group of people. Mostly it affects the lungs. The bacilli comes out from the lungs through the sputum to spread infection. The signs and symptoms are cough with expectoration, chest pain, evening rise of temperature, loss of appetite and weight. Haemoptysis also may occur in chronic cases.

Preventive measures: BCG Vaccine to be injected from age group of zero persons and environmental hygiene to be adopted. Nutritious diet to be given to gain the immunity power.

Vaccination Schedule
(Latest I.A.P. & U.I.P. Recommendations)

Age	*Vaccine*
Birth	B.C.G. + OPV
1½-2 Months (TIRPLE)	O.P.V. (POLIO) + D.P.T..
2½-4 Months	O.P.V. (POLIO) + D.P.T.
3½-6 Months	O.P.V. (POLIO) + D.P.T.
8-12 Months	Measles & Polio (5th dose)
15-18 Months	M.M.R. (Measles-Mumps-Rubella)
18-24 Months	Polio + D.P.T. (1st Booster)
2 years	Typhoid (Typhim VI) Booster is given every 3 years
4-6 years	Polio + D.P.T. (2nd Booster)
10 Years	T.T. (Booster). 5-10 yearly Hepatitis B Booster
HEPATITIS B Injection	Primary dose : 3 (Given at Birth, 1 month & 6 month) Booster at 10 year
H.I.B. H. Influenza B (Pneumonia/Brain fever)	3 Doses (Age < 6 months) 2 Doses (Age 6-12 months) 1 Dose (Age > 1 year) Booster after 6-12 months

Nutrition and Health Education for Pre-school Children

Various studies and surveys have revealed a high degree of incidence of malnutrition among children. This calls for active health education programmes to improve the food practices in the Community. Nutrition Education is concerned not only with what the individual knows but what he does not know about food and his diet. Thus, the emphasis in nutrition is not on change but on improvement of or adding to present food patterns. Nutrition education through children to the parents can be reached and the acceptance gained. The following are the stages in the Nutrition Education:

1. Create awareness among the children.
2. Attention.
3. Creating interest about the topic.
4. This interest must be followed by the urge or the desire to eat.
5. At this stage individual evaluates the information received and decides whether or not he wants to adopt it.
6. Correct method or items must be selected and should be put into action.

Approach

If we are going to work through pre-school children, it's better to work with groups for stimulating action, we can work through the working women's group which is formed in the village.

Methods and Media

In the selection of the methods and media the worker must keep in mind the characteristics of the group with whom he is to communicate. We are going to work through pre-school children, we can impart the nutrition education through dramas, kits, songs, action songs etc. For all these methods the theme should be based on Nutrition and Health.

Example

1. Songs on importance of vegetables, immunization, vitamins etc.
2. Stories based on nutrition and health.
3. Dance by using masks (mask should be the cut out of vegetables, fruits etc.)
4. Using charts.

Evaluation

Evaluation is very important to know whether we are going in a correct path or not, whether the programme is effective or not. Based on the evaluation modification can be done by using various methods or media.

Follow Up

To sustain interest, there should be constant follow-up. A sort of reinforcement is necessary. If the mothers feel that they are materially benefited by that programme, then only they can create an interest and put everything into action.

17

Common Childhood Illnesses

Good Health is the foundation of growth and development, and it is one of the prime responsibilities of the child care worker. Good Health mostly depends upon the absence of diseases, illness or deficiency. It is the physical and mental well-being of the child. A child can only be said to be healthy child if it has a healthy mind in a healthy body.

Children suffer from a number of illnesses during their early childhood years. They have less resistance to diseases than adults. So they easily get affected by diseases.

Pre-school children are mostly affected by communicable diseases. deficiency diseases and other minor illness.

Communicable Diseases

A large number of diseases children suffer from are due to infection. These diseases are called communicable diseases. Communicable diseases are spread or transmitted from one person to another person through saliva, excretion, air, water and/or bodily contact.

There are three stages in any communicable disease. They are:

1. The incubation stage,
2. The acute, stage, and
3. The convalescence stage.

The period from the time the germs enter the body to the time the symptoms appear is called the incubation stage.

The period of actual suffering is called the acute stage. After the period of acute illness he gets into the period of convalescence. This is the period of recovery.

The following are the common communicable diseases:

1. Common Cold

One of the frequent infections of the child is common cold. This is caused by cold virus. Cold is usually accompanied by running nose, headache, and light temperature and cough.

Treatment

Applying camphor oil over chest may give relief to cough. There is no special medicine of common cold except to make the child comfortable by keeping his nose with nose drops.

2. Diarrhoea

This is due to unhygienic condition and late introduction of supplementary and weaning foods. If the motion is watery and often it will result in diarrhoea. This will result in loss of minimal salts in the body. If the foods are not properly cooked it will also result in diarrhoea. Other causes are:

1. Eating roadside eatables.
2. Not using safe drinking water.
3. Poor personal hygiene.
4. Unhygienic bottle feeding etc.

Treatment

To treat diarrhoea oral dehydration solution is effective, cheap, readily available and easy to make. Oral dehydration solution can be easily prepared by mixing salt, sugar and water. This solution must be given little by little whenever the child is willing to drink. Fluids such as water from cooked rice, dal water, weak tea, lemon juice, coconut water, home-made salt-sugar solution etc. can be given to prevent dehydration.

3. Dysentery

Dysentery is bloody diarrhoea. The child complains of abdominal pain and the stools contain plenty of mucous and blood. Sometimes there is high fever. Doctor must be consulted immediately.

Treatment

In the treatment of dysentery, soft diet should be given. Fluids such as lemon juice, and coconut water can be given.

4. Mumps

This is a condition where there is swelling of the glands in the neck as a result of infection by virus. The child may have fever. He may not be able to eat anything because of the enlarged salivary glands.

Treatment

The child should be separated. Liquid diet is recommended.

5. Tonsillitis

This disease is caused by bacteria. Throat is affected. There may also be fever accompanied by cough.

Treatment

Gargling with hot water containing salt gives relief. Only liquid diet should be given as it is painful to swallow.

6. Ear Infection

It is common in children to have mild infections of the ear. Whenever there is earache doctor must be consulted.

Treatment

Applying hot pad and giving aspirin may give temporary relief.

7. Scabies

Scabies are caused by a female insect known as 'Itchmita'. It spreads from person because of lack of cleanliness, dirty clothes and general lack of hygiene. This insect is chiefly found in mud and filth and it gets into the services of our nails. Through our nails it spreads to other parts of our body. Generally this insect enters the parts of our body like, the thighs in between the fingers shoulders, arm pits, genital areas, buttocks, and upper part of the hand. Among children it may be found on the head and on the faces. The wound caused by this insect will produce itching, the itching may be severe in the nights. Scabies may spread rapidly as the water oozing out of the wound is in contact with other parts and also because we scratch with our dirty nails.

Treatment

Treatment consists of applying Benzyl benzoates emulsion as per doctor's advice to the whole body for three or four days after a bath. Keeping the body clean is a preventive measure. Children should not be allowed to play in dirty soil.

8. Measles

It is caused by measle virus. The virus is present in the secretions of throat, nose and mouth and the disease is spread through air. Children who inhale infected air will get it immediately. The symptoms include cold, cough, and fever. Mild fever is seen for the first one week. Then red rashes are seen throughout the body. If the child is healthy it will vanish in one week. Otherwise it will result in death also.

Treatment

One dose of measles Vaccine between 9 and 12 months may prevent this disease.

9. Chicken Pox

It is caused by the germ called variola minor. It begins with fever shortly, separate raised pink sports on head, face and waist. They increase in number rapidly forming nodules and blisters and then a crust within about seven days. The incubation period for the disease is 11-21 days.

Treatment

The pox may cause intense itching that makes the child very restless. By scratching it causes secondary infections. So the child's hands should be washed with soap several times a day.

10. Diphtheria

Diphtheria is a dreadful disease. This is a fatal disease caused by an organism known as corynebacterium diphtheria. It is a highly contagious disease caused by the bacillus. Children between the age of 1 to 10 are especially susceptible. The germs are usually carried by infected secretions from the nose or throat of a person who harbour these germs. The symptoms in the early case of diphtheria include mild-sore throat, the elevation of body temperature, and difficulty in breathing and swallowing. The child suffers from mild fever and cannot breathe easily. As the disease progresses, the child is not able to breathe.

Treatment

If proper treatment is not given, the child may die. This disease can be prevented by giving three doses of DPT before the baby's first birth day.

11. Pertussis

This disease is also called whooping cough. It is caused by a specific germs called '*Bordettella Pertussis*'. The first stage of whooping cough begins a week or two after exposure. During the first week the symptoms are safe as that of ordinary cold. After two weeks coughing becomes spasmodic and the typical whoop is heard. The patient's face becomes red and even bluish and the veins stand out on his head and neck as he struggles for breathe. By this time he becomes nauseated and may vomit. This disease lasts for three to six weeks. Children who are affected may lose weight and become severely undernourished.

Treatment

Giving three doses of DPT Vaccine before the child's first birth day will prevent the occurrence of this disease.

12. Tetanus

Tetanus is caused by the bacteria called clostridium tetani. This is a life threatening disease which is caused by a germ called clostridium tetani. These germs are found abundantly in soil or dust with horse manure. When there is a cut or open wound the germs penetrate into the body, grow and produce their toxin. Symptoms usually appear within five to ten days after the injury. When infected, the baby stops sucking milk because the sucking reflex stops. The baby cannot open his mouth. The jaws become rigid. The child also gets convulsions and when the convulsions become severe the body becomes arched.

Treatment

Giving two doses of TT Vaccine to pregnant mother will prevent the occurrence of this disease.

13. Poliomyelitis

This is also called childhood paralysis and is caused by a virus. The virus lives in the faeces of an infected person and is spread by contact or through contaminated water. Throat secretions can also spread this disease. This illness starts with fever. There will be mild cough and cold. There will also be pain in the legs and arms. Polio affects the brain, the spine, nerves and nervous system of the body. When this disease strikes it affects the nerves and related areas, and paralyses the hand or legs or both.

Treatment

Three doses of oral polio vaccine are to be given to the child during the first year.

14. Tuberculosis

This disease is caused by bacillus known as Mycobacterium tuberculosis. If affects in all the age group of people. Mostly it affects the lungs. It comes out from the lungs through the sputum through cough with expectoration, chest pain, loss of appetite and weight. There is prolonged low grade fever. If proper treatment is not given, the lymph nodes on the sides of the neck get enlarged. The wounds heal at one part while other such nodes begin to form. Tuberculosis can affect any part of the body like glands, lungs, brain and bones.

Treatment

BCG Vaccination usually given within a month after the birth of the child will prevent this disease. Nutritious diet to be given to gain the immunity power.

15. Typhoid

This disease is caused by the bacteria called S. typhi and is contracted by eating food or drinking water infected with the organism. The disease is accompanied by high fever and severe headache and can last for 3 weeks. The child may have diarrhoea. Typhoid has a tendency to relapse and so great care must be taken of the child.

Treatment

The intestines are inflamed and so only liquid diet is advisable. Nourishing soup and drinks and soft boiled food must be given.

16. Infective Hepatitis

This disease is also caused by a virus and is spread in the same manner as typhoid. There will be slight fever, nausea and vomiting with or without jaundice.

Treatment

Plenty of sweetened drinks and light boiled food should be given. The child should be made to take complete rest.

17. Worm Infection

Children often suffer from worm infections. The commonest worms found in human body are round worms, hook worms, thread worms and tape worms.

Round Worm: These worms are got by the child as a result of poor hygiene. Playing in infected soil, drinking impure water, eating contaminated vegetables etc., lead to infection. The infected child loses appetite, becomes restless and may develop protruding abdomen. If the worms are very large in number they form bunched and cause intestinal obstruction with abdominal pain and vomiting. Eradication of worms should be undertaken after confirming the presence of worms.

Hook Worms: These worms suck blood from the intestine. This results in iron deficiency anemia. This infection is acquired from walking bare foot. The larva from the soil penetrate the skin and enter the body. Children infested with hook worms complain of abdominal pain, nausea, heart burn, vomiting and loss of appetite. When infection occurs through skin, local inflammation and swelling at the site of penetration occur. Prolonged infestation leads to delayed mental and physical development.

Thread Worms or Pin Worms: They cause local irritation of the anus. Nails must be cut short and hands should be washed thoroughly with soap before earning food and also after going to the toilet.

Tape Worm: By eating improperly cooked pork and beef children get infected by this worm. Severe anemia develops and children complain of dizziness, headache, nausea, and abdominal pain. Children have to be dewormed after consulting a physician.

Other Illness

Children now and then suffer from minor illness which are not infectious. Neither are the result of deficiency of nutrients. These diseases do cause considerable discomfort to children. The most frequent of them include the following:

Fever: When a child suffers from fever, the temperature will be higher than the normal body temperature. The normal body temperature is 98.4°F or 37°C. Infections usually cause a rise in temperature. Generally fever is not a disease by itself. The child may have loss of appetite during fever. So all solid foods may be removed from his diet. The child's fever must be brought down by sponging the whole body with slightly warm water.

Colic: Colic is an acute intermittent abdominal pain, often associated in infants with the passage of gas, the infant cries with pain during an attack of colic. Common causes of colic are air swallowing, for example, thumb sucking, and an excess of carbohydrate and fruit juice causing intestinal fermentation and gas production. Some infants appear to be particularly susceptible to colic during the second and third months.

Treatment

Feeding at proper intervals avoid thumb-sucking. In an infant prone to colic, the quantity of sugar and fruit juice should be reduced. An acute attack of colic often responds to atropine methonitrate.

Asthma: Asthma is a form of allergy which occurs in those children who come from families where other members also have allergic disorders. Parents should try to find the cause of allergy and eliminate it. Medical help may be sought in severe asthma attack. Emotional problems can aggravate asthma. So parents should see that the child does not suffer from tension.

Treatment

All necessary preventive measures should be taken to help children enjoy the best health during their childhood. It is equally important that once the child gets ill, proper medical treatment should be given immediately.

Role of Pre-school

What can pre-school do to prevent childhood illness, communicable diseases and deficiency diseases in children? Children of pre-school years get easily affected by all these diseases. If not diagnosed and treated early it will be difficult to treat them later. Hence, it is the duty of the teacher in the pre-school to find out whether the child is suffering from any diseases. In fact the purpose of physical check up by the teacher every morning is to make sure that the child is healthy and not suffering from any illness.

If the teacher finds in the child any unusual symptoms she should immediately refer to the doctors and report to the parents. This fact of teacher will help the child immediate medical attention and treatment. For any symptoms of deficiency diseases she should talk to the parents to provide the child nutritious diet. Whereever it is possible she can also get the help of feeding centres and other nutrition programmes and child welfare centres.

Teacher should also provide proper and healthy atmosphere in the pre-school centre. Children should be taught to practice healthy habits of brushing, bathing, cutting nails, wearing clean dress, washing hands before and after eating, washing after playing outside, not to eat what is sold outside in unhygienic places etc.

18

First Aid for Minor Injuries and Common Ailments

An accident is an unexpected occurrence of an event which may involve injury. Majority of the accidents are preventable. If an accident has already occurred, immediate treatment has to be given, to the person who has met with an accident without any delay before medical help is obtained.

DEFINITION

First aid is the immediate treatment given to the victim of an accident or sudden illness, before medical help is obtained, with the following objectives of first aid are to:

1. Preserve life,
2. Promote recovery, and
3. Prevent the condition from getting worse.

GENERAL PRINCIPLES OF FIRST AID

The general principles of first aid may be summarized as follows:

1. The casualty must be removed at once from any source.
2. First aid should be confined to essential only.
3. Severe bleeding must be attended to at the earliest possible moment.
4. If a causality is found to have difficulty, in breathing or to have stopped breathing, the cause of this must be dealt with

artificial respiration, if needed commenced at once and continued so long as there appears to be any chance of restarting normal breathing.

5. Shock must be treated.
6. When a bone or bones are found to be broken, or it is suspected that they are broken, great care should be taken to immobilize the affected part so that the patient can be moved as quickly as possible, without danger of the broken bone becoming worse.
7. Pain must be relieved by supporting the injured part in the most comfortable position.
8. It must be remembered that a casualty is a human being who has probably had a terrifying experience and suffered a severe shock. If conscious, it is the duty of a person who renders first aid to do all in his power to gain the confidence of a casualty, by firm but gentle handling and to relieve his anxiety by convincing reassurance.

The following are the source of accidents at the pre-school level:

1. General Bleeding
2. Bleeding—Nose
3. Shock
4. Burns and scalds
5. Wounds and injuries
6. Fracture
7. Dog Bite (or bites of other animal)
8. Foreign body in the eye and nose
9. Fainting
10. Falls
11. Suffocation

General Bleeding

During the crawling stage and during the walking stage babies have a tendency to pull down things. Heavy and sharp objects may fall on the body causing injuries leading to bleeding.

Treatment

1. Lay the child down on the floor.
2. Apply firm pressure over a pad to the affected part and maintain until bleeding is controlled.
3. If venous bleeding from limb, apply pressure below wound. If arterial bleeding, apply a tourniquet above the wound.
4. When bleeding is controlled, apply a dressing and firm bandage.
5. Treat for shock.
6. If upper limb, place in a sling. If lower limb keep raised.

Bleeding Nose

Pre-school children mostly suffer from bleeding nose.

Treatment

1. Make the child sit up with head erect and bent forward.
2. Loosen all clothing at neck.
3. Ask child to pinch nose at junction of hard and soft parts.
4. Do not let him blow the nose. Apply a cold compress.

Shock

Electric points must be at a high level. So that children cannot reach them. They should be properly protected. Unused wall sockets must be covered with adhesive tape.

Treatment

1. Make the child lie down with the foot of the bed raised about 22 cm.
2. Keep him warm.
3. If conscious, give strong hot tea with plenty of sugar.
4. Avoid unnecessary handling of the child.

Burns and Scalds

Burns and scalds in the home often happen when a child too young to know the danger gets near to the stove and cooking pots. Child may play with a match box or pull over a lighted candle or oil lamp. Hot iron box, hot tea pot etc. Should not be kept on a table cloth. There is the danger of the child pulling the table cloth and along with it the dangerous objects too. These should be kept at a height which will be difficult for the child to reach.

Treatment

1. Immerse the part in cool water for at least few minutes. This will relieve the pain.
2. Do not try to remove clothing which is sticking to the burns. However, remove anything constricting, for example rings, bangles, shoes, belts, etc. before the affected part begins to swell.
3. Do not prick any blisters.
4. Paint exposed areas with gentian, violet, apply vaseline or acriflavine ointment, cover with sterile gauze or clean cloth and bandage.
5. Immobilize a burned limb.
6. Give weak tea or milk with plenty of sugar. If medical aid is delayed give dehydration mixture.

Wounds and Injuries

Knives, scissors, tools, needles, pins, broken glass pieces, razor blades, sharp edged objects or anything which may hurt children must be kept away from them. Wounds due to falls are also common among pre-school children as children play inside as well as outside in grounds.

Treatment

1. Wash wounds with clean boiled water and soap.
2. Remove any dirt or other foreign matter.
3. Wash with antiseptic lotion.
4. Apply acriflavine ointment, cover with gauze and bandage.
5. If extensive, give sulphadimidine tablets.
6. If dirty, dress every two days.
7. Give tetanus toxioid.

Fracture

Fracture may occur when children are playing in ground. During the crawling stage, babies may fall from top places.

Treatment

1. Place the child in comfortable position with injured part well supported.
2. Apply spirit and bandage. Remember to immobilize joints above and below fracture site.
3. Never attempt to set the fracture.
4. Treat for shock. Do not give anything to drink.
5. If open fracture cut away clothing, over wound, stop bleeding and cover with a dry, sterile dressing.

Dog Bite (or bites of other animals)

While going out, children should be fully supervised by adults as children do not know the safety rules. They should be taught the rules at an early age. Children must not be allowed to go near cows, buffaloes, dogs etc. and disturb them. For any bite the treatment must be given immediately.

Treatment

1. Wash wound thoroughly with soap, running water and antiseptic lotion.
2. Apply mercurochrome or tincture iodine.
3. Dress and bandage the wounds.
4. Give suphadimidine tablets.
5. Give tetanus toxioid.
6. Do not kill the dog. Tie and observe for 10 days. Consult the doctor.

Foreign body in the Eyes, Ears and Nose

While playing children have the habit of putting everything into nose and ears. Other children may throw sand or other things into the child's eyes.

Treatment

1. Prevent the child from rubbing the eyes.
2. Pull down lower lid to see if foreign body is there. If seen try to remove it by gently, drawing the corner of a clean wet handkerchief across the foreign body.
3. If not seen pull the upper lid downwards and outwards over the lower lid to remove the foreign body or stand backing the patient, ask him to look down, place a matchstick along the base of the upper lid, hold the eye lashes firmly between the thumb and forefinger and fold the eyelid over the matchstick remove foreign body. Don't try yourself to remove any foreign body from ears and nose. Take the child immediately to the doctor.

Fainting

If children are playing for long time with empty stomach fainting may occur.

Treatment

1. Loosen clothing at neck, chest and waist
2. Lay the child down with legs above the level of head or seat him down and lower his head between his knees.
3. Ensure a supply of fresh air.
4. On recovery, ask him to breathe deeply and give sips of water.

Falls

Because of climbing on furniture steps sliders, swinging, running, jumping etc. falls are common.

Prevention

1. Furniture must be kept away from children without disturbing their movements.
2. Children should be taught the rules at an early age.
3. Children should be fully supervised by adults.

Suffocation

It can occur if a child below one year sleep in a soft pillow, or is allowed to play with a plastic bag which he pulls over his head.

Prevention

Children must not be allowed to put plastic bags on their heads. There is the danger of suffocation when a child is unable to take out the bag by himself. The most common conditions leading to accidents and the method of prevention are also given below:

1. Children may roll off from their cots. If they are left unattended they should be protected by keeping pillows on both sides. It is better not to leave them alone on the cot.
2. Children should not be permitted to go near the oven while cooking. The steam or smoke may harm the child's lungs and eyes.
3. Children have a tendency to put small objects like seeds and flowers into their nose. They also have the tendency to swallow small objects. So, it is better to see that the floor is clean when the child is allowed to play on the floor.
4. Tub or open water tanks should not be near the house. Children are attracted by water and without knowing the danger, they may fall into the water.
5. Medicines should be kept out of reach of children. Medicines, especially pills may be attractive and handy enough to tempt the child to put them into his mouth. All medicine bottles must be labelled, so that even if the child swallows the medicine, the parents may be able to identify it. Similarly, cleaning fluids, powders, shoe polish, ink cigarettes, tobacco, paint sprays etc. must be kept away from children. Constant supervision of the children is essential to prevent accidents.

Activities

1. Take weight and height of children various age-group and compare with standard prescribed.
2. Study the food habits of children of various communities and find out their nutritional awareness and food habits.

3. Prepare some low-cost diet for pre-school age children.
4. Find out commonly found deficiency diseases among the pre-schoolers in your locality.
5. Locate some common childhood illness and suggest remedial measures.
6. Evolve some programmes to impart the Nutrition Education to parents.
7. Visit a hospital and identify the frequently reported illness among the children of 0 to 6 years of age.

19

Home Stimulation

Child is the precious gift of God. The child's learning experiences start from the home since it is the child's first and longest social environment in which it lives and develops into a wholesome human being. It is the home environment that promotes the value system in the child. The family introduces the social and physical world to the child. Bi-directional influences that exist among the family members shape the child's personality and future growth. Like parents, the siblings, grand parents and others at home influence each other. An enriched home environment acts as a stimulant in the development of the child. A challenging and stimulating home environment is the foundation stone in a child's personality development.

More insight in the area of home stimulation becomes essential today because of our changing social scenario. Breaking up of joint families, increasing number of nuclear and single parent families and rise in the number of working women had stolen or reduced the time spent by the parents with their children. Parents need guidance in spending their limited time more qualitatively with their children and thus provide a stimulating environment at home.

HOME STIMULATION

Any material or experience that energizes or vigours the child's activities and promotes its development can be termed as stimulants. A broad spectrum of these stimulants given at home to boost the child's development is called 'Home Stimulation'.

Stimulation refers to any toys or materials possessed or used by the child, a smile, verbal interaction of the mother or caretaker, songs, play, etc. In broader terms stimulation given to a child can be classified into before birth-pre-natal and after birth-post-natal.

Pre-natal Stimulation

A child's development starts from the first day of its conception. So stimulation becomes essential from its foetal stage itself. The stimulation given to the foetus through the pregnant mother is termed as pre-natal stimulation.

(a) Mother's emotional well-being/mental health/positive emotions

There is a direct relationship between mother's emotional status and foetal development. So listening to melodious music, enjoying the beauty of nature, reading books that gives relaxation to mind, meditating and exercising should be encouraged among pregnant mother. Research also proved that these act as stimulants for foetal development.

The love and care shown to the pregnant mother, acceptance of the child in the family are the major factors that influence the emotions of the mother. Better Inter-personal Relationship in the family act as an indirect stimulant for the development of the foetus.

(b) Diet

The next major stimulant is the quality of food taken during pregnancy. Nutritious foods taken during pregnancy helps for the better development of foetus. It fulfills nutrient requirements and fosters foetal growth.

Apart from these, regular medical check-ups, immunization given to the mother, her health conditions play a significant role in the development of the foetus.

Proper pre-natal stimulation helps the mother to have safe delivery and a healthy baby.

Post-natal Stimulation

Any type of stimulation given to the child after birth may be termed as post-natal stimulation.

During the post-natal period, whatever the material the child feels, sees, smells, hears, tastes, uses, and manipulates stimulate the child's development.

In the same way emotional expressions like a smile, hug or

kiss from parents, siblings, peer group neighbours also act as stimulant.

Based on the nature or type of stimulant, home stimulation at this stage can be categorized as (*a*) Stimulation through physical environment (materials), and (*b*) Stimulation through social environment (people).

Type of stimulations that could be given to the children from 0 to 6 both physical environment and social environment are given in tabular form for easy reference. These are only suggestive. Depending upon the requirements and the availability these may vary. At the same time we should remember that if the environment is simulative, development of the child will be quicker and wholesome.

Post-Natal Stimulation

Age (in months)	*Physical Environment*	*Family/Social Environment*
0-6	— Bright coloured toys, rattles, hanging toys etc. — Soaps/Oils/Talcum powders — Objects, materials that stimulate senses of the child — Music (Lullabies) etc.	— Breast feeding — Closeness of mother/Caretaker — Face-to-face interaction with the baby — Baby massage etc.
6-12	— Pull & Push toys — All other materials at home such as Kitchen utensils, Tables, Chairs, etc. — Soft toys — Musical instruments — Television — Anklet worn to the child — Accessibility to child's movement inside the home	— Breast feeding — Frequency of interaction with family members and their intensity — Visit of other people to home and their interaction with the child — Child rearing practices — Listening and responding to child's play activities
12-24	— Safe play environment	— Verbal interaction

(*Contd.*)

(*Contd.*)

Age (in months)	*Physical Environment*	*Family/Social Environment*
12-24 (1-2 years)	— Safe play environment — Varieties in toys — Books, Picture — Kind of materials at home — Occupation related materials, toys — Television, Computer and its frequency of use — Musical Instruments — Frequency of visit to Zoos, Parks, temples etc.	— Verbal interaction — Interpersonal communication in the family — Ways of expression of love by family members — Values, occupation, habits of family members — Frequency of visit to neighbour's home — Type of experiential content provided
24-36 (2-3 years)	— Availability and use of play materials, books, materials that child can see, use and manipulate — Chance for using, manipulating, destructing variety of materials — Frequency of visit to other places — Television, Computer at home — Safe play environment — Exposure to play centres, Day Care centres, etc. — Language used at home and neighbourhood — Socio-economic conditions of the family — Sensory Experiences	— Nature of communication at home — Child rearing practices — Frequency and chance of interacting with grand parents, relatives and peer group — Listening to stories from Parents, siblings, relatives, grand parents — Nature of Relationship between mother and father — Parental responsibility
36-48 (3-4 years)	— Exposure to materials at home, neighbourhood, Schools-frequency of use, manipulation — Rituals, ceremonies, functions celebrated at home	— Family size and atmosphere — Type of punishments given to the child — Nature of frequency of interaction with Peer group, family members and others

(*Contd.*)

(*Contd.*)

Age (in months)	*Physical Environment*	*Family/Social Environment*
	— Frequency of visit to other places and nature of freedom given to children in moving around — Involvement in household activities — Play environment — Exposure to 3 R's.	— Parental Education and occupation — Child rearing practices — Social relationships — Freedom given to the child.
48-60 (4-5 years)	— Quality of child's interaction with outside world — Nature and type of learning environment at home. — Place of Residence — Chances for aesthetic appreciation — Visit to garden, Zoo, Circus etc. — Child's opportunity to know about parents occupation — Accessibility to puzzles, and other learning kits.	— Parental responsibility — Discipline Techniques — Guidance from people at home — Interaction with neighbours, relatives, Peer group, schoolmates — Mental health of parents — Nature of freedom given to the child — Family Traditions

Bibliography

Arthur, Jersild, T., *Child Psychology*, Englewood Cliffs, N.J., Prentice Hall, Innc, 1961, Part IV.

Baller, Warren, R.(ed.), *Readings in the Psychology of Human Growth and Development*, New York, Holt, Rinehart and Wilson, 1965.

Bhatl Champa and Kohn Ruth, *The Exploring Child*, Gujarat University, 1968.

Bossard James, H.S. and Ellanor Stroker Boll, *The Sociology of Child Development* (4th edn.), New York, Harper & Row, 1966.

Brearley Molly and Elizabeth Hitchfield, *A Teacher's Guide to Reading Piaget*, London, Routledge and Kegan Paul, 1970.

Brown Roger, How Shall a Thing be called?, in Raymond, G. Kuthlor and George G. Thompson (ed.) *Psychological Studies of Human Development*, New York, Appleton Century Crofts, 1970.

Crow Lester, D. and Crow Alice, *Child Development and Adjustment*, New York, The Macmillan Co., 1962.

Elliot D. Landauet *et al.*, *Child Development Through Literature*, New Jersey, Prentice Hall, Inc, 1973.

Gesell Arnold and Frances L. Ilg., *Infant and Child in the Culture of Today: The Guidance of Development*, London, Hamish Hamilton, 1965.

Grace, J. Craig and Marguerite Kermis, *Children Today*, Prentice Hall, Englewood Cliffs, New Jersey, 1995.

Hess Eckhard, H. Imprinting, An Effect of Early Experience in Raymond G. Kublen and George, G. Thompson (ed.), *Psychological Studies of Human Development*, New York, Appleton Century Crofts, 1970.

Hilliard Ernes, R. *et al.*, *Introduction to Psychology* (6th edn.) New Delhi, Oxford and IBH Publishing Co., 1975.

Hurlock, Elizabeth, B., *Developmental Psychology* (4th edn.), New Delhi, Tata McGraw Hill Publishing Co. Ltd., 1976.

——, *Growth and Development*, Bombay, Tata McGraw Hill Publishing Co. Ltd., 1970.

John P. Dworetzky, *Introduction to Child Development*, West Publishing Company, New York 1990.

John W. Santrock, *Child Developmemt*, (7th edn.) Brown and Benchmark Publishers, Chicago, 1996.

Johnson Ronald, C. and Gene R. Medimus, *Child Psychology: Behaviours and Development* (2nd ed.), New York, John Wiley and Sons, Inc, 1969.

Jordan Thomas, E., *The Exceptional Child*, Ohio Charles, E. Merrill Books, Inc, Columbus, 1962.

Kuhlen Raymond, G. and Genor G. Thompson (ed.), *Psychological Studies of Human Development*, New York, Appleton Century Crofts, 1970.

Kuppuswamy, B., *A Text Book of Child Behaviour and Development*, Delhi, Vikas Publishing House Pvt. Ltd., 1974.

Laura E. Berk, Intents, *Children and Adolescents,* Allyn and Bacon, Boston, 1996.

Magary James, F. and John R. Eichorn (ed.), *The Exceptional Child: A Book of Readings*, New York, Holt, Rinehart and Winston, 1964.

Morgan Clifford, T. and Richard A., King, *Introduction to Psychology*, New Delhi, Tata McGraw Hill Publishing Co. Ltd., 1970.

Mussen Paul, H. *et al.* (4th edn.), *Child Development and Personality*, New York, Harper International Education, Harper and Row Publishers, 1974.

Netherington Mavis, E. and Ross, D. Parke, *Child Psychology: A Contemporary Viewpoint*, New York McGraw Hill Book Co., 1975.

Piaget Jean and Barbe Lnhelder, *The Psychology of the Child*, London, Routledge and Kegan Paul, 1973.

Smart, S. Mollie, and Russell, C. Smart, *Children Development and Relationships*, New York, The Macmillan Co., Oilier Macmillan Ltd., 1967.

Solberg Zubek, *Human Development*, New York, McGraw Hill Book Co. Inc, 1964..

Sparkman Brandon and Ann Carmichael, *Blue Print for a Brighter Child*, New York, McGraw Hill Book Co., 1975.

Warren Baller, R. (ed) , *Readings in the Psychology of Human Growth and Development*, New York, Holt, Rinehart and Winston, 1965.

Watson Robert , *Psychology of the Child*, Wiley Toppen Ltd., 1958.

Index

Acquiring Information 122
Adaptive Behaviour 176
Aesthetic appreciation 122
Aesthetic Standards, development of 125
Aggressiveness 83, 161
Aids to motor activity 78–79
Albinism 188
Alcohol 48
Altura 49
Anesthesia and Analgesia 49–50
Anger 94
Anxiety 95, 161
Approaches of 3
behaviouristic 3–4
cross-sectional 6
description on 4–5
field theory 3, 6
longitudinal 6
normative-descriptive 3–4
psychoanalytic 3, 5
Appetite 100
Artificial excitation 161
Ascendant behaviour 84
Attachment behaviour 83
Auditorily handicapped education for 196–97

Babyhood 59, 86, 94
beginning socialization 56–57
common play pattern of 82–83
Babyish Behaviour 100 (*see also* childish behaviour)
Backward child 172
causes of 174
characteristics of 173
educational provisions for 174
kinds of 173
Bedwetting 161
Behaviour Problems 160
ascendant 84
day dreaming 122
definition and meaning 172–73
enuresis 162
lying and stealing 166
masturbation 160
causes of 161
nail-biting 100, 165
stealing 166, 167
thumb-sucking 161, 163
toilet habits 154
Binet Simon Intelligence Scale 176
Binet, Alfred 2
Biological processes 4
Birth process 52
breech birth 55
cesarean delivery 55
complications 56
gentle-girth 54
instrument delivery 55
labour and delivery 52
natural and prepared child-birth 52–53
Bladder control 151
Blindness, causes for 184–85
Boredom 164
Bowel movement 154
Broken homes 161

Carrol, J.B. 118
Child development,
imagination of 122
nature of 1
reasoning and thinking 120
specialists of 2
stages 43–50
trends 86
Childhood illnesses 235–42
Asthma 243–44
chicken box 238

common cold 236
diarrhoea 236
diphtheria 239
dysentary 236–37
ear infaction 237
fever 242
measles 238
mumps 237
nose bleeding 247
pertussis 239
polio 232
poliomyelitis 240
scabies 237–38
tetanus 240
tonsillitis 237
tuberculosis 240–41
typhoid 241
warm infaction 241
Child's Emotions, features of the 98
Childish behaviour 98
Children with Special Needs 169
Children's Gangs, characteristics of 89
observation of 7–8
Climbing 65
Clinical manifestations 220
Clinical symptoms 204–05
Cognitive development 10–11, 104–05
Piaget's theory 104
reactions 106, 108
stages of 104–05
cognitive thought 110
concrete operations 109
pre-operation representation 109
Colic Pains 242
Colour concept 130–32
living and non-living theory 131
Compensatory Postural Adjustments 70
Concept formation 116
role of teachers in promotion of 134
stages of 117
Conceptualization 41, 135
Concrete Operational Period 104
Contraceptive foams 50
Couch, Jock 173
Creative activities 103
Creative thinking 122
Cretinism, factors leading to 178
Criterion referenced testing 27
Cumulative records 14
Curative measures 200–201
Curiosity 96

Deficiency diseases 225
kwashiorkor 203, 226
nutritional marasmus 226
protein-calorie malnutrition 226
vitamin 'A' 227
vitamin 'B' 228
vitamin 'C' 229
vitamin 'D' 229
Dehaern, Robert 173
Destructiveness 154
Development stages 43–50
Developmental Trends 86
Diphthongs 142
Discipline 157
DNA blueprint 45
Dramatization 146

Early Childhood 61–63
Eating Habits 151
Educational measurement 26
Educational programmes 187–89
Ego-Bolstering-Motivation 158
Egocentrism 84, 86
Embarrassment 164
Embryo period 44–45
Emotional development 94, 97, 100
childhood, characteristics of 98
common patterns 94–95, 102
common problems 102
factors 100–02
pleasent forms 96–97
Emotional stress 52
Emotionally challenged 198–99
Erikson 97
Essay type test 32
defects of 33
examination 33–34
Evaluation 18–19
aspects of 20
formative 23–24
purpose of 20
summative 25
types of 23–25
Exaggeration 166
Exceptional children 169

Exploratory play 82
Eye Blinding 100

Family adjustment 1
FAO 219
Fatigue 164
Female Reproductive System 42
Fertilization 41
Fetal development 46–47
Fetus period 46–47
First Aid 245
  burns and scalds 247
  dog bite 249
  electric shock 247
  fainting 250
  fracture 249
  general bleading 246
  general principles of 245–48
  nose bleading 247
  general principles of 245–48
  wounds and injuries 248
Floor Locomotion 73
Frequent crying 100
Freud, Sigmund 5, 164
Functional emancipation 72
Fundamental muscles 74

Gardening 64
Gifted children 170
  characteristics of 170–71
  educational provisions for 171–72
  identification of 170
Glaucoma 187
Gripping component 72
Gross muscular adjustments 72
Grossman 175
Group discussion 147

Habit-formation 151
  cleanliness 154–56
  discipline 157
  eating procedure 152–53
  sleeping habits 153
  toilet habits 154
Hall, Barton 172
Hall, G. Stanley 2
Health Education for Pre-school Children 223
Health and nutrition 203–24
Hearing impaired 189–90
Home stimulation 254–65
  pre-natal 254
  post-natal 254–57
Hunger 164
Hurst, R.J. Having 170
Hysterical Outbursts 100

ICMR Committee 221
Indoor activities 63
Infancy 59
Infant Babbling 139
Infections 207
Infestations 207
Infrastructural facilities 63
Initiative play 82
Instructional materials 172
Intellectual development 111–12
Intelligence 101
Intelligence level 144
Intra-uterine environment 47
Iron Deficiency 230

Jumping 65
Jungle Gym 64
Juvenile delinquencies 198
  symptoms of 199

Kulu, Samuel A. 169
Kuppuswamy 174

Lack of Appetite 100
Language development 12–13, 135–36, 142, 149
  factors influencing 144–50
  functions of 137
  role of teachers in 148
  stages of 138–39
Language disorders, types of 194–95
Language skills 141
Language-Behaviour 5
Large motor skills, activities for 77–78
Learning of words 139
Lewin, Kurt 6
Linguistic development 150
Linguistic learning 150
Logical thinking 121
Low-Birth-Weight Infants 56–57

Make-Believe Play 82

Malnutrition, ecology of 208–10
Manual control 74
Marasmus 203
Masturbation, causes of 160-61
Matching items 36–37
Maternal diet 52
Mathematical Index 74
Maturation 100
Measles 232, 238
Measurement 19–20
  devices 25
  prevention of Mental Retardation 180
  types of 19, 26–28
Mental manipulation 121
Mental retardation 175
  classification of 176–77
  clinical categorization of 177–78
  symptoms of 176
Microcephaly 179–80
Mongolism 179
Moral standards, development of 124–25
Motor behaviours 5
Motor Command 75
Motor development 10, 70
  aids for 78
  periods 70–76
  activities for 77
  eighteen months 73
  four weeks old 70
  five years 76
  four years old 75
  forty weeks old 72
  one years 72
  sixteen weeks of 71
  twenty-eight weeks old 71–72
  two years old 73–74
Multiple births 42
Multiple Speech and Language Disorder 195
Multiple-Choice Items 34
Muscular adjustments 72
Musical prodigies 77
Mutual masturbation 161

Negative-disintegrative emotion 94
Negativism 83
Neuro-motor maturation 72
Neuromuscular development 152
Night Blindness 227
Nightmares 161
Norm referenced groups 26–27
Nutrition knowledge 207–10
Nystagmus 186

Observation 14
Obstinacy 100
Organiemic experience 118
Orthopaedically handicapped 183
Ovum period 44
Oxygen deprivation 56

Parental control 162
Parental Love 160
Parent-child relationship 85
Parental development, adverse influence of 47–48
Pavlov, Ivan 4
Peer group 85
Periodical reports 16
Personal-social behaviour 5
Pertussis 231, 240
Phantasy 140, 143
Phenylketonuria 179
Physical causality 133
Physical development 58–59
  equipment for 64–66
    indoor play 65
    outdoor play 64
    pattern of 59
  promotion activities 65
  stages of 58
Physically challenged 182
Piaget, Jean 86, 104, 117, 133, 134
Piaget's Theory 104, 111 (*see also* Cognitive Development)
Poor Economic Status 206–07
Positive-integrative emotions 94
Post-natal stimulation 254
Post-term Infants 57
Postural skills 70
Power Test 28–29
Prenatal Development 41, 254
Pre-operational representation 109
  adverse influences on 47
Pre-school children,
  approaches 4–8
  feeding behaviour 205
  healths 205–07

low income 206
nutrition of 203, 218–20
nutrition equipment 218–20
problems of 205
Pre-schools in health education 223–24
Primary Circular Reactions 106
Problem solving 121
Prolonged Illness 144
Promoting physical development 63–65
activities 65–66
Psychological processes 4
Psycho-social theory of development 97
Puppet Play 147

Radiation 51
Recall Items 37–38
Recording observations 8
Reference system, types of 26
Reflective thinking 122
Reflex Stage 105
Regressive Response 163
Remand House 161
Revenge response 163
Rh Factor incompatibility 51–52
Riboflavin 221
deficiency 229
Running 65

Scabies 237
School Records 14
Scolding 161
Secondary Reactions and Schemata 106–08
Sedentary Balance 71
Self-confidence 89
Selfishness 84
Sensorimotor period 104–05
Sensorymotor Play 82
Sex antagonism 84
Sex education 151–55
Sibling relationships 85
Skipping and Hopping 65
Slide 64
Slow learners, teaching of 181–82
Smoking 48
Social adjustment 151–156
Social approval 83
Social development 80
factors in 84–86
pre-primary school role of 89–90
stages of 80–84
Social groupings 88
Socialization 87
Socio-Economic Status 101, 124
Special Assignment 172
Speech development 140–41
activities 201–02
Speech disorders 100, 148, 190
Speech impairment 190–91
Story Telling 145
Stuttering and Stammering defects 149
Suffocation 251
Summative evaluation 25
Swimming 66
Swing 64

Taxoplasmosis 51
Teacher made achievement tests 29–32
Tertiary Circular Reactions 108
Test contruction, principle of 29–30
Tidiness 154
Tonic-neck-reflex 71
Transitory character 99
Tricycling and Bicycling 65
True/false items 35
Trunk musculature 71
Tuberculosis 232, 240
Type of questions 38–40
Typhoid 241

Urination 154

Vaccination schedule 233
Van Riper 190
Verbalization 139
Viruses 51
Visual disease 185–86
Visually impaired 184–85
Vocabulary, growth of 139–40
Vocal mechanism 141

Water play 64
Watson, John B. 4
Welfare services 184
World Health Organization (WHO) 219
Worm infection 241
Wounds and injuries 248

Xerophthalmia 227

Yale University 3